FUTURE CAMPUS

Future Campus

© RIBA Enterprises Ltd., 2016

Published by RIBA Publishing, part of RIBA Enterprises Ltd, The Old Post Office, St Nicholas Street, Newcastle upon Tyne, NE1 1RH

ISBN 9781 85946 610 0
ISBN 9781 85946 716 9 (pdf)

British Library Cataloguing-in-Publication Data
A catalogue record for this book is available from the British Library.

Publisher: Steven Cross

Commissioning Editor:
Elizabeth Webster

Production: Richard Blackburn

Designed and typeset: Paul Tilby

Printed and bound: Page Bros, Norwich

Cover design: Paul Tilby
Cover image credit: Hufton & Crow

www.ribaenterprises.com

FUTURE

DESIGN QUALITY IN UNIVERSITY BUILDINGS

CAMPUS

Edited by **IAN TAYLOR**

Higher Education Design Quality Forum

CONTENTS

1 CONTEXT and MASTERPLANNING 1

2 SPACES 23

3 BRIEFING, DESIGN and CONSTRUCTION 81

4 VALUE and PERFORMANCE 113

FOREWORD

Universities exist both to create and to disseminate knowledge, playing a major role in innovation and in the transmission of ideas from one generation to another. The modern university takes many forms, with considerable contrasts in history, size and location, and in the balance between teaching, learning and research. Universities play a major role within their local communities in education, in their contribution to the economy and in generating a sense of pride and engagement. The built environment can include museums and art galleries, theatres and concert halls, as well as research laboratories, libraries and lecture halls. Most institutions have national significance and a large number both operate and compete at an international level.

The central argument of this book is that the physical space of the university and the quality of design of that space matter. They matter for the student experience of teaching and learning, for the effective pursuit of research and for institutional reputation. The present built environment of most universities shows the extent of the challenge of planning space effectively: heroic successes sit alongside occasional failures, both aesthetic and functional. The purpose of this book is to try to show:

- why good design matters
- how best it can be encouraged and procured, and
- how experience can be shared.

A number of themes emerge as particularly important.

First, although most universities have evolved into a mix of architectural styles and approaches as they have expanded, most do have a legacy of previous, often ambitious, masterplans. The best of these, and not least some of the oldest, reflect a clear conception of what a university is for, both pedagogically and socially. This book shows how masterplanning remains relevant to the modern university and, in a climate of often rapid change and growth, how difficult it can be to make a masterplan supple enough to endure.

Second, flexibility and sustainability need to be built in to projects as approaches to research and teaching evolve. This might involve creating new, or adapting existing, space to suit large, often collaborative, scientific research projects of international impact; creating specific spaces for expanding disciplines, such as Drama or Film Studies, and understanding how the modern student learns in spaces where the pedagogical and the social overlap and sustain each other. The specific issue of adapting historic buildings of high quality is implicit in a number of chapters in this book. Central also to the provision of space for the modern university is an understanding of the virtual world and of the scrambling of distinctions between home and institutional spaces for discovery and learning. A small but important aspect here is the continuing role of the university to provide residential accommodation and how this fits into a modern conception of higher education.

Third, is the aesthetic – where universities have long sought to create buildings that enhance their reputation. Many of the leading architects in each generation, and perhaps most of all today, have been involved in university design, often producing striking and innovative buildings.

Finally, the book draws out some of the 'nuts and bolts' issues of ensuring adequate budgets, value for money and utility, including methodologies for learning from buildings in use. Universities in many countries have expanded greatly over recent decades, with massive investment in the physical infrastructure.

This volume exemplifies the themes above, and others, by drawing on a wide range of case studies from different higher education systems. It also represents a very welcome collaboration between the Higher Education Design Quality Forum (HEDQF) and the Royal Institute of British Architects (RIBA) and I would like to thank the latter on behalf of the members of the former for helping us to bring the book to fruition. Particular thanks are also due to Ian Taylor and his colleagues for coordinating this volume with such skill, care and good humour. I hope it proves an enjoyable, informative and provocative read.

Professor Philip E. Ogden

Queen Mary University of London
Chair, Higher Education Design Quality Forum

June 2016

ACKNOWLEDGEMENTS & DEDICATION

I wish to thank Feilden Clegg Bradley Studios and the HEDQF for supporting the creation of this book, which I dedicate to the memory of Richard Feilden, co-founder of FCB Studios. Richard was a moving force behind the creation of the HEDQF in the 1990s when he brought together clients and architects in a bid to gain a better understanding of each other's needs, and was Chairman from 1995–2000. With the HEDQF now constituted as an independent charity, I hope that the book will help its work furthering the spirit of co-operation and learning between universities, professions and contractors involved in the creation of the physical estate for learning and research. I hope that the ideas exchanged here can reach a wide audience, and that the HEDQF can extend its efforts to share knowledge across all parts of the UK, Europe and internationally, at a time when there are political shifts away from integration. There is an ever-increasing need for collaboration: both between universities internationally, and between universities and their local communities.

Within FCB Studios I would like to thank Claire Hender for her liaison with the authors, photographers and RIBA Publishing and Joe Jack Williams and David Hawkins for contributions to Parts 3 and 4.

I would like to thank Sarah Busby, Elizabeth Webster, Richard Blackburn and Steven Cross at RIBA Publishing for their expertise in creating this book, and in particular Heidi Corbet and Michael Riebel for their work in co-editing Section 2/Changing Spaces, and all the authors for their enthusiasm and skill in presenting their thoughts and experience so eloquently.

HEDQF
THE HIGHER EDUCATION DESIGN QUALITY FORUM

HEDQF is a registered charity and exists to promote high-quality design in university buildings and facilities, in the belief that the quality of the estate enhances the student experience of teaching and learning, the effective pursuit of research and the process of public engagement.

The Forum pursues these aims through several means:

- visits to university buildings of particular interest in the UK and overseas
- dissemination of information on best practice and latest thinking through workshops, seminars and debates
- an annual conference on a specific topic.

The Forum also undertakes and publishes research relevant to promoting high-quality design in higher education. Research focuses both on innovation (looking forward) and lessons to be learned (looking back) from projects in terms of student satisfaction, research and teaching outcomes, as well as operational success over time.

Membership is open to all those in the UK and beyond with an interest in these themes and the intention is to maintain a balance between representatives from higher education (both academics and estates professionals) and those from architecture, design, engineering and construction.

HEDQF was established around 20 years ago as an initiative of the RIBA in order to promote a stronger understanding of issues affecting its clients and to promote good design in a fast-changing sector with high public visibility and impact. In 2014, the Forum decided, with the encouragement of the RIBA, to become independent, though with strong support for particular projects and initiatives (of which this book is the latest example).

The new organisation is governed by a board of 20 trustees, again with a balance from higher education and the design professionals. There are two categories of membership: Founder Members who have made a substantial contribution to the set-up costs of the new organisation and Ordinary Members who pay an annual subscription. Associate membership is also available to, for example, funding bodies, research councils or other professional bodies. All members are encouraged to play an active role in the Forum and to suggest and organise themes for visits, debates and research. A number of officers and sub-committees take particular responsibility for membership, finance, research, events and conferences.

The Forum welcomes new members and enquiries should be made to admin@hedqf.org

AUTHOR BIOGRAPHIES

PART 1

TOM KVAN

Tom is Pro Vice Chancellor (Campus and Global Developments) at the University of Melbourne, in which role he provides leadership in the alignment of academic and research strategies with opportunities for campus developments. From 2007–15 he was Dean of the Faculty of Architecture, Building and Planning in Melbourne, during which time he led the establishment of the Melbourne School of Design and delivered an award-winning building to host the graduate school. Tom is internationally recognised for his pioneering work in design, digital environments and design management. He is the founding Director of LEaRN (the Learning Environments Applied Research Network), delivering multidisciplinary research on learning and architecture.

PHILIP E. OGDEN

Philip is Chair of the Higher Education Design Quality Forum. He is Professor of Human Geography and Senior Adviser to the Principal at Queen Mary University of London. Over the last 15 years he has been closely involved in the development of a number of major new buildings at Queen Mary for research, teaching and student residence. His academic interests focus on demography and urban change in Europe and the Caribbean, and he has published widely on these themes.

RUPERT COOK

Rupert joined ArchitecturePLB in 1998, becoming a Director in 2003. He has led projects in university, commercial, arts and cultural sectors and is currently leading several university masterplans. His strong interest in sustainable developments is demonstrated by his recent involvement in the practice's first Passivhaus project. He is a trustee of the HEDQF, a Civic Trust Awards judge and a visiting critic at a number of schools of architecture.

PART 2

JONAS NORDQUIST
Jonas is Director of the Medical Case Centre, Karolinska Institutet and the Associate Director of residency programmes at the Karolinska University Hospital, Sweden, and affiliated to the College of Medicine, University of Qatar and the Wilson Centre, University of Toronto. He was in charge of the visionary and strategic briefing for the Future Learning Environment Project at Karolinska Institutet between 2009 and 2015, and is currently involved in several learning environment projects around the world.

HEIDI CORBET
Heidi is a Partner at Hawkins\Brown Architects where she has led a variety of projects across the education sector from more traditional teaching and learning environments to multi-use building typologies with social learning spaces, such as the Hub for Coventry University. Heidi co-edited Part 2 with contributions from Hawkins\Brown Partner Oliver Milton and Researcher Michael Riebel.

IAN CALDWELL
Ian graduated as an architect from the University of Strathclyde in 1977. His early career in private practice, local and central government included schools, historic buildings and national museums and galleries. In 1989 Ian joined Deloitte, after which he was Director of Estates at Sheffield Hallam University, Imperial College London and King's College London. He is the past Chairman of HEDQF and is now an independent consultant advising on university and other projects.

IAN GOODFELLOW Ian is Deputy Chair of the Higher Education Design Quality Forum. As a Partner at Penoyre & Prasad he has led on a wide range of award-winning HE projects including libraries, research and creative industries facilities and new schools for business, mathematics and architecture In addition to his work in the HE sector, Ian is also responsible for the practice's sustainability strategy and implementation and is committed to a genuinely pragmatic approach to low energy design.

PART 3

GABRIEL AEPPLI Gabriel is Professor of Physics at ETH Zurich and EPF Lausanne, and a division head at the Paul Scherrer Institute, also in Switzerland. After taking his BSc, MSc and PhD in electrical engineering from MIT, he spent the majority of his career in industry (NEC, AT&T and IBM) and was subsequently Co-founder and Director of the London Centre for Nanotechnology, Quain Professor at University College London, and co-founder of the Bio-Nano Consulting Company.

FIONA DUGGAN
Fiona is Founding Director of FiD, a London-based consultancy set up in 2006 to work with organisations and institutions undergoing change. Using a combined background in architecture and organisational psychology, Fiona works at the place where users and buildings meet, seeking ways in which the design and use of space can support change.

ANDY FORD
Andy is Director of the Centre for Efficient and Renewable Energy in Buildings (CEREB). He was a Founding Partner of 'Fulcrum Consulting' which became famed for low-energy building design and sustainable masterplanning. He has had a long interest in research, innovation and knowledge. He was awarded the IMechE Built Environment Prize in 2008 and an honorary doctorate by Herriot-Watt University in 2012.

IAN TAYLOR
Ian is a Partner at Feilden Clegg Bradley Studios with particular expertise in masterplanning and the design of cultural, university and school buildings. He has worked on 14 RIBA Award winning projects, two of which have been short listed for the Stirling Prize. He leads the Research and Innovations Team in the practice, and has been involved in the development of sustainable design guidance and post occupancy evaluation methodologies.

PART 4

JULIAN ROBINSON

Julian is Director of Estates at the London School of Economics and Political Science, responsible for the development and implementation of estates strategy, policy and performance. Formerly he was Project Director at Queen Mary University of London. Projects delivered include a new medical school and students' village at Queen Mary and the Saw Swee Hock Student Centre at the LSE. The LSE was named AJ100 Client of the Year 2014. Julian is also Deputy Chair and a Trustee of the Higher Education Design Quality Forum.

JOANNA ELEY

Joanna is an architect and Director of Alexi Marmot Associates, specialising in understanding building users and their needs, and advising on strategies for briefing, space use, post-occupancy evaluation reviews. She is a RIBA-accredited Client Adviser, and a facilitator for HEDQF post-occupancy reviews. She has carried out extensive research and technical writing for many public organisations, including CABE: Creating Excellent Buildings – a Guide for Clients (2003) and Client Conversations for the RIBA (2013).

MIKE ENTWISLE

Mike is a Partner at BuroHappold Engineering where he leads their Education Sector work. He has an exceptional range of knowledge and experience of building and environmental design, focusing particularly on user-centred design and

real world building performance. He has led the engineering design of university buildings at Cambridge, Oxford, Exeter, Bath, Bristol and London. An acknowledged expert in the field, he has written technical articles and is a regular speaker at industry events.

KENN FISHER

Kenn is Associate Professor of Learning Environments at the University of Melbourne and Director of Education at Woods Baggot. He has practised in learning environment planning, design and research locally, nationally and internationally for over three decades. He was Head of the OECD Centre for Effective Learning Environments in Paris in 1997/8, and has consulted to UNESCO and to educational sectors in Australia, Asia, the Middle East and Europe.

ELEANOR MAGENNIS

Eleanor is a Chartered Architect with 25 years' post-qualification experience. She has spent the last 16 years in higher education, leading on Strategic Planning of the estate, effective space management, innovative learning/academic space design, post occupancy evaluations and championing equality and diversity. At the University of Strathclyde she was a major driving force in their £350 million estates strategy and currently she is Head of Space Planning at the University of Glasgow.

INTRODUCTION

Ian Taylor

We need to share experience,
learn and develop new ideas.
We need universities.

This book is about creating places that enable effective and enjoyable teaching, learning and research. Set out in four parts, it aims to identify issues through the life cycle of our university environment that need our critical attention. From the first idea through to demolition, decisions made about our environment impact on its effectiveness in meeting our needs. There is a cycle here that historical reflection should help us to analyse – a cycle which the construction industry and clients should learn more from to inform our decision-making.

The creation of the Future Campus must learn from precedents, and in particular look at recent experiences in changing the use of existing buildings and the successes of newly designed projects. This book is about sharing ideas to inform better briefing, design and use. It is about an approach to creating a future based on firm understanding in order then to reach out towards potentially inspirational and visionary solutions.

The book includes the views of university academics, estates directors, architects and engineers involved in the creation of settings for university life: it looks backwards in order to look forward and it reflects on successes and failures in order to inform the future. It encourages long-term thinking, and gives guidance on issues to consider in the creation and life of a building project, to help support better learning, more effective research and a happier university community.

Through consideration of projects and research in the UK, Australia, Scandinavia, the USA and Asia, the authors investigate issues that impact on design quality and the future performance of the university. *Future Campus* is divided into four parts:

PART 1: CONTEXT AND MASTERPLANNING

- What is the future role of a campus, what physical estate is needed, what future needs will define it?
- How might universities relate to their neighbouring communities?
- What processes can be followed to create an estate vision?

PART 2: SPACES

- How can pedagogical aims be defined adequately to influence spatial requirements?
- What emerging spatial typologies are resulting from new requirements?
- How can spaces be more flexible, support greater demand, and improve outcomes?

PART 3: BRIEFING, DESIGN AND CONSTRUCTION

- Can changes in the briefing process help clients define their requirements better?
- When should sustainability targets be set?
- Does continuity in engagement improve outcomes?

PART 4: VALUE AND PERFORMANCE

- How should projects be valued?
- How can feedback be sought?
- What lessons can be learned?

Each part of the book is introduced by those with university experience, with reflections on the topic by a Pro Vice Chancellor, a research academic, a Professor of Physics and a Director of Estates, bringing experience from Australia, Scandinavia, Switzerland and the UK.

This client view is an important feature of the book – a focus on how spaces work in use and about how good briefing, excellence in design and responsive operation can deliver exceptional results that improve educational practice and research outcomes, raising the profile of the university.

In a period when the ever-developing use of IT is changing learning and teaching methodologies, it is important to understand how the physical estate can provide opportunities to enhance online resources and communication. This can be in IT-enabled settings or in complementary spaces that offer a different type of environment where human and physical interaction is facilitated through comfort, character and atmosphere. The need for characterful and flexible space is therefore as pressing as ever. The character of the university estate has a direct impact on student and staff admissions and retention; how the estate provides environments that enable successful IT integration into teaching and learning practice, alongside complementary functions, will define the next ten years of university development.

This book describes how emerging changes to traditional teaching spaces could meet future needs, and asks if the university estate's current focus on social learning needs to change further in the future. The imperative to provide maximum benefit through the use of minimal environmental and financial resources demands a focus on long-term value and performance. There is an increasing need for universities to offer robust, attractive and comfortable settings for as yet undefined uses, alongside very particular functions: for learning and ideas exchange through project and team endeavour. There needs to be debate both on how these spaces are arranged and connected – public to private, inclusive to exclusive – and on social, staff and educational organisation within universities to re-establish a synergy between buildings, technology and the university community.

It is human interaction that the physical university offers, and those with the best facilities and character to retain their staff and encourage interaction and the exchange of ideas will be the most successful.

For further information on issues raised in this book, reference materials, and additional case studies visit the HEDQF website at www.hedqf.org

context and masterplanning

The framework that guides the development of a university estate should primarily reflect the ambitions and character of the institution, building on the opportunities of its context and enhancing the specialisms which it offers.

Funding challenges and the opportunities that the internet offers tertiary education are two major factors changing the requirements of the physical estate. The student experience, and the quality of teaching and research, impact on reputation. The strength of the people and the place will still determine where academics and students choose in a world where everything is more closely connected by electronic communication.

Universities need to establish priorities for investment, and building designers need to understand the context in which new spaces need to operate.

Tom Kvan's observations on the current context facing university development raise questions about the timescales for masterplanning and suggest that additional or alternative strategies are required to address the fast rate of change.

Guidance on issues to be addressed, and how a strategic framework might be manifested are set out in the masterplanning section by Philip E. Ogden and Rupert Cook.

1.1 CONTEXT

Tom Kvan

OPINION

Driven by budgetary uncertainties and marching to managerial timelines, we easily forget the context within which campus developments take place. We start then by reminding ourselves that there are two purposes that guide and inform our thinking about university campuses:

1. the overarching academic purpose or vision of the institution
2. an attitude to the academic community that uses the campus.

Campuses take many forms, from the urban assemblage of extant buildings to custom-built compositions on greenfield sites. In considering 'campus planning', it is helpful to recognise that we can identify two distinct conditions with different demands:

1. there are those large bounded campus territories that can be regulated by the university, or
2. there are campuses composed of discrete buildings located in an urban fabric controlled by other agencies.

Most often, the term 'campus planning' refers to the former, as the term came to be used in the early to mid-20th century as nations and communities invested heavily in expanding the tertiary sector and allocated large tracts of land to such purposes.

Universities also vary widely in scale. Some campuses are large communities of users – often with many tens of thousands of people present each working day, campuses can be the size of small towns. Likewise, their operating budgets would place them as significant stock-traded businesses and the commensurate capital investments are significant. Regardless of size, campus development is a matter of technical consideration as well as social, with the facilitation and nurturing of an academic community. For example, Thomas Jefferson expressed this explicitly in 1819 when he sought to bring sense and order to the University of Virginia by conceptualising it as an 'academical village'.[1] The University of São Paulo recognises this with the election of a mayor (prefeita) for their campus[2] who is a voice for the considerable population of users.

Today, this population is highly mobile. Students and staff flow around their countries, regions and the world, choosing their place of study by comparing attributes and experience. Universities are under pressure to distinguish themselves: to differentiate their offerings to students and their experience, to ensure better graduate opportunities and to be good employers. The delivery of buildings and creating a future campus is a risky and expensive activity. Of course we need careful planning, proper risk management and strong project control. The problems arise when those aspects of delivering a future campus take over. With risk comes opportunity; a project in which risk is fully managed-out is often so sterilised that the product is anodyne.

CAMPUS PLANNING, HISTORIC PERSPECTIVE

While universities and institutions of higher learning have very extensive histories, we can identify in the 19th century the emergence of our modern understanding that distinguishes between two discrete models. One model was articulated by John Henry Newman[3] as having a singular focus on teaching, drawing on 'universal knowledge' in an ecclesiastic and monastic tradition. The other model is that of a purpose-formed research institution, as exemplified by Humboldt's framing of the pursuit of knowledge through personal discovery.[4] This distinction can be observed not only in academic agendas and institutional visions but also in the practices of campus planning. In different nations, these two images take different priorities: in Britain, it is the Newman model that has been the

popular image of a university with the associated typology of a cloistered quad; while the typology for the Humboldt model is the research bunker, the building camouflaging the activity within, rendering it anonymous.

As higher education expanded in the third quarter of the 20th century, institutions were mandated to develop with particular missions as framed by these two models. Thus, campuses were planned with a clarity of purpose and supported by a funding scheme that was stable (at least at the beginning). Campus development was undertaken with focus and intent at a time when urban or town planning had emerged with confidence as a management technique that served government and industry well, building from the post-war practices of managerial planning and industrial delivery. It was in this context that the 'masterplan' came to be the tool to guide the many steps needed to deliver the academic campus.

Framed in this model of practice, Dober wrote that campus planning was 'the premeditated guidance of the amount, quality and location of facilities for higher education so as to achieve a predetermined objective. The objective is the plan.'[5] Academic infrastructure was then delivered against this plan. Buildings were identified for their particular purpose in serving an aspect of academic activity. The masterplan controlled each step along the way.

To support the scale of design and delivery of these campuses, a number of mid-century professional journals published regular articles documenting practice and advising on approaches. One broadly referenced body of this work

is that by Mildred F. Schmertz published in *Architectural Record,* compiled into the text 'Campus planning and design'.[6] In this, each building is an object on campus described by type and function, each built according to the masterplan, although she notes that 'A building or building group which is conceived as part of an overall design for campus function and growth tends to serve purposes beyond the mere provision of necessary facilities.' Here she recognises that the plan, once executed, is subverted by users and consideration given to these other uses.

THE ACADEMIC MISSION TODAY

In the Newman model, the university was conceived with the monastic court as the genus, isolated from the chaos of daily life. Exiting the academic quad meant stepping into the secular disorder of the civic realm, the contrast underlining the division of the two worlds. Each component of the university, likewise, is of its own world; as buildings were constructed, the inward mission was given priority and value judged by the delivery of that mission. With this framing, campuses were created as bounded and isolated territories and buildings on those campuses were impenetrable.

The globalisation of education has encouraged universities to shift towards a shared – rather than divided – understanding of the continuum of teaching and research. Whether universities engage in more or less of the two components, both play a role and the interaction between the two is increasingly important.

As education access has expanded and higher education is no longer accessible only to a privileged few, society's expectations of a university have changed. Whether funded by private or public means, universities are playing more proactive roles in their immediate contexts while delivering on their broader missions.

Universities recognise that their campus is the place where it can engage with their communities and thus deliver on a broader and more public mission. In 2006, the University of Pennsylvania adopted a strategy formulated two years earlier, the Penn Compact, to focus the university on addressing major and complex global challenges, but it also explicitly articulated the responsibility the university has to its local community in doing so. This strategic vision was translated into a campus development strategy, 'Penn Connects',[7] to align the university development initiatives with the needs of the immediate community as well as the city of Philadelphia.

The strategy recognised that decisions on land use, building design or academic delivery has social, employment and physical consequences for the urban context of the university. Through this, Pennsylvania has created community benefits from underused land and has added impetus to the city's sustainability outcomes while also opening academic engagement. This illustrates how, together with its web presence, the campus has become an important contribution to the public face of a university as it engages with different sectors of the wider community.

At the same time, certainty in university funding has been eroded in many countries, including the UK, and capital investments are increasingly challenging to budgets. As the academic sector becomes increasingly closely managed, many universities now require extensive business cases to be prepared to support proposed campus or academic developments. Commensurate with this is a greater focus on short-term returns that challenge the traditional time horizons of academia.

THE LEARNING EXPERIENCE

A major campus-user community is the student body; for many institutions, students are the primary users and significant sectors of campuses are typically dedicated to them.

Students' needs are often focused on safety, connectivity and 'accommodating activities'. The students' perspective is often captured (and dismissed) in the phrase that the campus is a 'suitable setting for world class research and teaching'.[8] Learning is portrayed as being achieved through planned and delivered teaching activities, rather than something experienced and developed.

What role does a campus and its buildings play in learning? This is something we have been researching in our work at the University of Melbourne in our Learning Environments applied Research Network (LEaRN). Here we have looked at the learning outcomes for primary, secondary and tertiary students and the places in which they learn.[9] The work considers both formal and informal spaces. For example, we have followed medical students as they learn in corridors while taking part in ward rounds, thus informing how we might better design corridors as essential learning places.

It is clear that tertiary environments contribute in several ways. At all levels, learning progresses through the encounter with, and testing of, ideas. While there are often well-publicised exceptions, the vast majority benefit from learning with others. Likewise, those who teach benefit from structured engagement and support to deliver their teaching, not least from periodic contact with students. As Glyn Davis says, 'Group discussion reminds us that knowledge is always an argument about evidence – we need to hear a range of viewpoints, including those we will not accept.'[10]

The campus experience also plays a role in cohort progression from adolescence to adulthood. All societies and cultures develop mechanisms to guide and develop young people; campuses are a contemporary space in which such development occurs.

The physical environment in which the learning takes place is more than a passive context; it can be engaged as an active teaching tool. This can be accomplished at the level of a building, as was achieved in the Melbourne School of Design[11] (see pages 146-151) but more broadly by using the campus as such. For example, many campuses use their landscaping to catalogue plants for use in horticultural teaching. The idea can be used to support broader learning by enabling disciplinary practice to be observed, for example by glazing parts of lecture theatres to allow casual observation from outside. This can be extended to facilitate contact across disciplines, thereby allowing

5

students to encounter one another. This has been one of the more positive outcomes of the open-work areas, particularly in the library and the atrium of the Melbourne School of Design. In part, this prepares students for their futures, as they use their acquired knowledge in conversations with one another.

Taken further, the building illustrates that the campus is a laboratory; a platform for research as well as for learning. Through this, students become aware of the research culture that underpins their learning experience. For the student, a campus that is one of research and teaching risks being impersonal and unengaging. Supporting the academic mission usually means creating a place that supports the student in learning about the fullness of the academic activities that support the exploration and development of knowledge rather than the delivery of universal truths.

A PLACE FOR WORK

While the primary purpose of a campus may be considered to be an academic environment, it is a workplace for a diverse workforce of all those who engage in and support the academic enterprise of teaching and research, as well as a place for visitors. The diversity of the community and the many non-academic activities are of increasing importance to a university's success. Thus, the literature about workplace planning and design is relevant on campus and is explored in detail in Part 2.

Contemporary workplace planning differentiates modes of work, typically highlighting and contrasting the range of participation from individual through to a team, with their work spanning transactional repetitive activities through to those which are creative and indeterminate. A popular characterisation of academic activity is that of the reclusive don, a solitary contemplative writer in the humanities, for example. Increasingly, however, it is teamwork in and across the STEMM (Science, Technology, Engineering, Mathematics and Medicine) and humanities areas of knowledge that drives progress.

It is the type of work engaged in rather than the discipline that distinguishes the type of workplace needed. The campus can provide a range of such spaces too, from contemplative courtyards to social participation. Workplace design recognises the importance of promoting social opportunities as well as ensuring appropriate, safe workplaces to support a particular task.

THE VIRTUAL AND THE PHYSICAL

All campus users – students, staff and visitors – live their lives physically and online. So much of our daily work today is facilitated online (banking, social interaction, entertainment and culture) that physical place is intertwined with the digital for many of us, especially those of younger generations.

The advent of online and digitally enabled learning has prompted many to suggest we are at the threshold of a major revolution of higher education. Undoubtedly, online resources and capabilities are shifting the experience of students, teachers, administrators and researchers. Library footprints have shrunk as journals are delivered digitally to the desk and the future of the lecture hall is questioned. On campus-based universities, online resources and experiences now complement and supplement the academic experience of students and staff.

Likewise, much of our activity is now time-sliced, with multitasking ever more prevalent. This is antithetical to the cloistered heritage of the campus. Every teaching academic will be familiar with the experience of being challenged by a student during a presentation or discussion as they use online sources to add to their information. Used constructively, this is a powerful teaching too – for example, through flipped learning models.

As online resources and capabilities have expanded (including delivery of research materials, teaching tools, etc.), universities have considered the role of a campus as a complement to the digital or virtual world. Both share common goals; the literature of human–computer interaction shares vocabulary and aspirations articulated in urban design literature. Both speak to the need to clear places (physical or on screen) in which people/users engage in meaningful activity that develops value through such an activity.

What is clear from our experience in the dynamic is that it is difficult to anticipate and predict where the technology will take us, but also that the human interaction that underpins learning and development remains much needed. These matters are developed further in subsequent chapters of this book, in particular by Jonas Nordquist in Part 2.

THE ROLE OF A CAMPUS TODAY

Much has changed since the distinction was articulated between teaching and research in 1852, including changes in our trust in the certainty of knowledge. In particular, higher education has become more accessible to a greater portion of the population in every country, a transformation facilitated both by changes enabling more students on campuses but also by the growth of online education. These changes have led to a fundamental shift in the experiences and expectations of students and their perceived relationship to the university.

In 1997 Peter Drucker, the academic and management consultant, observed in an interview that '30 years from now, the big university campuses will be relics. Universities won't survive. It's as large a change as when we first got the printed book.'[12] He referred to the 'totally uncontrollable expenditures' of education that have led to the cost of education rising very rapidly. Contributing to this escalation of costs has been institutional spending on buildings and property as a competitive advantage. Drucker noted that 'the college won't survive as a residential institution. Today's buildings are hopelessly unsuited and totally unneeded.'

Our experience has not borne out Drucker's predictions, although perhaps it is too soon to take this measure. Instead, we observe that although digital and other modes of facilitating learning have developed, the demand for large lecture halls has not disappeared. While attendance at timetabled subject lectures is observed to be declining, it is striking that special lectures regularly fill the largest lecture halls available. Audiences continue to gather to hear remarkable speakers, desiring to collocate to share the event, as they do in other performance experiences such as music and theatre. From this, we have come to reassess the purpose of the campus, and anticipate that the primary focus of our campus will be to emphasise social and informal spaces above formal spaces. Even though almost all lectures are available online, the power of collective participation means that co-presence is desired.

At the same time, principles and patterns of higher education funding have changed. Where capital funding for construction may have been available and sufficiently reliable to allow for forward planning, most universities are now faced with balancing demands for such resources in the overall operational demands, including development of teaching and research. Projects progress in a more opportunistic manner as funding becomes available either through targeted capitalisation programmes, research successes or philanthropic gifts.

The event of 'going to campus' and the university experience are changing for all campus users but the social and human experience of sharing purpose and knowledge does not change. This is recognised in almost every campus plan: for example, 'The core purpose of the campus is to produce an environment in which world class research and teaching thrives'.[13] Recalling Dober's framing of the purpose of planning,[14] this formulation is less deterministic in that there is no longer a 'premeditated guidance of the amount, quality and location of facilities …' but now a search for the experiential rather than the delivery of fixed inventory.

Challenged by the uncoupling of location from access to resources that is enabled digitally, we seek a renewed role for a campus and its inventory of buildings and spaces. Shared goals for online sites and the physical is that they are 'sticky',[15] a term used for web pages that attract and keep viewers. For many campuses – particularly urban campuses – a challenge has been to keep students engaged with the opportunity to share the learning experience. Such stickiness is achieved in a number of ways: for example, in quality working spaces for the times between scheduled events (tutorials, sports, lectures) and in spaces that support teamwork and with high–quality network access complemented by location-bounded network licenses for specialist software.

As teaching and research institutions, we keep in mind the multiplicity of ways in which a campus can be a teaching tool or a research platform. Many institutions state that their campuses are living labs, places in which research is carried out, whether on the physical fabric or by engaging the community in collective enquiry. This extended use of the campus as an academic tool is essential not only to apply the capital investment to greater ends but also as a means for the university to act on its leadership role in society. In such contemporary social concerns as sustainability, responsible trading and equity, the campus plays a part as a place to develop ideas, test actions, educate the next generation and demonstrate positive interventions. The role of the university as a good client is best demonstrated by the decisions made on the campus through the commissioning of buildings as well as their maintenance and use. We have a role not only to apply best practice in design and construction, as described in Part 3, but to show the way, using evidence to inform our decisions in Part 4.

THE CAMPUS DEVELOPMENT FRAMEWORK

The mid-20th century surge in universities was informed by the management principles prevalent at the time where the delivery of complex projects were guided by explicit plans that sequenced expenditures, established prescriptive design standards and diagrammed spaces according to an ordered narrative. Teaching was a process, learning occurred according to plan. As the challenges on campuses become operational rather than establishment and as the certainty of sequential funded is removed, developments and change are influenced by numerous factors.

In a contemporary academic context, there is a growing distrust of corporatisation of academic life. Students and researchers seek opportunities for innovation; the globalisation of academic opportunity, as a prospective student or employee, has led to choice that is informed by the quality of the work or study environment. The adherence to masterplanning becomes more challenging and perhaps questionable. The implication of the term is that we have a shared and firm grasp on the progress of development through specific planning decisions and that we can master the outcome to an overall intent. With the changes in funding streams and their unpredictability in delivering capital or the pace of change in delivery technologies and their adoption in teaching methods such as increased laboratory work via computer, such certainty is eroded.

The campus masterplan is necessarily prepared in a linear manner, proceeding from statements of aspiration, moving to the framing of principles, identification and testing of needs through planning parameters to specification and documentation with a final plan issued some 24 or 36 months after the first steps and then frozen for the next five-year cycle. Often a decade has passed between decision-making and consequent action. Typically, a campus planning officer or estates manager (to use two culturally and temporally specific terms) will have a shelf of serially superseded documents.

There is also the question of what happens when the masterplan is completed. In Schmertz (1972), for example, we read in section 3 of the library for Boston University by Hoyle, Doran and Berry, with the presentation entitled 'A major library fulfils the masterplan for Boston University central campus', a planning scheme prepared by Sert, Jackson and Gourley. The title of the section raises the question, what do you do after 'fulfilling a masterplan'?

The reality is that most campuses are seldom completed, directed instead by a rolling series of masterplans that each, in time, becomes irrelevant or superseded. As a consequence, the campus is illegible, difficult to navigate and frustrates a core aspect of contemporary university ambition – that of engagement with a wider community. Although most campuses have removed significant portions of their fences and gates, they remain impenetrable to many.

Bringing together the disparate fabric of a campus that has been delivered through various initiatives and often in response to local needs, perhaps guided by architectural typology and material use, campus plans have in recent years sought to bring together the campus experience and create some coherence for its users. Typical of many campus ambitions, the Planning Principles stated by Case Western Reserve[16] summarises contemporary conditions and therefore the needs of planning well:

- to unify the campus
- to create campus identity
- to foster living, learning and discovery
- to focus outwards.

All campuses respond to their evolving surroundings. If the campus is dispersed across an urban context, planning attends to dispersal, identity and integration to the strategies of the urban governance and management. Distinction between the urban experience and the campus interior must be managed, because often the purposes are distinctly different. Those institutions that have control over discrete and bounded campuses have a particular opportunity in which the experience can be managed both inside and out of the buildings and continuities developed to increase the value of the campus experience. As described in the accompanying case study of the Melbourne School of Design, this context was exploited so that the campus ground plane flowed through the ground floor, encouraging people to move through and participate vicariously in the academic life in the building, thus creating the opportunity to share knowledge and thereby value the disciplines explored within. The masterplan becomes redundant, an anachronism of a corporate attitude.

THE ACADEMIC MISSION GUIDING PARTICULAR PROJECTS

Increasingly, universities are recognising the importance of academic diversity, collectively engaged in support of innovation, supported by a vision that reaches into community engagements and social impact beyond the fence or walls. These expanded horizons guide our thinking in campus projects. A common approach to masterplanning is to set out the matters that need resolving. A typical list of these issues may include traffic, identity, lighting, streetscapes and open spaces. These are the knowns that must be addressed but in themselves are insufficient to support the innovation needed.

At the University of Melbourne we recognised that these were indeed aspects to consider but in themselves do not relate to our academic purpose and priorities. In structuring an approach for the next five years, a period aligned to the university strategic plan,[17] we have formulated a development framework in which we address five themes pertinent to this mission:

1. Technology and tradition: how is the academic experience changing as technology asserts itself?
2. Synergy and innovation: how does campus experience support innovation through collaboration and intersections of knowledge?
3. Quality experience: ensuring we realise a supportive workplace for a diversity of users.
4. A culture of inclusion: addressing our strategic aim to make a university a place for all, not only its members.
5. Space and places: translating spaces into places, including 'spaces between' and addressing both the online and the physical.

As opportunities arise in coming years, each will be assessed to deliver on the five dimensions of campus experience and purpose, thus delivering a campus that has been guided in its evolution, rather than masterplanned.

The campus presents to the community a statement about the institution, either distinct and exclusive or fully merged into its surroundings. It is the physical manifestation of a larger statement of the institution's role, as is the online presence that an institution presents. Thus, campus planning is part of the range of strategic thinking that an institution undertakes, such as planning curricula, research infrastructure, personnel policies and web presence. For many institutions, the campus is one of several strategic tools in recruiting appropriate staff and students, and ensuring that they find their workplace sufficiently rewarding that they decline offers to take their expertise elsewhere. The campus is therefore a key tool to fulfilling the vision of a university and supporting the academic purpose. Recognising that each step must be executed under the best project planning principles, the overarching guidance cannot be framed in rigid and prescriptive plans; the academic context is evolving too rapidly.

1.2 MASTERPLANNING

Rupert Cook and Philip E. Ogden

The campus masterplanning process provides the opportunity for an academic institution to reflect upon its history and heritage, to assess its current condition and needs and to create a vision and prepare for the future.

Brandeis University, Master Planning Scope, 2000

The idea of the planned campus is, in many ways, at the heart of the development of the idea of the university. Although many contemporary institutions bear the marks of uncoordinated developments in relation to periods of rapid growth in research and student numbers, most now recognise the need for strategic planning of their estates. Competition in terms of reputation, the pursuit of research funding and student applications means that universities in the UK and in many other countries have been investing heavily in their built environment. This investment has provided a major opportunity for universities to respond to changes in pedagogy and research practice, to embrace the consequences of the information revolution and to address environmental challenges and the desire for greater public engagement.

Architecture and design have responded to these challenges with notable enthusiasm, producing buildings of distinction that make an important contribution to the public realm and often compete with the best new architecture nationally.

The central challenge is whether, given the rapidity of expansion and pressure on budgets, and with the rate of change being so fast, planning is sufficiently robust to ensure that some of the great university buildings over the last two centuries are matched in the future.

This chapter sets out the key factors that lie behind the masterplanning process and how it fits within wider institutional governance.

PLANNING THE RELATIONSHIP BETWEEN FUNCTION AND FORM

The idea of planning the relationship between function and form dates back to medieval European universities which, as for example in the case of Oxford and Cambridge, brought together the classic combination of teaching, residence, dining hall and chapel around a central open space. This model was adapted to the American environment from the early colonial days[18] where the monastic model gave way to a 'campus' of separate but related and planned buildings, more open to the outside world. Harvard, Yale, William and Mary, Princeton (the first university to which the term 'campus' was applied), and the University of Virginia in the 17th, 18th and 19th centuries laid the groundwork for future conceptions of the university's estate. Joseph Jacques Ramée's 1813 plan for Union College in Schenectady, New York, was the first comprehensively planned campus in the USA,[19] since much used as a point of reference, not least by Thomas Jefferson in the University of Virginia soon afterwards (1817–26).

In Britain, the expansion beyond the medieval universities in England and Scotland during the 19th and early 20th centuries produced a variety of physical responses, determined not least by location. To what extent does the campus of today reflect previous attempts at masterplanning? The picture is mixed. In London, where space was constrained, the new 19th-century institutions such as UCL, King's College or Queen Mary were characterised by one particularly impressive new building – by William Wilkins, Robert Smirke and E.R. Robson respectively.

UNIVERSITY OF YORK UK

The University of York, UK founded in 1963, is a good example of a planned university (designed by RMJM) adapting its founding principles to future expansion as the university grew in stature and size. Its expansion on to a new site at Heslington East in the early 21st century has been guided by a masterplanning process. The university has aimed to create a single campus and maintain a high-quality rural landscape setting in a largely car-free environment, and 'the strong integration of activities – research, teaching, business, social, sporting, leisure and residential. We intend the campus to be secure, distinctive and publicly accessible.' University of York, Estates Strategy, 2013–20

▶ Figure 1.1

These developments found echoes in continental Europe, for example the universities of Graz or Lund.[20] Outside London, there has been considerable variety of experience, with what became the great 'red-brick' institutions[21] often planned on an impressive scale – Alfred and Paul Waterhouse at Manchester in the 1870s, for example, or Birmingham's grand collection of buildings by Aston Webb and others from 1900.

By the 1960s, the wish to expand meant that new universities were created, taking the number of UK institutions from 22 to 46 and the number of students from 108,000 in 1960 to 228,000 in 1970. The new campus universities – Sussex, York, University of East Anglia, Lancaster, Essex, Warwick and Kent – were all created between 1961 and 1965, each to a plan.[22] Sussex, designed by Basil Spence, has the only Grade I listed buildings from that period.

In other longer-established institutions, expansion led to perhaps the least happy period for university architecture, with poorly designed buildings, especially for expanding research and teaching in science, springing up. Oxford and Cambridge were not exempt from these challenges, with each having science areas of pedestrian and muddled design.

Subsequent expansion, particularly by giving university status to former polytechnics and other institutions and, especially from 1997 expanding the number of students admitted, has dwarfed earlier growth and thrown the need for adequate planning into sharp relief. By 2013/14, the total student population at over 140 university institutions had risen to 2,299,355.[23] There was an increase of 32.5% in postgraduates and 14% in undergraduates since 2000/01, with a considerable increase in those coming from overseas. This has been matched by unprecedented capital expenditure. Between 1997 and 2011, UK higher education institutions spent £27.5 billion,[24] generated through a number of financial sources. Part of this was based on external borrowing, part on internal surpluses and part on direct grants for teaching and research infrastructure from the funding councils.

In many other countries in the developed world, universities have also expanded greatly and produce regularly updated masterplans. The USA and Australia abound with examples of institutions planning expansion carefully, but so too do countries in Latin America and the Far East, notably China.

THE PROCESS OF MASTERPLANNING

In surveying these diverse examples, current masterplanning of the university estate may be seen as being driven, therefore, by ten principal factors.

1. The increase in competition among universities, where buildings and facilities are given new prominence in the search for a successful market "brand", has increasingly led universities to seek out the best architects to deliver high-quality and innovative buildings.
2. The increase in student numbers and associated changes in funding – in the UK, for example, fees charged directly to students both from within (most of) the country and from overseas – has given fresh prominence to the idea of student satisfaction. This includes not only high-quality teaching spaces but also libraries, facilities for sport and well-designed common learning spaces and good residential accommodation.
3. Investment in research has greatly expanded the need for new build in the leading universities, including major scientific collaborations with external bodies.
4. In both teaching and research, the estate needs to be adaptable to future changes in pedagogy and research practice, not least in information technology.
5. Specific provision for 'growth' subjects, such as business and management, law, or medicine and the life sciences.
6. A greater sense of public engagement within local communities, not least through museums and galleries owned by universities and through public art.
7. The need to ensure compliance and sustainability, and adequate future maintenance.
8. The need to ensure efficient space utilisation to help underpin financial performance.
9. The development of many universities as global institutions, attracting overseas students but also increasingly building overseas campuses, often with local partners.
10. The need to consider the residential estate and the extent to which external providers reduce the need for universities to engage directly in provision.

We shall discuss the importance of masterplanning within institutions below, but it is also of vital importance with respect to a number of external bodies. These include external lenders, who have financed much recent expansion; and, though their significance has been reduced of late as universities have increasingly become masters of their own fates, external funding bodies (such as the HEFCE, Higher Education Funding Council for England, and its Scottish and Welsh equivalents in the UK) in giving capital grants and applying governmental policy on sustainability. Such was the case, for example, with the CIF (Capital Investment Fund) grants allocated to English universities in the first decade of this century, where demonstration of masterplanning and effective management of the estate was essential.

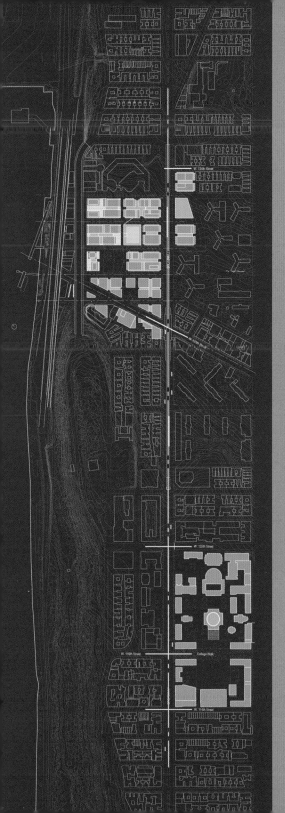

◄ Figure 1.2

THE LOCAL CONTEXT

Local planning authorities also need to be reassured that individual planning applications are both set within a general institutional plan and have been considered in relation to local planning frameworks. Within this context, too, the importance and sometimes protected status of historic buildings can have a major effect on the planning process. Nor should the possibility of local opposition to new development be underestimated, for the urban campus, neighbours, landowners and adjacent businesses and institutions vie for attention and land. On a greenfield campus, similar concerns overlap and extend to include ecology, landscape and views, and greenbelt policy. Hence the question of when to enter into public engagement on the masterplan needs to be considered, particularly around commercial sensitivity when leading to

EXAMPLE
COLUMBIA UNIVERSITY MASTERPLAN RENZO PIANO

Columbia University provides a good example of both masterplanning underpinning the foundation and expansion of a distinguished university and also the perils of further expansion in a local urban environment. Originally founded in 1754, the Morningside Heights campus in New York was designed along Beaux-Arts principles by McKim, Mead and White, following Seth Low's late 19th-century vision of a university campus where all disciplines could be taught in one place. The university also owns extensive residential property for staff and graduate students in the vicinity, as well as two dozen undergraduate halls of residence. Controversy was sparked in 2002 when a new $7 billion masterplan for the Manhattanville campus in West Harlem by Renzo Piano and Skidmore, Owings & Merrill proposed taking over new land. Although eventually approved in 2009, there was considerable and sustained local opposition by residents and others. The first buildings have now been completed.

disposals or acquisitions, through either growth or consolidation. Too soon, with too much on the table can confuse; too late then the only option is to object rather than influence.

As an independent major institution the university can sit uncomfortably between central and local government. Add to that wider European initiatives and potential for funding partnerships and the picture is complex and changing. It is against this background that the local picture for each university unfolds. The relationship between university institution and local authority in the UK varies greatly. Some older universities have a proud heritage of stewardship, evidenced through the commissioning of high-quality buildings, although some have not always maintained this path. The newer UK universities often enjoy a much closer relationship with their local authorities, born out of their technical college and polytechnic heritage, which had strong links to local education delivery.

Universities can, of course, be important partners in regional growth and regeneration, and often the university masterplan may be seen in a wider context.

As Charles Landry observed, 'The city is an interconnected whole. It cannot be viewed as merely a series of elements, although each element is important in its own right. When we consider a constituent part we cannot ignore its relation to the rest.'[25] For example, in London, the University of the Arts relocation, at a cost of £145 million, has been part of a vast scheme for urban regeneration at King's Cross/St Pancras, which also includes the £650 million Francis Crick Institute for biomedicine.

At the Olympic Park in Stratford, planning a higher education presence is very much part of a masterplan to integrate cultural, residential and economic activity. Similarly, in Manchester, the University of Manchester, Manchester Metropolitan University and the city planning authority are working closely together on an integrated regeneration of a substantial chunk of the central city.

As with all future planning there is a dichotomy, balancing private benefit and the public good. For a university, which has clear public benefit, there are also private interests and needs. In an ever-more competitive higher education environment, the concerns of privacy and commercial confidentiality, often motivated by competitive advantage, need to be tempered with public good. When considering long-term aspirations and impact on the campus, its planned future and the options available, a period of private considered reflection is needed before telling the wider world. Working in isolation, while simpler, will give little opportunity for support from key external bodies. So the question is not whether to engage or not, but when. This sits alongside the question of what is the nature and purpose of the engagement. And is it a longer-term relationship and not one born out of short-term aims?

It is a network of interrelated interests, not simply a pyramid from national to local that informs the strategic picture for an individual university. This network brings complexity, but it also puts a greater burden on the clarity of the masterplanning project from inception through to completion. However, by involving others there is potential to

unlock opportunities not available by acting alone. With pressure continuing on efficiencies, finding the right partners helps, for example, to exploit space for the full year. Partners extend to NHS Trusts, and beyond to charitable foundations such as The Wellcome Trust and Sainsbury Family Trusts; to private organisations, for conferences, sports and wider events; and to international partners, whether private enterprise or arts and cultural institutions, with many universities holding rare and designated collections.

ESTATES MASTERPLANNING AND CORPORATE PLANNING

The way in which these pressures are handled is determined to some degree by type of institution. It is worth recalling that the balance of research versus teaching varies considerably (the proportion of institutional income that derives from research, for example, varies within multi-faculty UK universities from around 70% to almost zero); that the size of institutions varies greatly; and that location, history and rate of growth bring different flavours to the masterplanning process.

Central to how the process proceeds is the link with institutional vision and strategy. Most universities publish a corporate plan, revised periodically, in which investment in estates and facilities is explicitly recognised and is also implicit in wider targets for growth. Much of the thinking around estates development is long-term and therefore the masterplan has a significant role to play in persuading senior members of the university – Vice Chancellors and their deputies, Deans and Heads of Schools – that thinking carefully about

15

EXAMPLE
CRICK INSTITUTE

The Crick Institute in London, due to open in 2016, is a good example of the way in which estates development must adapt to changing university research practices. It is also an important element in the wider commercially driven masterplan for regeneration in the King's Cross area. The principal partners comprise major universities (UCL, King's College London and Imperial College London) and the Medical Research Council, Cancer Research UK and the Wellcome Trust. Architects HOK and PLP Architecture have designed a notably innovative building. Total investment is in the region of £650 million and, when completed, it will employ 1,500 staff of whom 1,250 are scientists. The location near major transport hubs, including the Eurostar terminal at St Pancras and many other scientific, educational and cultural buildings (for example, the British Library, King's Place and the University of the Arts London) give the project a head start.

Whether this building embraces its context by becoming a welcoming public presence in the area in the way the UAL building does further to the north will be demonstrated when it opens. While the public will be able to see into its large central atrium, it will need a strong outreach programme to encourage interaction with the public.

▶ Figures 1.3 and 1.4

space, understanding the importance of good design and ensuring future flexibility, and budgeting appropriately for the estate, is a central part of strategy.

Certainly there is ample evidence that this is being taken on board.[26] The University of Oxford, for example, has recent, or soon to be completed, buildings by major international practices, including, among others, Zaha Hadid, Herzog & de Meuron, Rafael Viñoly Architects, WilkinsonEyre Architects, Rick Mather Architects and Dixon Jones.[27] This approach is reflected in the award of architectural prizes to university schemes – for example, the *Architects' Journal*[28] records that four of the top 20 UK clients winning RIBA prizes in the last ten years were universities, and that the RIBA Client of the Year was Manchester Metropolitan University. It also reflects an international trend towards the appointment of 'star' architects to bring a particular gloss to image and reputation, though as the examples quoted above show this is not an entirely novel phenomenon.

If masterplanning is to lead to results on the ground, integration with financial planning is essential. Two aspects are significant:

1. Full engagement in developing business cases for investment with the academic community who generate the activity.
2. Making sure that estates planning is fully integrated with the financial management of the university, with an agreed approach to the development of surpluses and external financing.

The detailed implementation of a plan depends not only on reacting to internal aspiration but also helping to shape that aspiration by the application of good practice from elsewhere. This may include the links between space and pedagogy, and the ways in which students behave and learn on the campus; for example, in relation to developments in information technology.

Equally, a good masterplan also helps the institution to manage compliance and maintenance and develop robust targets for environmental performance (as in the example of Lancaster University, which developed a specific masterplan for what one might call the nuts and bolts of services and environmental performance).

PROJECT GOVERNANCE
PROJECT SET-UP, MANAGEMENT AND BRIEFING

The normal proposition is that the estates and property team within a university commission a masterplan from external consultants. Rather like a brief for a single capital project, the masterplan will need to be defined in scope. A balance needs to be struck between being specific and limiting the outcomes versus being open to unexpected solutions emerging during the process. The scope of a masterplan can vary hugely, ranging from the development frameworks for major new districts (for example, north-west Cambridge), to supporting organisational change, to spatial capacity studies that increase density in discreet parts of the campus.

The university will know the critical areas within a physical campus and organisationally that need to be

▼ **Figure 1.5** *The University of Oxford: The Blavatnik School of Government by Herzog & de Meuron sits in the delicate historic context of the Radcliffe Infirmary quarter redevelopment. The long double-glazed window above the entrance frames the view across to the Neo-Classical Oxford University Press.*

addressed and resolved through the masterplan process. These should be clearly stated.

The brief

A succinct briefing paper developed by the 'project board' (see below) setting out the concerns, keeping in mind the ten principal factors (see page 13) and setting out the vision for the institution. The vision should state the ambition of the study, for example:

- To complete the campus.
- To improve the sense of place.
- To increase density, for example more research space or greater intensity in the use of teaching and learning spaces.
- To overcome poor connectivity.

In addition, an outline of the scope should be stated and should include:

- Timescale for the study to be completed and what is the plan period, for example 15–20 years?
- An explanation of engagement required within and external to the university.
- How will the masterplan be reviewed, for example every 5+ years?
- How will the masterplan accommodate change?
- Does the masterplan need to be approved or adopted by the planning authority?

Continuity with the project briefs

There should be a connection into project delivery, including:

- How the masterplan should be communicated to individual project teams and what aspects can be delivered in individual projects, whether major or minor.
- Explain expectations about phasing, decant and whether there is flexibility over phasing.
- Infrastructure (often identified separately to capital works).
- Impact on facilities management and running costs.

The team

A masterplanner does not come in one size or shape but may have an architectural, urban design, landscape or planning background. How a team is formed and responsibility for coordinating multiple inputs needs to be considered. Typically, there is a single source appointment and an architect leading the team brings a wider educational focus, rather than, say, a town planner or urban designer. The choice of lead will depend on the type of study required. Project management may be a combination of internal or external and benefits come with each. There is accountability from an external consultant, who is dedicated to this project, which avoids the complexity of ongoing day-to-day distractions for an internal project manager, though of course many universities have capable and strong project management skills within existing teams.

Cost, viability and value

A quantity surveyor normally covers this; however, a masterplan study will also often include valuation and potential acquisition or disposal of sites. A valuer may be involved and universities often retain these separately. The costing of a masterplan against the likely timescale is critical. On completion of the masterplan, which plans over, say, a 15–20 year period, there will be a need to consider how to make adjustments for changes in market conditions.

Engineering

Services, infrastructure, highways, energy use and many more are concerns for a masterplan. Note, however, that a masterplan is informed by detail, yet must not get bogged down in it. Keeping the inputs and recommendations at a high level distinguishes the study as a masterplan, rather than as a series of feasibility studies for the implementation of projects.

The project board: engagement, management and decision-making

To ensure the masterplan develops and delivers the aims of the university strategic plan, it is vital that the university develops a clear strategy for the leadership and development of the masterplan, as there is always much to cover, often to a tight timescale.

Responsibility for decision-making

This is the project champion, lead or sponsor. He or she will ultimately be responsible for signing-off the brief, signing-off on the options to be explored and reporting to the university governance. The person may well be a board member or a member of the executive. They will have ownership of the budget, have got buy-in to the aims and objectives, and fully understand the vision to be achieved.

EXAMPLE
QUEEN MARY UNIVERSITY OF LONDON

Queen Mary University of London, founded in the 1880s and a member of the Russell Group of research-intensive universities, has pursued a policy of sharp growth in both student numbers and research over the last 30 years. Located on tight urban sites in inner London, the 1985 masterplan for the main campus (top right) has been used to guide each new building and by 2015 almost all of the buildings envisaged in that plan have been brought to fruition. Two of the most recent – a new Humanities Building (£25 million) and a new Graduate Centre (£39 million), both by WilkinsonEyre Architects – were the product of careful development of business plans with the academic schools and part of an integrated approach to capital planning. Along with other buildings, for example a student village by Feilden Clegg Bradley Studios and a new medical school building by Alsop Architects, good architecture has helped to redefine the institution, both internally and externally.

▲▲ Figures 1.6 and 1.7

▲ Figures 1.8 and 1.9

Participation in decision-making

This may well be a 'project board', involving estates and property, academic, student and professional services representation: a sounding board for the project sponsor, made up of representatives of the wider institution. Where key partners are involved in the masterplanning, then they are likely to be represented here. It is possible to have third-party representation at this level who does not have a direct interest in the project. Their role would be to challenge and support while bringing new skills to the existing group. This could be via peer review from another institution, an independent advisor or RIBA Design Advisors.

Consultation

Wider consultation should be informed by the Gunning Principles:[29]

- Consultation must take place when the proposal is still at a formative stage.
- Sufficient reasons must be put forward for the proposal to allow for intelligent and timely consideration and response.
- The product of consultation must be conscientiously taken into account.

There will be numerous other considerations. How does the board consult at a wider level? Will the university want their consultant team to manage this? Will the project board members lead this engagement through workshops with a wider group of academics, professional services and students? Does the representation reflect current faculty and wider institutional lines, or could this be organised as a delivery group, responsible for ensuring the masterplan covers all relevant aspects of the university's vision? For example, the board has a role in disseminating, commenting on scope and preferred options and chairing sounding boards for specific aspects of the developing proposals.

Informing those affected

How will this be carried out? What should be said at each stage? Social media and online have been successfully used by institutions to inform wide groups. Representative members of the group who are participating in decisions should also be responsible for disseminating and ensuring representation of areas of interest. For example, the Student Union representative would need to work with a wider group, consult them and discuss and debate responses to particular challenges thrown up by the masterplan study.

INPUTS AND OUTPUTS

For the masterplanner, there are a number of baseline pieces of information which are either essential or informative in creating the brief. These form the hard data from which to develop the masterplan. Part 3 discusses the process of brief development. The table here provides an initial checklist of inputs and outputs.

Baseline data required for a masterplan

The following list provides some guidance to the background needed:

The academic ambition

- Corporate plan and detailed academic plans, as the aim of the masterplan is to align the academic and corporate vision with the estates strategy.

The historical context

- Historical context: importance of tradition and heritage and including current and past masterplans.

The existing estate

- The physical estate; plans of buildings, sites and infrastructure: accurate, up-to-date survey or asset plans which are linked to the space database.
- Space Utilisation Survey (SUS): combining intensity and frequency of use, normally needed in the UK for the annual Estates Management Statistics (EMS) returns for each university.
- Building condition, for example rating buildings on a scale from A–D (A = new, D = poor condition).
- Surveys including topographical and ownership (for example, in the UK Land Registry plans). Not just to understand ownership and tenure, but to consider whether acquisition on non-contiguous parts of the campus could be assembled to create a better campus over the longer term.
- Electronic management systems, rather than simply electronic record files. This is a developing area, known as 'Geo-Spatial BIM', a hybrid of GIS data and Building Information Modelling.[30]

- Ongoing projects: work currently being undertaken on site, from small refurbishments, summer works, infrastructure and agreed and budgeted works for the immediate future.

Infrastructure and sustainability

- Servicing and energy use, including EPC/DEC certificates for all buildings.
- Water, waste, recycling, deliveries and logistics. Where and how do these happen?
- Sustainability: in the UK the Carbon Reduction Commitment (CRC) defines overall targets for buildings and wider use, such as purchasing. However, some are being much bolder: for example, the University of California has pledged to become carbon neutral by 2025, becoming the first major university to accomplish this. [31]

Outputs

The range of outputs from the masterplanning process may include the following:

Spatial strategy

- Spatial strategy, size of estate, uses and needs, including teaching and learning, research, public engagement and professional services space needs.
- Space typologies and standards, for example cellular, open (sqm/person per space type).
- An assessment of space in relation to assumptions on growth, business cases and external funding opportunities.

- Guide to space use/interfaces with internet learning.

Building and site planning

- Commentary on existing buildings, and how far they are suitable for conversion and re-use, or need replacement.
- An assessment of heritage assets.
- Capacity for new build and expansion.
- Ownership, boundaries and neighbours, and the potential for acquisition and disposal.
- Townscape audit, connections, landscape, prioritised projects and improvements.
- Routes, levels, highways, logistics and parking.
- Public realm and public arts strategy.
- Design codes to define critical principles which will define how new buildings and spaces should be designed. This could cover issues such as building uses and location, relationship to landscaping and external space, façade design, heights, circulation, ground floor uses, character and materials. How prescriptive these are will depend upon the circumstances of the site and the approach of the institution. Ambitions rather than rules may provide greater flexibility to tackle future change (as discussed earlier by Tom Kvan on pages 3-9).

Infrastructure and sustainability

- Infrastructure: power, water, IT and other services.
- Sustainability criteria and targets.

A completed masterplanning exercise, which reflects the future ambition of the institution and meets the aims of the vision developed through consultation, is clearly an asset for the institution and should be disseminated widely.

Typically there are several audiences for the masterplan, some requiring a non-technical guide to the masterplan, which excludes any commercially sensitive and confidential information, and then the full version is available for those who will work to implement the plan.

CONCLUSION

The 'Idea of a University' was a village with its priests. The 'Idea of the Modern University' was a town… 'The idea of the Multiversity' is a city of infinite variety… [32]

The university sector continues on a journey from inward 'village', through 'ivory tower' and the glorious isolation of the elite, towards the joint aims of broader access and raising achievement. This has meant huge growth in the sector, opening up higher education while to some degree maintaining an idea of retreat from normal life to reflect and grow through learning and research.

Universities, as complex institutions, increasingly play a crucial role in their local, national and international environments in terms of economic and cultural, as well as educational, leadership. This is the task for a masterplan: to plan for this change.

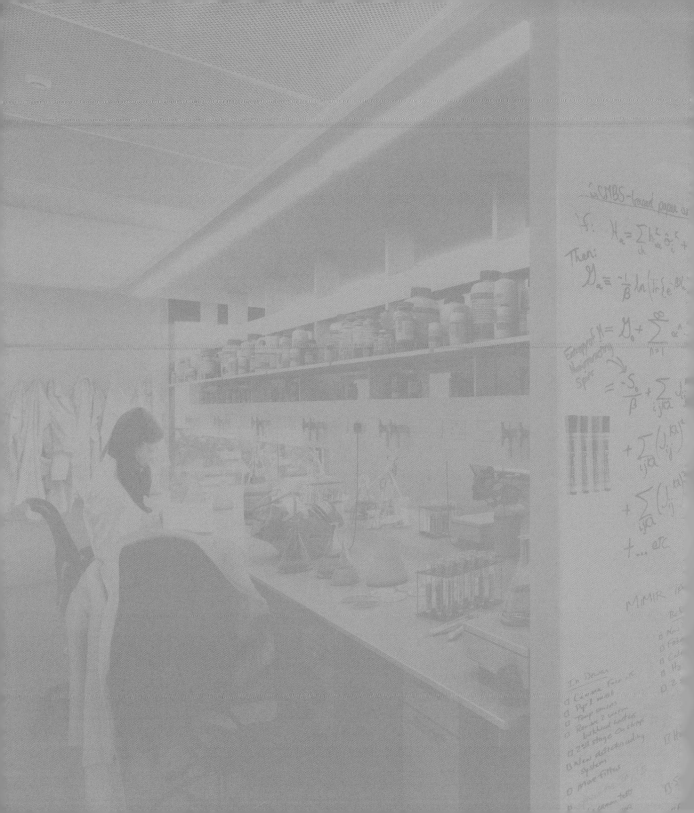

spaces

A university arises out of interrelationships between ideas, people, artefacts, technology and space. Spaces for thinking and socialising overlap with teaching and research. Spaces need to work in many different ways to enable this community of learning to develop to embrace new technologies and communication styles.

2

University spaces have always developed over time to embrace and facilitate new equipment, mixed media and communication technologies.

The rate of change is now fast, and the numbers joining the university sector across the world ever-increasing. This section investigates current changes and themes that are developing in how spaces might respond to these drivers. It is introduced by Jonas Nordquist's plea for better-detailed understanding of the spatial needs of learning environments before design is commenced.

Spaces, authored by Heidi Corbet, Ian Goodfellow, Ian Caldwell with Oliver Milton and Michael Riebel, considers how changes in the relationships between academics and students, and the artefacts, technology and specialist needs of their working lives, are altering the demands on the range of university spaces described – changing functional priorities and influencing spatial form.

2.1 TEACHING AND LEARNING SPACES

Jonas Nordquist

OPINION

The aim of this introduction is to provide a perspective on the process of developing learning spaces in higher education. The development or redevelopment of learning spaces must be considered from an overall perspective of the intended curriculum experience and curriculum alignment. The core message is curriculum alignment: all physical learning spaces must always be analysed, evaluated and developed in order to align with a current or emerging curriculum.

An analogy is made between the development of technical devices and the development of learning spaces; software and hardware developers have to work together on a specific product in order to make it work. Curriculum developers (software developers) do not always coordinate well with developers of physical learning spaces (hardware developers) and as a consequence we all too often find a clear misalignment between emerging curricula and physical learning spaces. Many new buildings might have a modern shell but remain a 'museum' of old-time ideas about teaching and learning inside.

It is suggested here that the educational input into the very early stages of any project – the visionary briefing – is key: a creative, iterative briefing process led by educational experts, who have a central responsibility to articulate educational performance requirements of learning without going into design or technical issues too early.

HARDWARE AND SOFTWARE DEVELOPERS: THE MISSING INTERFACE

According to Biggs and Tang,[1] curriculum alignment may be defined as the connection between all aims and learning objectives, teaching and learning activities and the assessment of an educational programme. The aim is to strive for maximum consistency throughout the system and clear objectives should state appropriate levels of understanding rather than report on topics to cover: teaching methods should be chosen on the basis that they lead to realisation of the objectives, and assessment tasks should be created on the basis that they address exactly what the objectives state that the learners should be learning.

What is lacking, though, from the conversation about curriculum alignment is the connection to physical and virtual learning spaces. What kinds of learning spaces are needed in order to implement a specific curriculum?

A traditional discipline-based curriculum is based mainly on lectures. This requires specific physical learning spaces, i.e. lecture halls. However, many universities are putting more emphasis

In different industries software development typically works with 'interface specifications' which allow different developers to work on their part of the product independently. As long as every team sticks to the agreed interface definition, each separate part will fit together smoothly. Thinking about the interface also means understanding that complex systems can work well and still remain flexible.

What is often missing in developing physical learning spaces is the active collaboration between the software and hardware developers.

on active learning and collaboration while the physical learning spaces supporting new curriculum ideas often remain as they were, based on ideas about teaching and learning as simple transfer of information.

It is therefore key that educational performance requirements are an input into the visionary brief of a project. This responsibility rests on educational and academic experts. Briefing processes must be designed in order to accommodate for this and it is particularly important to provide this input in the early stages of visionary and functional briefing. Architects and building consultants will then work (like hardware developers) on design solutions that align with the educational performance requirements. Most likely

this is an iterative process and it can be anticipated that the roles between the software and hardware developers might overlap to some degree, but it is central to make sure that both groups are at the table from the very early stages. The educational performance requirement as articulated by the educational experts is one of the driving inputs into the project; not just implicitly assumed by the hardware developers.

CONTEMPORARY EDUCATIONAL CONCEPTS FUNDAMENTAL TO VISIONARY BRIEFING

There is limited research on how physical space impacts on learning in higher education.[3] It is therefore difficult to use evidence-based design principles in the visionary briefing process, and so an alternative educational theory-driven approach to learning space design is proposed here.

Independent of a specific learning theory, there are at least three principles that are common property in the current global discourse driving curriculum development in higher education:

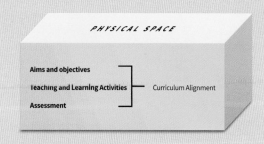

▲ **Figure 2.1** *Aligning curriculum with physical space*[2]

| Learning theory | ⟫⟫ | Curriculum model | ⟫⟫ | Central principles | ⟫⟫ | Performance requirements of spaces | ⟫⟫ | Building program applicable to all scales |

▲ **Figure 2.2** *The process of creating an interface specification; software and hardware alignment*

- Dialogue: learning is an active process. Learners need to be engaged in conversations between themselves as well as between teacher and individual learners.
- Visualisation: to access and build on previous knowledge and experience. The ability to visualise, articulate and verbalise previous knowledge and experience is therefore important.
- Peer-to-peer learning/collaborative learning: there is good evidence that peer-to-peer learning enhances and enriches the individual learning experience. Students may also reach a deeper understanding with the help of peers rather than studying alone.

These three principles (or others, as long as they are derived from educational theory) can function as a first step in interpreting and communicating the underlying research in education to developers of physical learning spaces. Curriculum developers must in simple and concrete terms create the 'interface specification' of a curriculum and the kinds of learning space that are needed. The designers (the hardware developers) of learning spaces must be able to clearly understand such principles in order to translate them into a proper building programme and design.

THE NETWORKED LEARNING LANDSCAPE

The networked learning landscape model[4] used the idea of a learning landscape[5] combined with the new technology enabled opportunities for learning in four scales of settings in which particular kinds of learning activities can be organised: classroom, building, campus and city (the integration into the overall urban landscape). The model is a framework to get a better overview of different kinds of learning spaces and how they interconnect[6] (see Figure 2.3).

A specific curriculum often requires more than one kind of space and it is therefore important to be aware of how spaces in the networked learning

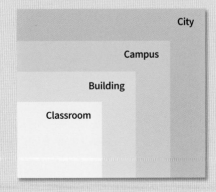

▲ **Figure 2.3** *The networked learning landscape*[7]

landscape are interconnected and can be mutually supportive. The model helps us to understand and analyse the scope of several projects presented in the literature,[8] many of which tend to have too limited a focus on only the spaces between classrooms within a building, or on classroom scale alone, with no discussion of how such spaces interconnect across scales and constitute a networked learning landscape.

FOUR COMMON DISEASES TO AVOID IN DEVELOPING NEW PHYSICAL LEARNING SPACES

As stated earlier, all physical learning spaces must always be analysed, evaluated and developed in order to align with a current or emerging curriculum. But if we do not pay proper attention to this central message, we might be affected by diseases. The causes of the diseases are the same: lack of access to, and understanding of, underlying educational theories, and lack of recognition of scales and their interconnection.

1. THE POWER OF UN-SURFACED UNDERLYING ASSUMPTIONS OF LEARNING

No, or too few, 'software developers' are involved in the project in early stages or get involved too late. What constitutes contemporary and emerging curricula is therefore left to the designers only or other stakeholders from the client organisation – not primarily involved in education. Their underlying assumptions on learning will then drive and define the educational framing of the project. Consequently – unfortunately – we can see many new projects around the world simply reflecting old-time curricula; the new spaces are already at inauguration 'museums' in terms of the design of learning spaces reflecting the history of education rather than the future. This is particularly evident on the classroom scale.

The solution to this disease is: involve software developers in very early briefing stages.

2. METHODOLOGICAL FETISHISM

This disease is an obsession with educational methods. A clear symptom and indication of this disease is when universities are marketing their educational strategies via *specific methods*, such as a university or a specific school in a university defining its offering as a Team-Based Learning (TBL) school or a Problem-Based Learning (PBL) school.

More and more contemporary discussion is moving towards a blended approach to curriculum development, meaning that a building must be able to accommodate more than one specific method. It is therefore critical to avoid situations where an obsession with specific prescriptive teaching methods is driving the building programme, rather than more general principles underlying these methods.

It is a clear responsibility for the software developers to avoid this disease in the visionary stages of briefing and base the educational vision of educational theories rather than individual methods.

3. 'WHAT'S NEW ON THE EDUCATIONAL CATWALK?'

The next disease is closely related to methodological fetishism, namely the sensitivity to the latest of the educational trends. Many schools are trying to keep up-to-date with contemporary education, which is of course honourable. This might, however, become a problem, particularly from a building perspective, if the different 'seasons on the educational catwalk' on international conferences will drive specific schools' curricula.

The vaccine for this particular disease is to base the building programme on specific educational theoretical principles – as above – instead of prescriptive requirements for individual methods. Principles based on contemporary educational theory change at a much slower pace compared with new 'methods of the educational catwalk'. Many such methods tend to be rather short-lived fads.

4. LACK OF INTEGRATION BETWEEN SCALES – ISOLATIONISM

In some projects the shell of a building is given far more attention and focus than the inside, sometimes to communicate the vision and aspiration of a university. Without any doubt this is one important aspect of developing new buildings. To recognise the interconnection between the four scales of a building and make sure that a specific vision cascades down to the remaining three scales is strongly encouraged. It is important to avoid developing new buildings that look innovative from the outside, just to be aligned with old curriculum models and ideas about learning on the inside.

Innovation and development of the shape and form of a building cannot be isolated to the 'shell' scale, but must instead be integrated with the other three scales.

CONCLUSION

In the device industry, hardware must be compatible with software in order to create new functional products that are successful in the market.

Similarly, in buildings, physical learning spaces must align with contemporary and emerging curricula in order to be successful for teaching and learning in universities.

Ultimately, software developers (the curriculum developers) need to be much more actively involved in developing physical learning spaces together with hardware developers (the designers of the spaces) in an iterative and creative process with a clear curriculum alignment in mind.

2.2 CHANGING SPACES

*Heidi Corbet, Ian Caldwell and Ian Goodfellow
with Michael Riebel and Oliver Milton*

This section is very consciously a collaborative piece. There is such a diverse range of spaces within our universities we felt it appropriate to draw on a number of authors who are working within the sector, along with ideas from other sectors. This reflects the fact that universities commission buildings not just for teaching, learning and researching but also for living and working, and are increasingly producing these in collaboration with the commercial and industrial sector.

There has been a huge shift in the way we teach and learn. Boundaries are so blurred between working/learning and our social/home lives that they are often interchangeable and this has a big impact on the way we design buildings.

Changing Spaces explores the types of teaching and learning spaces we need to provide. What follows is an exploration of what future and emerging space types might be. These are broad and varied, and reflect the increasing importance of the student experience. This shift has also spawned a number of new hybrid building typologies such as 'one-stop shop' type student centres and innovation centres.

Before we explore this further, it is important to reflect on how our approach to a few key questions can influence the design.

▲ **Figure 2.4** *Cooper Union New York: the successful integration of a large and complex academic brief into an urban context.*

ICONOGRAPHY OR PERFORMANCE?

There can sometimes be conflicts between character and functional performance – especially in situations involving the retention of existing historic buildings or where a building needs to have significant presence in a campus. Recent years have seen a trend for universities to commission iconographic buildings, often by renowned architects. But if a 'signature building' approach is adopted this could also have limitations. Highly bespoke buildings may have less flexibility than a building focused on providing innovative learning spaces. That is not to say that such buildings do not work or do not have their place on campus, as they could often be highly successful in attracting leading researchers and funding. It is all a question of how we measure performance and value. Do we want to provide innovative spaces which improve learning outcomes or drive up our presence in a crowded international market? Without significant design investment it may be difficult to deliver both.

Some universities have a legacy of listed structures which are part of its historic fabric. These can be expensive to maintain and difficult to convert, but can also provide important iconic landmarks for the university. Here a 'best fit' approach should be adopted, avoiding complex retrospective installations of servicing and finding alternative, more compatible uses, such as collaborative learning. This additional constraint often means less efficient spaces but can also add character and identity.

HIGHLY DEFINED OR ULTIMATELY FLEXIBLE?

Highly specialist spaces will, by their nature, have limited flexibility as they are characterised by their specific functional requirements. However, even within these limitations there has been extensive development in terms of furniture and specialist fittings, which can allow for changes to the 'settings', but these come at a cost.

Providing flexibility is a dilemma There is a risk that in attempting a high degree of flexibility, there will be a compromise when compared with a space designed for a single specific use. No one can predict future changes in technology, which has a huge impact on the design. Flexibility also requires more space to allow for differing layout configurations.

LOW-TECH OR TECH-DEPENDENT?

Advances in technology have played a big part in the expansion of learning opportunities. They have transformed the way we interact with each other and how we learn. How much should we invest in the hardware that we provide to support learning? Technology can sometimes define the spaces required (for example TEAL – Technology Enabled Active Learning) and that can prove tricky; the future is unpredictable and

▼ **Figure 2.5** *Kings College London Learning Centre, BDP*

▼ **Figures 2.6 and 2.7** *Coventry University: flexible lecture theatres - Arup Associates*

▼ **Figure 2.8** *Harvard University technical enhanced learning space, Shepley Bulfinch*

▼▼ **Figure 2.9** *Cooper Union, New York, Morphosis - wireless connection enables working anywhere*

technology is expensive. Defining spaces by technology often requires additional technical support and could lead to future obsolescence.

We now expect all areas of the campus to be connected through wireless networks but this also extends out into wider communities. The increasing use of mobile devices provides improved flexibility and reduces the need for specialist furniture and equipment. However, charging devices can still be an issue and the ever-increasing reliance on WiFi increases the demand on our infrastructure.

SECLUSION OR INCLUSION?

Learning is becoming less a singular endeavour and more a shared collaborative experience. This is aptly demonstrated by the democratisation of traditional teaching spaces to promote dialogue and, more importantly, the rise of social learning spaces across the campus. But have we gone too far? Social learning space is in high demand and its provision is still increasing but we need to ensure we are catering for differing learning styles. A balance needs to be struck with the provision of personal space to ensure this is not forgotten/undervalued in this wave of change. How do we get this balance right?

SINGLE USE OR MULTI-FUNCTIONAL?

Spaces have been traditionally analysed by type or function. More recently, we have seen a move away from traditional categorisations of space in response to social, pedagogical and economic changes. The university curriculum is constantly shifting to meet emerging trends, new technologies and market

demands and this affects the spaces and places required to support the teaching, learning and research.

There is also a blurring of boundaries between learning and social spaces as we now recognise that technology allows learning to happen virtually anywhere. This can be seen as a positive shift in the way we approach future developments; allowing greater flexibility to balance constantly pressurised space requirements through shared use.

Perhaps it is time for us to re-think briefing based on activities needed to support the curriculum, as developed in Part 3.

▼ **Figure 2.10, 2.11 and 2.12** *The Why Factory TU Delft – MVRDV : multi functional space*

TYPES OF LEARNING SPACES

Space can be categorised in a number of different ways.

Our intention is not to replicate well-publicised research in detail but to provide an overview of the different space types which may be required, working from the more specific to the more generic typologies.

Rather than looking at traditional space typologies, this has therefore been approached from a broader perspective, categorising spaces as:

- Specialist
- Teaching
- Collaborative
- Personal.

This frees up any preconceptions about these spaces as traditional 'rooms' and it encourages us to think of the activities we need to support.

There is an increasing hybridisation of spaces which are more flexible and can support many differing activities. For example, a lecture theatre with swivel seating can offer opportunities for collaborative learning, so it can be said to be multi-dimensional.

Flexibility is to be encouraged; as courses and curriculum changes develop over time, the physical estate will inevitably lag behind. The ability to utilise space in alternative ways allows the university to be swifter in responding to the curriculum needs. We outline the characteristics of spaces and then explore further how these may be multi-functional on pages 32 and 33.

SPECIALIST

Spaces which have specific functional/performance requirements typically: laboratories, lecture theatres, workshops, serviced studio spaces

Their limited spatial flexibility can lead to under-utilisation. To counter this they need to become more flexible and/or more intensively used. Additional flexibility can be provided through flat floors, more open orientation and use of furniture. Group sizes are typically medium to large.

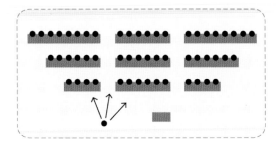

TEACHING

Spaces for the exchange of ideas: there is a move away from tutor- to student-centred learning, a transformation to more open participatory layouts, and the emergence of collaborative learning. This typically increases space standards and the need for increased flexibility, with TEAL. Group sizes can range from small to medium.

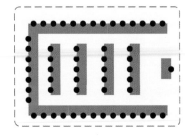 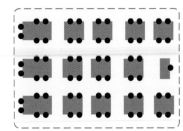

COLLABORATIVE

Spatial settings that foster a balanced dialogue between students and teachers, and also peer-to-peer learning. This may describe spaces where student groups meet for collaboration or where tutors engage with students informally.

Layouts can range from small group working spaces (either fully or partially enclosed) to larger open areas – the 'kitchen table' approach to larger social learning spaces.

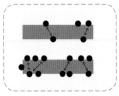 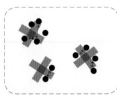 

PERSONAL

Spaces for independent learning a place of retreat, reflection and quiet study. Traditionally, these would be reading rooms in libraries or bedrooms. Contemporary settings now utilise furniture to define these zones in many different spaces. This has led to a new breed of specialist furniture. We are just as likely to utilise public spaces such as coffee shops to provide this activity because, for most people, retreating from the usual workplace and setting is sufficient distance to create this environment. For quick tasks, drop-in points can be provided to allow for rapid access to the internet/resources.

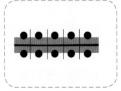 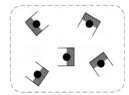 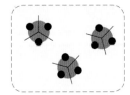

▲ **Figures 2.13** *Types of learning spaces*   ▶ **Figures 2.14**

THE HYBRIDISATION OF SOCIAL AND LEARNING ACTIVITY

Space types are not only merging into hybrid typologies but there appears to be a trend towards larger spaces, utilising furniture to define boundaries/zones which has created a new spatial paradigm. Furniture can provide the 'setting' to define both space and use in a way which would not have been conceivable 20 years ago. It should not, however, be seen as a panacea – specialist furniture can be expensive and the more complex it is, the less flexible it becomes. Mobility and standardisation of components are key in maximising the adaptability of space.

▶ Figure 2.15

SPECIALIST

A The Centre of the Cell in the Blizzard Institute, London by Will Alsop. Specialist education facility.

B New Biochemistry Building, Oxford, by Hawkins\Brown. Combination of write-up desks in a large atrium with collaborative break out spaces.

C Manchester School of Art by Fielder Clegg Bradley Studios. Specialist art facilities in open plan studios shared across departments and used for crits and social events.

D Aga Khan University, Faculty of Health Sciences learning studio, Karachi spatial concept by 'Spaces that Work'. Specialist medical lab for dissection that alllows for personal and colllaborative learningseating and can be configured in a traditional auditorium and other tutor-centred teaching arrangements.

COLLABORATIVE

E The Learning Hub, Singapore by Heatherwick Studio. 56 class rooms for collaborative learning.

F Learning Hub, Coventry, by Hawkins\Brown. Open plan arrangement for personal and collaborative learning.

G Super lab, Metropolitan University London, by Pascall+Watson architects. Specialist facility that combines flexible personla and collaborative workplaces.

H Vennesla Library and Cultural Centre / Vennesla by Helen & Hard Architects. Library that combines personal group learning spaces, specialist workplaces together with an auditorium in one large organic mono space.

TEACHING

I The Rolex Learning Centre, Lausanne by SANAA. Auditorium in student centre.

J Connect lecture theatre seating by Burwell Deakins Architects. Lecture theatre with seating that allows for collaborative learning/group discussions.

K Node chair by Steelcase. Can be arranged for personal and collaborative learning situations as well as for tutor-centred teaching configurations.

L TU Delft, The Why factory by MVRDV. Large mono-space with auditorium, group and personal learning spaces, smaller classrooms under the auditorium and an area for model storage.

PERSONAL

M Humboldt University Library, Berlin by Max Dudler. Central reading room.

N Cornell Library of Fine Arts by Wolfgang Tschapeller. Library intermixed with personal learning spaces.

O James B Hunt Jr. Library by Snohetta, North Carolina State University. Large learning commons with specialist resources, an open plan auditorium and areas for personal and collaborative learning.

P Refurbishment of Pearl Library at Rhode Island School of Design by Monica Ponce de Leon. Existing specialsit library was equipped with 'colossal pieces of furniture' that allow for an auditorium, break out spaces, social learning spaces and personal learning pods.

SPECIALIST / Pod

A

COLLABORATIVE / Building

E

TEACHING / Circulation arts

I

PERSONAL / Library

M

B Central atrium

C Central double-height space

D Lab

F Learning commons

G open plan workspace

H Building

J Lecture theatre

K Any space

L Foyer

N Library

O Information commons

P Library

BREAKING BOUNDARIES

What is clear from recent experience is that there is a shift away from the traditional model of spaces and ownership (with spaces being owned by faculties or departments) towards a greater variety of more flexible shared spaces which respond to the increase in collaboration and peer-to-peer learning. This allows for departmental expansion and contraction, and provides increased opportunities for interaction and serendipity through shared use of space.

Success is not just governed by the types of space we provide but how we treat their interfaces – blurring the boundaries between uses through dispersed social learning creates activity across the campus.

PROVIDING VARIETY AND BALANCE OF SPACES

While pedagogy will continue to evolve, there will be a need for the types of space covered here. Research is becoming more specialised, so it is unlikely that we are looking at the death of the mono-dimensional space. We are likely to see the continuing rise of more open collaborative learning areas. Clustering differing space types together can provide flexibility without making every space multi-functional.

We should take care that the shift to collaborative spaces is balanced with smaller personal spaces – we all need somewhere to retreat to for more intensive/quiet work. Getting this balance right may take time as a collaborative culture develops. We should consider a Soft Landings programme for new innovative environments. This would allow us to 'fine-tune' spaces as users settle into their new environments and use them in ways we had not anticipated when we designed them – such as a change in configuration, additional furniture/equipment, etc.

Space standards are constantly under review and optimising utilisation rates should come not just from within the estate but looking more widely into community/industry to provide compatible opportunities to learn and share knowledge, training and experience.

We must also not forget the 'softer' aspects of this in terms of design quality, the creation of places which inspire and engage people, whether it be through building form, furniture or materials or more intangible aspects such as character, light and feel.

INNOVATION AND CHANGE

How far should we innovate? Should we go back to low-tech?

In terms of innovative learning space and new technologies can be problematic but if successful there are great benefits in being ahead of your peers. Encouraging research and testing into the design of learning spaces, gathering feedback from students and staff can foster ownership and engagement in a longer-term project. Greater collaboration through interactive learning requires compatible connectivity. Experience has taught us that building capacity into the infrastructure is where money should be focused. Mixing high- and low-tech approaches allows for a mix of working styles and appeals to a wider range of users, and can add a richness and texture.

FUTURE-PROOFING

We need to recognise that spaces are temporary; they will need to adapt and change over their lifetime. If we approach projects with a longer-term view, we can devise sustainable strategies which will safeguard the future. This need not be expensive or specialist, and in many ways concentrating on efficient layouts, plan depths, good lighting and ventilation strategies is the most effective approach for long-term planning. We can reasonably assume that the trend towards greater mobility in technology will continue. Complex and expensive multi-use partitioning, interactive systems and multi-functional spaces should be carefully considered during project planning because, on large-scale projects, technology and pedagogy may have already moved on by the time the buildings are handed over.

We should think holistically about space provision. Look for new and interesting opportunities; consider more conversions of existing structures. Many post-war buildings are very robust concrete-framed constructions with generous ceiling heights and convert very well to provide contemporary learning spaces.

New extensions can provide any highly specialist requirements. A more pragmatic approach may be to make some key strategic decisions at 'shell and servicing' level – such as providing generous well proportioned spaces, while allowing for future flexibility in 'scenery' and 'settings'; accepting that there is a long-term strategy and setting aside some funding for refresh.

▲ **Figure 2.16** *James Stewart Centre for Mathematics, McMaster University, KPMB Architects. Juxtaposition of the new and the traditional. Tactile blackboards provide opportunity to capture those 'lightbulb' moments*

IS THIS THE DEMISE OF THE PHYSICAL ESTATE?

The way we learn is constantly shifting due to changes in pedagogy and is shaped by the advancing technology which allows for learning to happen in many different environments, often remote from the institutions themselves. If taken to its logical conclusion, we could argue that the university estate could actually reduce in scale if Massive Open Online Courses (MOOC) take-up increases, as technology makes these virtual connections more viable. However, students choose universities on the basis of a wider 'life' experience, so while obviously the 'formal' curriculum – the teaching, learning and research on offer – is important, this may

well be gauged alongside other factors such as the environment in which it is delivered, and the personal contact and experiences which are important to our lives. The quality and variety of learning spaces could be the differentiating factor in student decision-making. It could set the university apart and demonstrate a value in the 'student life' experience at a time when attending university is a major investment. It is therefore more likely that the estate may be extend out of its traditional campus boundaries creating satellite hubs and links with community where students can be supported in their online learning, as outlined in Jonas Nordquist's networked learning landscape (page 153).

IMPACTS ON SPACE

The following sections look at a variety of spatial functions where spaces and their furniture and equipment arrangements are developing in response to the changing patterns of student life, learning and research described above.

Each space type is analysed to see where they are still required to deliver very particular specialist functional performance for research or teaching requirements, and where they are becoming more hybrid, encouraging overlapping uses and enabling potentially more collaborative work styles alongside the requirements for personal study.

TEACHING: FLAT ROOMS AND LECTURE THEATRES

There is a quiet revolution taking place in the design of teaching spaces to reflect changing pedagogies. The lead for this has come from Australia and the USA, with the adoption of these facilities growing in the UK.

IS THERE A FUTURE FOR THE LECTURE THEATRE?

Lecture theatres provide an efficient method for teaching, but the traditional raked lecture theatre with fixed rows of seats has its limitations for student engagement and may be replaced in part by digital means. Many traditional lecture theatres are inefficiently used through the calendar year owing to their rigid use, with university conference offices tasked to fill them with external bookings during quiet periods.

Lecture theatres are still being designed and built, with recent high-quality examples by BDP at Edinburgh Napier University Business School, the Investcorp Building at the University of Oxford and the Hong Kong Polytechnic University School of Design's Innovation Tower (both by Zaha Hadid).

However, given the unpredictability of the future, flexibility in provision of facilities is key. An obvious question for a new lecture theatre must be whether a permanent rake is essential or whether other flexible options can be provided. 21st century students demand seats with a worktop in front of them for their laptops and tablets. With retractable seating for all or part of the lecture theatre, combined with appropriate acoustics and lighting, a lecture space such as that being designed for King's College London at Bush House can be designed to be flexible for other uses, such as graduation, performance, music and drama.

The Collaborative Lecture Theatre, developed at Loughborough University and at Queen's University Belfast, enables both formal lectures and interactive group work. Other options include the semi-circular, horseshoe or elliptical lecture theatre, common in business schools, with a fixed work surface, a very shallow rake and moveable swivel chairs.

The technology demanded in lecture theatre continues to grow. Adequate wireless connectivity is crucial, as are electrical power sockets or recharging facilities. Mobile phone apps facilitate student/lecturer interaction; a lecture theatre of 400 students may easily have 800 devices connecting wirelessly.

Teaching walls have to be increasingly flexible. In subjects such as mathematics, there is a discussion about the use of blackboards rather than whiteboards, and today's lecturers may well wish to use three or four media during their session that need as much flexibility as possible.

Finally, why have large dedicated-space lecture theatres? For occasional large-scale events, there are examples of other large open flexible spaces being used, such as in the libraries at TU Delft and at WU in Vienna.

FLEXIBLE TEACHING SPACES

Flexibility is an essential part of future teaching room design, whether it is the ability to subdivide large rooms to smaller ones or to support TEAL or Advanced Learning Classrooms (ALCs) which allow a combination of teaching from a lectern in the centre of the room with interactive work around tables using different media. The Royal Melbourne Institute of Technology (RMIT), for example, has a range of such spaces of different sizes and shapes focused on different styles of learning.

▶ **Figure 2.17** *Edinburgh Napier University Business School, BDP*

▼ **Figures 2.18 and 2.19** *The Investcorp Building, St Antony's College, Oxford, Zaha Hadid*

▲▲ **Figures 2.20 and 2.21** *Hong Kong Polytechnic University School of Design's Innovation Tower, Zaha Hadid*

▼ **Figure 2.22** *The Collaborative Lecture Theatre, developed at Loughborough University and at Queen's University Belfast, Burwell Deakins*

▶◀ **Figures 2.23 and 2.24** *TU Delft Library, Delft, Netherlands. Architect: Mecanoo Architecten. South elevation with cone and turf roof. The library interior can be used for large gatherings and special events*

◀ **Figure 2.25**
Library, WU in Vienna,
Zaha Hadid

◀ **Figure 2.26**
UNSW Australia
Business School 'the
Place' by Woods
Bagot, University of
New South Wales,
Australia

◀ ▼ **Figures 2.27**
and 2.28 *'Flipped*
Classroom', UNSW,
Australia

The 'Flipped Classroom' at the University of New South Wales, Australia, offers students a space where teaching is by a facilitator rather than a lecturer, guiding group discussions or providing individual attention for students who are expected to have prepared for the sessions by watching podcasts and reviewing online background materials.

Outside scheduled class times, the space is available 24 hours a day for brainstorming, presentation rehearsals and group projects. The space is found to support improved academic results and improve the soft skills increasingly expected from graduates – negotiation and collaboration, idea generation, problem-solving, working under pressure, presentation skills, leadership and project management.

The ultimate technology-rich room is the Harvard Business School HBX Digital Deck in which the lecturer stands in the centre of a room of 60 screens, each used by a student in the programme who can all interact with each other. Expensive to build and maintain, it also relies on all the students having the same quality and speed of bandwidth at their home base.

learner-generated   teacher-guided

DEMONSTRATING AND APPLYING

TRYING AND TESTING

presentations

games
simulations

experiments

conferences

authentic
problems

eportfolios
(showcase)

creative
projects

**NOW
WHAT?**

EXPERIENCE

blogging

**SO
WHAT?**

WHAT

video
lectures

eportfolios
(reflective)

websites
and blogs

REFLECTING AND MEANING-MAKING

research
literature

social
media

wikis

podcasts
and videos

EXPLORING CONTENT AND CONCEPTS

learner-generated   teacher-guided

LEARNING:
LIBRARIES AND HUBS

In recent years, recognition of the significant benefits social interaction has on learning outcomes and student wellbeing combined with developments in IT has led to a major shift from individual-based learning to more dynamic and collaborative models.

Students now learn wherever they feel comfortable, both on and off campus. On campus, students expect the same level of quality and choice they find on the high street, which is leading to the provision of high-quality, comfortable, adaptable environments where they can access information, interact with one another and use a variety of supporting spaces, services and technologies. From large-scale 'learning commons' to small intimate corners for focused, quiet, personal study, there is an ever-increasing variety of these non-designated spaces appearing throughout campuses.

Often physically located at the heart of modern campuses, the library is generally now where research and technical support services are located and more social and student support services are often co-located. The on going migration from print to electronic collections will continue to release spaces currently occupied with book stacks for use for individual study and social learning. Libraries are likely to remain an important focus for learning and student interaction at the heart of many universities.

At the University of Kent's Canterbury campus, the central Templeman Library is being extended and remodelled to include large-scale teaching areas, extensive social learning spaces and a café off a major new student concourse.

Social learning spaces are now one of the primary attractions for students when choosing a university. Universities with multiple campuses, predominantly found in larger cities, are more likely to follow an ever more decentralised model in the future, where a network of 'learning commons' is spread throughout the built estate supported by strong online support rather than one central library.

EXAMPLE

TEMPLEMAN LIBRARY EXTENSION & REFURBISHMENT
UNIVERSITY OF KENT.
PENOYRE & PRASAD

The new extension to the Templeman Library provides a wide range of high-quality spaces for collaborative and individual learning. Extensive research, using methods including time-lapse photography, full-scale prototyping and interactive workshops, explored how students study in different settings and informed the interior design and furniture selection.

▶ ▼ ▲ Figures 2.29, 2.30 and 2.31

VIRTUAL LEARNING HUBS?

The development of the Open University in the UK and, more recently, the rapid rise of MOOCs have been heralded as a revolution that would move higher education from bricks to clicks. Neither has yet posed a significant threat to 'physical' universities. MOOCs might have opened academic content to a wider audience but do not fundamentally challenge the traditional campus as a place. One of the key problems that plague them is the very low rate of participants actually completing the course.

The explanation is obvious and simple: learning is not only a formalised cognitive process but a holistic social experience where the face-to-face contact with tutors and fellow students is indispensable. Contemporary educational methods emphasise collaboration and interactive learning which fundamentally relies on face-to-face interaction. Digital media may support but cannot replace this experience. The role of proximity is central to the contemporary theory of successful knowledge work. Due to demand from students to have places to physically meet and study together,

online university providers are now creating learning centres.

The outcome of this demand could produce a new physical typology: this could create a new higher education space where interested students meet and discuss their online course experience but potentially without one single HE umbrella institution: similar to co-working spaces, these Virtual Learning Hubs could be small in size, simply equipped and run by the learning community itself. This would fit into contemporary educational concepts where self-directed learning in a collaborative environment is of central importance.

◄ **Figure 2.32** *Dublin Institute of Technology's masterplan for its major new Grangegorman Campus development positions a large new library at its heart.*

▼ **Figure 2.34**
Percentage of students completing university courses in the UK.

▲ **Figure 2.33**
Medical Education Building, Columbia University, New York, Diller Scoficio and Renfro. The building is conceived of as a 'vertical campus' with all the social learning and public spaces fully on display, forming a dynamic and expressive 'study cascade' over many floors.

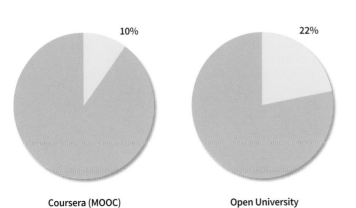

University courses completed in the UK (%) (source Simpson 2010)

10%

22%

88%

Coursera (MOOC)

Open University

UK Average

STUDENT CENTRES

Recent years have seen a merging of the traditional Student Union with recreation centres to create new student centres – dynamic places with a wide range of facilities catering more closely to contemporary lifestyles and technology demands.

These new centres also have appropriate retail and health facilities adjacent and may provide a 'one-stop shop' for student advice and access to careers services. These centres may then link to, or incorporate, other specialist facilities such as libraries (discussed in the previous section, within the student centre. It is broadly recognised by universities that this new breed of student centre plays a significant role in the recruitment and retention of students.

Looking at the trends, recent examples show a considerable overlap between activities, with flowing, flexible, creative spaces in a variety of forms from bars to cafés to restaurants, including support for outside events and conference activities. Amenities and programmes often overlap with academic, sports and recreational facilities. The Saw Swee Hock Building at the London School of Economics, completed in 2014 by O'Donnell + Tuomey, is a good example of a new form of student centre, housing an events space, nightclub, pub, learning café/restaurant, gym, multi-faith prayer space, advice centre, careers service, large meeting space and rooftop café and terrace (see case study in Part 4, (see pages 162-167).

The Hub at Coventry University provides a dynamic new heart to the student campus and includes large-scale 'learning commons' and social spaces alongside student support spaces.

In the USA, this coming together of wide-ranging activities has led to some very large and complex buildings with major facilities and spaces co-located. In the UK, this form of co-location can present problems due to different funding regimes and the historical division between the university and the Students Union. However, there are examples where this has been achieved. The John Henry Brookes Building by

▲ **Figure 2.37** *New School Student Centre, New York, SOM architects*

Design Engine Architects at Oxford Brookes University incorporates student services, the Students Union, teaching spaces and a new library all gathered around the forum, a vast social learning area surrounded by cafés and retail outlets.

Minimisation of dedicated space and greater innovation in flexible design solutions is facilitating the use of spaces for multiple functions, e.g.

while food or drink serveries always have to be dedicated spaces, these can be closed off from the adjacent spaces for those to be transformed into activity spaces. In addition, buildings that in the past would not have provided space for student activities are now being designed to be able to do this in addition to other uses. Recent buildings, such as the MMU Business School and the

Mathematical Institute by Rafael Viñoly Architects at the University of Oxford minimise the amount of dedicated space and enable areas to flow and connect into other spaces, with moveable furniture, facilitating a wide range of other activities to take place, such as student clubs and society events.

RESEARCH AND LABORATORIES

The ways in which universities provide space for research is evolving.

Laboratory buildings are expensive assets that are often made redundant by rapid changes in research techniques, funding or priorities. Each institution has a different response to these challenges but some common themes are emerging. In this section three of these main themes are explored:

1. The shift from wet to dry research.
2. The increasing emphasis on collaborative research environments.
3. The need for laboratory buildings to be flexible.

THE SHIFT FROM WET TO DRY RESEARCH

Traditional 'wet' laboratory work is being replaced with bio-informatics and computational research in 'dry' laboratories. This provides an opportunity to review how buildings are designed for research, and both reduce the cost of buildings and produce buildings that are better suited to flexible collaborative and interactive working. 'Dry' laboratories are less space-hungry and cheaper to provide than traditional 'wet' research space.

Given the changes in research towards more computational work, with less use of traditional laboratories, many universities are looking for 'wet' labs with improved utilisation and the ability for researchers to use wet and dry labs flexibly, as and when it suits their research.

'Hot-benching' allows researchers to make use of a bench space as and when they need it. This only works when laboratory management policies are in place to support hot-desking and when specialist equipment can be shared. This is common practice in industry but more unusual in academia.

Encouraging as many secondary activities as possible to be located within a shared 'core' facility reduces the overall need for laboratory space. This requires a change in culture for many academic users. They are used to the idea of bidding for equipment on the back of research grants, etc., and not making use of specialist equipment (and the space it takes up) as shared/centralised facilities.

COLLABORATIVE RESEARCH ENVIRONMENTS

Traditional laboratory buildings do not typically generate a particularly collaborative working environment. They contain many divided spaces, research groups often work behind closed doors, and the ability to meet colleagues or to share facilities is very limited.

Modern research benefits from a collaborative environment with new avenues and explorations being born out of the ability for researchers to meet, collaborate and work together – formally or through serendipitous encounters.

Buildings should be organised to facilitate this with a generosity to circulation spaces and a focus on social spaces as the heart of successful research facilities.

Traditionally dry research or 'write-up' work was carried out in a quiet, separate area, which was space-hungry and inflexible. There is still some need for this type of space in academic institutions where this culture is ingrained. However, not everyone expects a desk to work from: some work at home, some prefer to work in a canteen or at a shared informal break-out space.

The relationship between different types of space is also critical. By removing the traditional relationship between wet lab and write-up, opportunities for interaction and efficiencies are generated through the management of researchers around a building.

EXAMPLE
MAX PLANCK INSTITUTE FOR BIOLOGY OF AGEING COLOGNE, HAMMESKRAUSE ARCHITEKTEN

The layout and organisation of the building fundamentally enables a collaborative research environment (demonstrated on the upper floor plan). Offices and specialist labs – the more quiet and sensitive space types – are located around the perimeter of the building. Laboratory clusters sit inward, creating a quiet corridor relationship with the perimeter offices but are open to guests and other building users within the central atrium space, which comprises transparent meeting rooms. The extensive use of glass maximises visibility between laboratories, offices and public activities within the atrium, fostering cross-collaboration between departments and further allows for science to be the showcase of the building. Bridges within the atrium allow for horizontal circulation between individual lab clusters, connecting the varying research departments.

▶ ▲ ▲ **Figures 2.38, 2.39 and 2.40**
Max Planck Institute for Biology of Ageing, Cologne, Hammeskrause Architekten

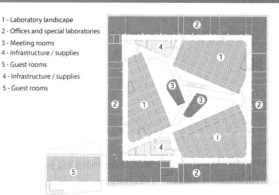

1 - Laboratory landscape
2 - Offices and special laboratories
3 - Meeting rooms
4 - Infrastructure / supplies
5 - Guest rooms
4 - Infrastructure / supplies
5 - Guest rooms

UNIVERSITY OF EXETER
LIVING SYSTEMS INSTITUTE HAWKINS\BROWN

At the Living Systems building at the University of Exeter all wet laboratories have been stacked to minimise horizontal services distribution and simplify the services strategy. The open lab clusters have been designed to enable all of the benching to be removed wholly, or in part, providing flexibility for the placement of equipment and workspaces. Services are zoned to reduce downtime when labs are reconfigured; central aisles are serviced from overhead. To improve space and operational efficiency, equipment trolleys are used to allow rapid changes in use and user. Overhead services, not fixed to the benching, are used to allow rapid adaptation of the lab to accommodate workspace and equipment configurations.

▼ Figures 2.41 and 2.42

FLEXIBILITY IN
LABORATORY BUILDINGS

The nature of scientific research is constantly changing and evolving. New methods, equipment and technologies require different spatial and servicing configurations. New groups will join a research community and bring with them new demands on space. Flexibility in laboratory buildings should be thought of across many different scales, from the basic building location through to the detailed design of furniture, fixtures and equipment (FFE) and controls.

GETTING THE BASICS RIGHT

Campuses need to be planned through a strategic masterplan that considers adjacencies, site-wide infrastructure, deliveries, public realm, community links and building entrances.

PLANNING TO A GRID

Planning laboratory buildings to a well-tested grid will help ensure that they can be re-planned in the future.

STRUCTURE AND SERVICES

Careful resolution of the structure, servicing strategy and the building's infrastructure is critical to allowing for easy re-planning of spaces. Floor-to-floor heights should be designed to accommodate intensive servicing requirements and improved access. Floor loadings should be designed to allow for a degree of future flexibility. Cores are ideally best located to one side of the building to maximise usable floor plates.

MECHANICAL AND ELECTRICAL SERVICES (M&E)

The locations and flexibility of primary plant can have a major impact on flexibility. It is important that there is sufficient grid capacity, space and control flexibility in the plant areas to allow for minor changes in the use of the building, and that consideration has been given to how the plant would be adapted or replaced in the event of a more significant change in the building's location.

FURNITURE, FIXTURES AND EQUIPMENT (FFE)

Research buildings require extensive FFE. The design of this element has a big impact on their ability to be re-organised. The use of mobile laboratory furniture can help research spaces be more flexible on a day-to-day basis.

TESTING AND INTERROGATION

The process of testing assumptions and layouts through the design stages and continually reviewing the impact of emerging technologies is critical in ensuring a building's future flexibility.

EXAMPLE
PHYSICS DEPARTMENT
UNIVERSITY OF OXFORD,
HAWKINS\BROWN

DESIGN OF COLLABORATION SPACES
The design of interaction and collaboration space requires careful consideration. These spaces are harder to get right, because how they are used is less predictable and they are spaces that are new and untested for a department. At the new Experimental and Theoretical Physics Building, a number of typologies were developed to describe collaboration spaces. For each space we considered numbers, activity, the time people would spend in the space, location in relation to circulation routes, the anticipated nature of the collaborative working, etc. These spaces have become the focus for the department and are fundamental to its success in forming new research threads.

▲ Figures 2.43 and 2.44

CREATIVE DESIGN STUDIOS

Studio workshops are typically space-hungry and often very specialised, defined by the equipment they require to support creative activities. This in turn dictates the spatial, environmental and safety requirements, making them potentially inflexible. Heavy workshops are often found tucked away in basements due to noise and scale of equipment. With emerging technologies, such as 3D printing, there is an opportunity for some of these to be located more prominently, to act as a shop window and provide inspiration and insight into the creative processes undertaken within.

FOSTERING A CREATIVE CULTURE

Studios should foster inspiration, creation and exploration of ideas, debate and exhibition. A good studio culture is important to stimulate debate and critical thinking. Allowing students to express their ideas and to 'own' their space is important. However, studio space is at a premium with student numbers increasing and courses competing for limited resources, so justifying providing students with dedicated studio space is going to be an increasing challenge.

We need to re-think how we provide these spaces so that we create an open studio culture where spaces can be appropriated and shared by students without losing the benefits. The challenge is to support studio identity without creating 'silos', which can make studios insular.

Allowing a suitable framework or 'scenery' for the students and tutors to make the space their own but not so bespoke as to make it unique is the key factor. This openness and cross-fertilisation of ideas better reflects the collaborative working practices within the creative industries.

Robust finishes are important, as they allow for change and minimise maintenance but also reinforce the idea that these spaces are experimental and help promote the creative and often messy work as students explore materiality and form.

An open-plan 6m x 6m grid with break-out spaces on each floor allows for each unit to reconfigure layouts according to their diverse range of needs.

▲ Figure 2.45

◀ **Figures 2.46 and 2.47** *Existing spaces*

▼ **Figure 2.48** *Image created from a 3D scan of the space at the Bartlett School of Architecture UCL.*

EXAMPLE
BARTLETT SCHOOL
OF ARCHITECTURE UCL

A strong unit-based culture is being given a new home; one which aims to foster dialogue between units. The original 1960s cellular building, is characterised by long corridors, is being extensively remodelled and extended.

▲ **Figure 2.49** *The ideas for the new studios have been tested in the temporary fit-out for its decant space in a large warehouse on Hampstead Road, allowing experimentation in terms of subdivision, storage servicing and space*

▼ **Figures 2.50 A and B** *The result of this process has informed the approach to furniture and transparency. Studios are open to the circulation space; staff are interspersed throughout the studios. As the floor plan and image (below) illustrate, social spacesocial spaces double as exhibition areas; engagement is encouraged by hosting crits adjacent to breakout areas*

SHARED RESOURCES

Multi-use of space and zoning of activities based on public, privileged or private uses can allow many activities to co-exist with higher utilisation, but this also requires greater management.

If we can stop thinking of spaces as being departmental, free of any territorial restrictions, this can provide huge opportunities for shared resources. This needs to evolve out of agreement of how spaces will be managed. Co-location of resources with other specialist disciplines can bring benefits in terms of shared use of spaces/equipment and this can in turn encourage exploration of new materials/ techniques and dialogue and skills shared between different disciplines.

EXAMPLE
LARGE PERMEABLE OPEN STUDIOS AND SHARED WORKSHOPS

University of the Arts London, Stanton Williams workshops (see right) are not department based and students are encouraged to explore new materials. Time slots are negotiated with primary users gaining priority access. Open studios help foster collaboration both between students and disciplines.

▶ Figure 2.51

▼ **Figure 2.52** *Manchester School of Art, Feilden Clegg Bradley Studios*

▼ **Figure 2.53** *School of Architecture Cornell, OMA*

TECHNOLOGY

Portable technology has already freed up restrictive layouts for vast areas of fixed CAD workstations. Increasing use of WiFi allows for use of standard tables/benching which can be more easily reconfigured. Clusters of more specialist facilities can be dispersed and shared/bookable.

ARTS COLLABORATION

Universities are linking up with other institutions/providers to foster closer relationships with the arts. This can have a mutual benefit: allowing students to experience working in high-quality professional environments, while at the same time providing commercial funding to support their facilities.

EXAMPLE

CREATING INNOVATIVE SPACES

The Hasso Plattner Institute of Design at Stanford or 'd.school' ran a five-year experiment in their design studios, which investigated how space can support the creative process. They designed, prototyped and tested ways of creating space and furniture, and analysed how these influenced the way in which students work. Their findings have been published in a book *Make Space*, which has useful insights, tools and templates to help others adopt similar strategies for designing spaces to foster collaborative work and develop their own culture and identity.

EXAMPLE

SCHOOL OF ARCHITECTURE, UNIVERSITY OF GREENWICH HENEGHAN PENG

The crit space forms the heart of the School of Architecture. It is adjacent to the central circulation spine and overlooked from many points inside and outside the building, thus encouraging passers-by to join the crit sessions.

▼ Figure 2.54

▼ Figure 2.55

UNIVERSITY OF PORTSMOUTH COLLABORATION WITH THE NEW THEATRE ROYAL
PENOYRE & PRASAD

The University of Portsmouth and the New Theatre Royal joined forces to create a new cultural and creative hub in the city centre for interdisciplinary and creative exchange between the two institutions and the community. On land adjacent to the Grade II Listed New Theatre Royal, a new extension houses a state-of-the-art flytower, back of house facilities for the theatre, highly specialised drama and music teaching facilities and TV studios. Both institutions share a new entrance and foyer, opening onto a 100-seat performance space in the heart of the scheme, where the new and old buildings connect.

◀ Figures 2.56 and 2.57

▲ **Figure 2.58** *University of Westminster has recently reopened its historic Theatre; venue of the Lumiere brothers first public showing of moving pictures in Britain refurbished by Tim Ronalds Architects*

The University of Westminster recently re-opened their historic cinema which had long been converted into a standard lecture theatre. Now a fully functioning cinema supporting all film media, it allows film students to present their work in a full cinema but it is also open to the public with screenings aimed at the independent film audience.

In London, much of the current growth in the creative and cultural industries is centred around the redevelopment of the Olympic Park at Stratford. UCL and Loughborough University are both creating London Campuses, focusing on the digital and creative industries. Like many others, they are attracted by the legacy of London 2012, which brought huge data connectivity to a historically underutilised part of East London, and the vision for the future to create a unique place for creating and making and allowing ideas to blossom and businesses to grow; fostering creative talent and creating jobs for the community. Opportunities are further strengthened by the new UCL East Campus, and the Olymicopolis development, which brings together Departments of the University of the Arts London alongside new outposts of the V&A museum and Sadlers Wells.

INNOVATION AND INCUBATOR SERVICES

There are no general definitions for an 'incubator' and an 'innovation centre'. However, it can generally be said that while an innovation centre describes a building typology, an incubator can be defined as a programmed space that forms part of a larger architectural complex.

An incubator space is usually managed by a particular organisation with the aim to provide opportunities for start-ups to develop innovative ideas into commercially successful products.

An innovation centre typically describes a larger architectural complex which houses companies that have passed the start-up stage and show further growth potential; in fact, innovation centres usually incorporate incubation spaces. Incubators and innovation centres are often run by private companies or by government agencies. In conjunction with universities, innovation centres and incubator spaces serve as a platform to commercialise academic research, often in collaboration with private companies. While innovation centres can comprise very expensive specialist facilities, an incubator often is a simple space that provides economic shelter for young graduates to take the first commercial steps outside the academic realm.

INNOVATION CENTRES

As different as these two architectural tasks appear, the overarching principle is the assumption that innovation needs a specific place that fosters collaboration between universities, the government and private economy; but first and foremost between groups of inspired like-minded people. The innovation centres in Obidos, Portugal, and at the Universidad Católica de Chile have defined an external appearance that is strong enough to create identity but abstract enough to not appear as a pretentious corporate headquarters. Internal layouts emphasise the collaborative spaces as the key element of the innovation centre.

At Here East, in London (see page 61), it is the activities within the building which are exposed to the public rather than an iconographic form. Innovation centres are a relative young typology and it will be interesting to see how these architectural concepts evolve. The unconventional approach of Here East with both its broad mix of uses, and its "living façade" shows true potential to push the boundaries of this new typology.

EXAMPLE
THE INNOVATION CENTRE
OBIDOS, PORTUGAL, JORGE MEALHA

The building consists of an elevated quad with flexible office space above a large public plaza where tenants can meet, and which is surrounded by facilities that include workshops, a restaurant, meeting rooms and other communal spaces. The project uses a strong abstract language to frame a space for innovative collaboration.

► ▼ Figures 2.59 and 2.60

UNIVERSIDAD CATÓLICA DE CHILE ALEJANDRO ARAVENA

A similar approach is followed in Chile by Alejandro Aravena, who designed a monumental sculptural innovation centre for the university. While the exposed concrete establishes a strong geometrical presence to the outside, the inside consists of a loose arrangement of open spaces around an atrium and is characterised by the soft materiality of dark wood.

◄ ▲ Figures 2.61 and 2.62

EXAMPLE
HERE EAST LONDON,
HAWKINS\BROWN

This large innovation centre (1,150 000 sq ft) in East London reuses the former press and broadcasting centre of the Olympic Games for a large agglomeration of companies and universities that include state-of-the-art facilities for the UCL robotics institute, the London campus of Loughborough University, BT Sport and a wide community of co-working spaces. Instead of using architectural form to create visual identity, Here East turns inside-out and populates its edge, its 'soft crust', with artisan shops, maker workshops and – most prominently – studios for artists, designers and craftspeople on an existing gantry formerly used for

technical equipment. The main interaction space is a large yard and a 950-seat auditorium, both aimed at providing a communal space to foster and boost collaboration. Everything is designed to interlink, internally and externally.

▲ ▼ Figures 2.63 and 2.64

INCUBATOR SPACES

The importance of nurturing young creative start-ups by providing infrastructure and advice finds its expression in a multitude of incubation programmes provided by a mix of private and public companies and institutions. Universities play an important role here. Almost 25% of London incubators are financed by universities to provide a test bed for innovative ideas and to turn knowledge into commercial success by cooperating with the private industry. Incubators build up reputation via the number of successful spin-offs and compete on global indices such as the UBI (University Business Incubator) index.

While technically speaking incubators are different from co-working spaces, they share the same design principles. The latter often incorporate mentoring elements but generally are serviced office providers that generate most of their money from rents, while incubators tend to be financed by external institutions. Common to all incubators are the following characteristics:

1. It is a privileged space: start-ups have to apply to be part of an incubation programme. Expert committees decide on whether or not a particular start-up fits into their programme and has commercial potential.
2. It is a temporary space: often incubation programmes provide space only for a limited amount of time before start-ups either move on to larger premises or – in case of failure – give up.
3. It is a managed space: universities organise events, try to foster internal and external collaboration and give strategic and operational advice. Incubators often have mentoring programmes that are supported by a wide range of public and private organisations.
4. It is an economically sheltered space with low rents and seed funding programmes.
5. It is a shared space without ostentatiously expressed territory.
6. It is a flexible space that can easily be adapted to individual needs and the dynamics of the single start-ups.
7. It is a serviced space: start-ups are provided with all necessary infrastructures and resources, either free or at very low costs.
8. It is a collaborative space where like-minded people work along, with and inspired by each other.

Point 8 describes the central concept: an incubator space is about meeting people, collaboration and mutual advice. Community is at the heart of each incubator space. In this sense, the 'social design' is as important as the spatial arrangement.

Incubators are by definition permissive places. Their biggest asset is being a platform for informal open communication. An incubator space therefore needs a clear strategy where members can casually meet and discuss without having to interrupt other members at their desks. Meeting provisions, lounges and coffee machines/kitchens etc., serve this function but will need careful consideration to locate them strategically.

Incubators are dense, intense spaces with bustling collaborative activities. Several studies show that for effective 'knowledge spillover' people need to work in close proximity so that random exchanges of information can lead to successful cooperation. Desks can be arranged in dense, spatially efficient grids.

Due to its specific programme, every incubator will be different. However, as teams will only stay a limited amount of time, the space needs to be as flexible as possible, ideally open plan without many partitions and as much visual integrity as possible.

Naturally, this shifts the design focuses towards flexible partitions and furniture. The key design task of an incubator space is to select and arrange the right furniture. Desks may need to provide the ability to lock away a laptop or other personal belongings.

Incubators need to provide an abundance of visualisation opportunities in the form of white boards, displays, large screens, projectors, pin boards, etc., which should be as flexible as possible. This allows teams to collaborate better and provides the opportunity for spontaneous discussions.

Incubators need to create a strong identity; as imaginative places, which have an individual formal language. Co-working spaces are often designed in a collage of diverse styles carrying a clear message: 'I am not a commercial office, I am different' without emulating large corporate changes in workplace design.

EXAMPLE
INCUBATOR SPACES

A good example for collaborative furniture is the leaf desk designed by Studio TILT. It is flexible, nurtures good communication and allows high seating densities.

▲ Figures 2.65 and 2.66

EXAMPLE
CHA:COL

This 'kennel' was commissioned by K9 Ventures, a specialist for venture capital focused on emerging tech firms. The brief was to design a space on a very tight budget that visualises the very concept of an incubator space: intense collaboration on a limited time scale. CHA:COL designed a 'furniture kit' which exactly fits into one shipping container. The space needed to be inspiring for tenants but it also needed to feel transient. 'The space was required to be bare bones in order to encourage incubated graduates to leave. Nobody should feel comfortable enough to stay for long.'

▲ Figures 2.67 and 2.68

EXAMPLE
HUB WESTMINSTER

Hub Westminster was designed, set up and managed by Architecture 00, who saw this as an opportunity to demonstrate its ability to design a collaborative space and to conceptualise its daily practice. The large open space is structured with mobile furniture and miniature 'houses' for meetings. It can be arranged for daily co-working activities and all forms of events. The purpose-designed desks have chamfered edges to facilitate cooperation and allow for high-density seating. The Hub accepts only social enterprises as members and is part of a worldwide Impact Hub network. The experience shows that – as most members work in similar areas – the density can be much higher than in any commercial office without social conflicts; the likelihood of unforeseen synergies is quite high.

▲ Figures 2.69 and 2.70

INCUBATOR FURNITURE

UCL Advances and Camden Town Unlimited commissioned Hawkins\Brown to design a 'business incubator'. Due to the restricted budget and the brief that required maximum flexibility and openness, the design stripped the project space to the bone and focused on the design of bespoke desks that are lockable and space efficient. Larger 'furniture', in the form of wooden pods, allow for more privacy.

▲ Figures 2.71 and 2.72

ARCHITECTURE 00/OPENDESK

An example of workspace furniture designed and available through the Opendesk platform using digital fabrication technology, where furniture designs are available to be downloaded as digital files and made locally – on demand anywhere in the world.

▲ Figure 2.73

STUDIO TILT

Studio TILT focus its designs of co-working spaces and incubators on simple furniture that either give structure to the space or serve a particular purpose, i.e. take over the function of a separate room.

▼ Figures 2.74 and 2.75

▼ **Figure 2.76** *Studio TILT, club at The Leathermarket, London Bridge*

EXAMPLE
SECOND HOME

The co-working/incubator space, Second Home, aims to push the limits of what can be achieved with a mid-range budget. Designed by SelgasCano, the reused warehouse space in London's East End uses acrylic sheets as an economic means of maximising transparency and design identity – especially in the café space, which curves out onto the street, creating a strong presence to the outside and inside. The layout is very dense but is not too claustrophobic because of the transparency between spaces. The co-working space also features extensive use of greenery in the form of hydroponically cultivated plants and a central event space with a table that can be retracted into the ceiling.

◀ ▲ Figures 2.77, 2.78 and 2.79

ACADEMIC WORKPLACES

Academic workplace design has not substantially changed within the last 100 years. The single office space with a desk, shelves and a small meeting table still dominates the academic workplace culture as a spatial typology and – quite importantly – a social model. It provides room for privacy and research focus, which is traditionally valued high in the academic world. As a consequence, academic staff tend to resist open-plan office arrangements or any other form of layout that deviates from cellular office space.

Academic workplace design offers a huge potential for space efficiency. Up to 28% of a university's area is taken up by office space. A study at Loughborough University came to the conclusion that the academic staff spend only 30–40% of their time in the office. The meeting provisions within the cellular offices – set up for mentoring students – are even less used and, due to the rising numbers of students, not large enough, so additional meeting facilities have to be provided to accommodate bigger groups.

When Delft University of Technology (TU Delft) had to move to a smaller building, a 15% reduction of academic workspace provision was achieved by open-plan arrangements and hot-desking. This was combined with a post occupancy evaluation (POE) of the usage which then led to further optimisation. An interesting feature of the refurbishment of TU Delft was the concept that students and academic staff would share the same workspace.

Along with space efficiency, enhancing collaboration and communication culture is the other key driver for a trend towards open-plan workplaces. While academic workspace seems to be frozen in time, commercial office design has already undergone a radical change towards more collaborative environments. The same applies to teaching and learning facilities. Students are expected to collaborate, and open-plan 'learning commons' have become part of the learning and teaching DNA. The situation at a university is a paradox: while students embrace new collaborative ways of working and learning outside of traditional spatial typologies, their tutors work and research in a traditional office environment. The space allocation per

▲ **Figure 2.80** *Academic space, TU Delft*

student in the UK has been decreasing constantly over the past decade, while the space provision for academic staff has not changed very much.

It is, however, too simple to dismiss resistance against open-plan academic workspace as conservative and transfer a model derived from commercial office design and student culture into academia. It needs to be stated that beyond all trends three points are fundamental to the academic workplace:

1. The need to focus without external distraction.
2. The need to store and easily access resources such as books, files, etc.
3. The need for private meeting space between tutors and students.

Any design that does not address the above is likely to fail. Unfortunately, these requirements form part of a complicated amalgam of social status, office design and territorial thinking which is difficult to disentangle.

It is not helpful that the debate about academic workspace orbits around the issue of whether or not open-plan is an appropriate approach.

In most industry sectors the design approach has long since moved beyond the binary argument for or against open-plan environments. In the activity-based scenario, model employees can choose spatial settings for different types of work. The gain of space efficiency can be reinvested into generous arrangements for meeting rooms and break-out spaces.

EXAMPLE
RESEARCH CLUB PILOT
LOUGHBOROUGH UNIVERSITY

Loughborough University undertook a pilot of a 'club' for mainly PhD researchers and junior academics. A former divided-up part of the Freeman Centre was converted into an open-plan space that offered a differentiated set of workplaces, including cubicles for concentrated work or phone calls. The result was positive and most of the participants liked the atmosphere and communicative culture. Interestingly, the cubicles were hardly used and the more senior participants preferred to carry out concentrated work at home. One of the key lessons learned from the club was that the researchers valued the improved quality of space; if open-plan design is well designed and offers good space, it is easier for researchers to accept the loss of privacy.

▲ **Figure 2.81** *Research Club Pilot at Loughborough University*

HARROW CAMPUS
UNIVERSITY OF WESTMINSTER

The University of Westminster commissioned Hawkins\Brown to refurbish the ground floor of an existing block at the Harrow Campus (Faculty of Media, Art and Design) to house a new workspace for the Faculty Hub, comprising the Dean, heads of departments and student registry. The existing space comprised outmoded cellular offices for individuals and groups. The challenge was to provide a series of different space typologies within one open-plan office: workspace for management that required a more secluded work zone, hot-desking provision, formal and informal meeting space and break-out space. Differing levels of privacy were therefore required.

Specially designed joinery items were used to provide extensive storage, divide the space and provide enclosure to create open, shared and more secluded areas.

The push for a more open-plan way of working was driven by the appointment of a new Dean of School. Although there was some resistance among staff about moving away from cellular offices, most recognised that the increased flexibility, transparency and allowance for future growth within a new high-quality space was a marked improvement to their workplace.

▲ **Figures 2.82 and 2.83** *Faculty Hub, University of Westminster - Hawkins\Brown*

KING'S COLLEGE LONDON

Consultation with staff and students is key to development of all the facilities at King's College London, but particularly important for academic workspaces. Following a period of consultation and development, an Academic Hub pilot project was constructed in line with the following spatial principles:

- to provide an academic home for 30–50 occupants: academic and administration staff, post-graduate research students and visiting collaborators involved in teaching, research and enterprise activities
- to ensure a good mix of individual and collaborative settings: offering choice and variety to support a wide variety of work styles
- to maintain a balance between open and enclosed space: catering for both solo and group activities
- to accommodate both live-in and drop-in users: where low-mobility suggests more live-in and high-mobility suggests more drop-in.

The pilot project was occupied and tested by selected departments for a number of weeks and, while the scope of the project was limited, it provided key findings which were fed into the future fit-out of buildings recently acquired by the University.

Academic workspace will remain a contested subject within the changing higher education landscape. There is no solution that fits all and it is not possible to transfer models from commercial office design 1:1 to the academic world. More than any other field, academic workplace change starts with a socio-cultural self-reflection exercise. It often needs an event (e.g. a fire at TU Delft) that 'initiates' the discussion. In reality, change – and especially large-scale change – defies logical rules and simple management actions.[9]

EXAMPLE
LOUGHBOROUGH UNIVERSITY'S SIR FRANK GIBB BUILDING
AUKETT SWANKE

The need for privacy in an academic workspace will stay an issue no matter how interestingly and smart open-plan layouts are designed. In this case, hybrid layouts might be a solution that yields good results. Here, each academic has their own small study, located off a shared open space that includes an array of break-out areas and additional storage, as well as a kitchen and a printer hub. In addition, there are a number of bookable meeting rooms. The occupants carry out most of their office-based activities in the studies, with the communal areas being mostly used for informal meetings. Staff report a high level of satisfaction with their new environment, and the support it offers for conducting individual concentrated work, as well as fostering interaction.

◀ ▲ Figure 2.84 A, B and C

STUDENT HOUSING

STUDENT 'HOTELS'

Student housing back in the 1950s was mostly well designed, with good social facilities to support the academic community. However, as student housing became self-financing, low rents became the priority and the quality dropped, with basic student study-bedrooms and large soulless developments becoming the norm.

Thankfully, the pendulum has swung back again in the last decade and high-quality, well-designed residences at a competitive rent are now considered essential for the recruitment of students, particularly from overseas.

While universities still fund some schemes, there has also been substantial involvement by private sector companies who, in seeking to differentiate their provision, have introduced new facilities akin to those found in hotels and contemporary interior designs, which has now percolated across the sector and raised student aspirations.

This also allows the university to compete in the tourist and conference markets, attracting business for undergraduate rooms during vacations to bring in extra income.

In addition, with the cost pressures for staff in seeking accommodation in major cities, many universities are providing residential accommodation in order to recruit new staff on a global basis, as well as for visiting academics, often in joint schemes with student residences.

PERSONALISED SPACES

The study-bedroom is designed as a private but carefully planned room with a combination space, standardised and built-in furniture and en-suite bathroom. The size of the bedroom varies: those in the USA tend to be larger than the UK, while in Hong Kong and China they are minimal with more space given to the shared social area.

In the UK, en-suite room sizes are typically between 11 and 13 sqm; however, some recent schemes, such as the Christina Miller Hall at Herriot Watt University, Edinburgh have seen the room sizes increase to 15 sqm, which enables the inclusion of a three-quarter double bed.

Accessible rooms may be used as double bedrooms when not needed for disabled students. Modularisation of bathrooms is very common and wet rooms offer the most efficient use of space and improved maintenance. Often, storerooms will be provided for luggage or other items not needed in the study-bedroom, in order to maximise study space.

Furnishings will vary between providers; many schemes now provide digital screens on the wall with TV services, particularly those which have conference lettings in vacations. Wireless internet and plentiful power provision is critical. Good quality environments do not necessarily have to be more expensive; and indeed, finishes can be robust, softened and personalised by furniture and colour.

COMMUNITY

The student experience is much more than just academic study; meeting new friends and developing new interests are all factors in housing selection. Ensuring that bedrooms are comfortable, well finished and provide a good environment for study is not only critical, it is now expected. These spaces also need to be connected to a wider community that provides support and security for the students.

Outside of the study-bedrooms, shared social spaces allow for meeting new friends, socialising, learning and sharing experiences. Canteens/cafés and lounge areas provide places for students to socialise. Students need to feel they are part of the university but not defined by it; so providing outdoor landscaped spaces, which support the

development of a community, creating a style and identity to reflect that this is a contemporary home rather than an institution, and providing a mix of accommodation types, can allow students greater flexibility to dip in and out of campus activities. Some universities in the USA even have pet-friendly rooms.

Housing types varies, depending upon location and catering provision. City centre schemes may be less complex as they have connections to the city's services. More peripheral schemes will include communal social facilities – perhaps a lounge, bar, coffee or dining area and shop – but may also include study areas, project rooms, computer facilities, gym and music practice rooms.

The university may co-locate other facilities, such as community

outreach, a health centre and dentist or student enterprise workshops, which has the advantage of joining the residential accommodation and other academic support facilities closer together. In traditional college-style accommodation, there may also be library and teaching facilities.

▲ **Figure 2.85** *Christina Miller Hall, Edinburgh, RMJM Architects*

Rooftop Studios

8 Bed Unit

◀ ▼ **Figure 2.86** *Study-bedroom typologies: Hawkins\Brown for Campus Living Villages RVC BH*

1 bed flat

Large single bed

Private bathroom and kitchenette

Full height glazing

Two adjacent standard units

Large single bed

Full height glazing

Sliding partition screen with adjacent room

EXAMPLE
WESTFIELD STUDENT VILLAGE
QUEEN MARY UNIVERSITY OF LONDON,
FEILDEN CLEGG BRADLEY STUDIOS

A variety of external spaces and social environments were created within this development of 1,200 rooms in concrete-framed buildings of varying height and cladding materials. All interior finishes and standards were similar but the number of bedrooms per flat varied from one to 12 sharing a kitchen.

▶▼ Figures 2.87, 2.88, 2.89, 2.90, 2.91 and 2.92

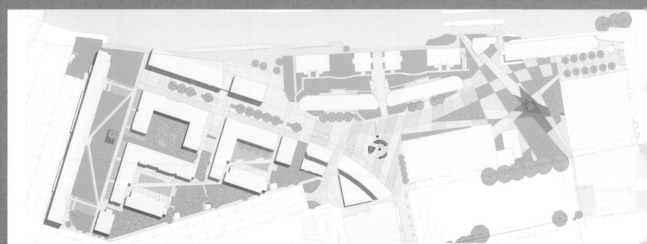

EXAMPLE

TIETGENKOLLEGIET
ØRESTAD, COPENHAGEN,
LUNDGAARD AND TRANBERG

Tietgenkollegiet, Ørestad, Copenhagen, puts community at the centre of student life, spacious rooms overlook a landscaped courtyard. Shared kitchens are generously sized and allow for living and informal study.

◀ ▲ Figures 2.93 and 2.94

EXAMPLE

BIKUBEN STUDENT RESIDENCE COPENHAGEN, AART ARCHITECTS

Bikuben Student Residence, Copenhagen, where the study-bedrooms and the common rooms are connected in a double spiral around a courtyard which provides direct contact and views into the common spaces while supporting privacy in the students' studio flats.

◀ ▲ Figures 2.95 and 2.96

HEALTH AND WELLBEING

Wellbeing is hugely important. Close proximity to sports facilities is becoming more common, promoting a healthier lifestyle. External spaces need to be well-designed, providing recreation and events spaces, picnic areas and good WiFi, allowing for outside study in good weather.

Other shared resources, such as small bookable training rooms, allow time on campus to be productive. Good pastoral care through on-site managers attracts students and provides vital support when pressures mount. We are moving towards a more hotel-style model of accommodation; most already offer students a concierge to collect mail. In time we might also offer repair and laundry services with collections on-site, cycle storage and car-parking facilities.

HOUSING TYPES

Many housing types are used. The cluster-flat still remains the most prevalent and single en-suite bedrooms share a common kitchen/dining area. The number of bedrooms varies to give options for students and is influenced by the needs of conference business and site constraints, with schemes often designed to reflect the look and feel of private housing.

CREATING AN IDENTITY

With land values at a premium perhaps we should look at more sustainable options such as refurbishment of existing buildings, imaginative re-use of which can reinforce connections with the city and offer possiiblities to combine with other uses.

EXAMPLE

HAWKSHEAD CAMPUS HATFIELD, HAWKINS\BROWN

Cluster-based flats at the Royal Veterinary College. Five bedrooms per flat. Full-height windows offer good lighting to rooms and ventilation is via perforated panels to provide security to the predominantly female residents.

◀ Figure 2.97

EXAMPLE

MILL JUNCTION JOHANNESBURG, CITIQ PROPERTY DEVELOPERS

In Mill Junction, Johannesburg, affordable housing was developed to meet a critical need (50% of students drop out for financial reasons). Eleven-storey concrete grain silos and 63 shipping containers were converted to create beds for 375 students.

◀ Figure 2.98

EXAMPLE

TRINITY COLLEGE CAMBRIDGE, 5ᵗʰ STUDIO

The recent refurbishment of William Wilkins' 1825 New Court at Trinity College Cambridge has created improved residential accommodation, social and teaching spaces. The architects, 5th Studio, applied strong environmental design principles to upgrade performance alongside provision of improved services and comfort levels – similar in approach to their earlier work on the 1960s Wolfson Building, but applied in the more challenging context of these Grade I Listed buildings.

▼ Figure 2.99

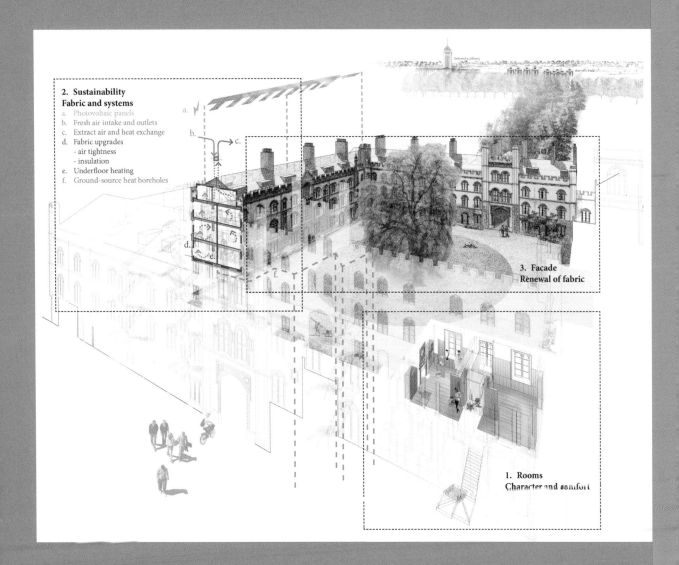

2. Sustainability
Fabric and systems
a. Photovoltaic panels
b. Fresh air intake and outlets
c. Extract air and heat exchange
d. Fabric upgrades
   - air tightness
   - insulation
e. Underfloor heating
f. Ground-source heat boreholes

3. Facade
Renewal of fabric

1. Rooms
Character and comfort

COMMUNITY SPACES

Universities are reconnecting with their local communities. The traditional Oxbridge college with the porter at the gate is changing as universities are collaborating with a wide range of partners at local, national and international level to support their research, to meet widening participation objectives and to support enterprise, employment growth, innovation and economic regeneration. In recent years this role has strengthened and universities have consolidated their important role in supporting the future economic wellbeing of their communities.

Universities meet these objectives in different ways, from carrying out activities off-campus through partnership links, to bringing outside organisations and school children onto campus. Universities are becoming much more transparent and open, which may raise conflicting issues between security and health and safety on the one hand and outside visitor groups on the other. Technology enables research and teaching to take place across organisations; the cost of major scientific equipment and facilities is such that sharing is increasingly common and there is a wish to support enterprise with students in addition to innovation with research.

SPECIALIST FACILITIES

Collaboration on specialist facilities is growing. The Francis Crick Institute (see page 19) is a world-class cancer research facility in London created by three universities (Imperial College London, King's College London and University College London), the Medical Research Council and two medical charities (Cancer Research UK and the Wellcome Trust), while the Carnegie Pavilion in Headingley, Leeds, is a dual-use cricket ground for Leeds Beckett University and Yorkshire Cricket Club. In the arts, Portsmouth University has worked in partnership with the New Theatre Royal on a joint redevelopment (page 56) where students work with industry experts in facilities that include a theatre and television studio, flexible teaching spaces, music practice rooms and offices.

OPENING UP SCIENCE AND IDEAS

More established universities have world-famous art and museum collections, which are a research and a teaching resource often well used by local communities. Modern facilities focus on showcasing current and future research.

Designers of new buildings therefore need to be conscious of the university's strategy and the need to plan access to new building projects.

Other universities have taken the university out of its own estate into the community – the Tinderbox talks at Strathclyde University are an example which aims to replicate 18th-century coffee houses as 'hotbeds of comment, debate and the exchange of new ideas'.

SCIENCE GALLERY TRINITY COLLEGE DUBLIN,
RKD ARCHITECTS

The Science Gallery at Trinity College Dublin, supported by
Google, which aims to showcase the research work of the
university. It has become a major attraction and is being
successfully replicated through Science Gallery International
(SGI) across the world, including London, Bangalore and
Melbourne.

▶ ▼ Figures 2.100 and 2.101

77

LINKS WITH SCHOOLS

Universities have relationships with schools for many reasons. Early years childcare provision may be provided on campus, as for example the award-winning day nursery at the University of Edinburgh and, at later years, universities have widening-participation programmes to encourage school children's interest in higher education, particularly in subjects such as the sciences, medicine and mathematics, and in areas where participation may be low. Every university will have its own strategy; some have relationships with neighbouring schools and work with them, while others sponsor academies, such as at UCL and King's College London Mathematics Academy, the latter a sixth-form school which combines mathematics teaching in its new building with students benefitting from other lectures and activities on the main campuses.

Running programmes on campus may have implications for design, as scientific facilities become more transparent, a trend seen with other university spaces. Some institutions provide dedicated facilities on campus which may double-up for other uses. King's College London has an experimental teaching facility at its Strand campus, which enables other higher education organisations to use it; while the Faculty of Computer Science and Mathematics at the Technische Universitat München has imaginatively used its art budget to create two full-height parabolic slides in the central atrium leading to a workshop at the base.

In Camberwell, London, the Maudsley Charity has built ORTUS, a well-designed

▲ ▶ ▶ **Figures 2.102, 2.103 and 2.104**
ORTUS, London, Duggan Morris

and flexible building with learning, event and meeting spaces available to its partners South London and Maudsley NHS Foundation Trust, King's College London and King's College Hospital, and also for external booking, located as a stand-alone building at the edge of the campus facing a residential area. 1,500 sqm of event space can be divided into 15 different room configurations and income is fed back into the charity's activities. A café on the ground floor serves the building and is open to the public with access to a landscaped sitting area outside.

Key is the external environment and the physical connectivity to the city.

briefing, design and construction

Making a building creates a focus on the future. The idea of 'the project' needs to harness enthusiasm, an optimism that we can influence our environment to create better places for learning, more cohesive communities, innovative research and greater universities.

Engagement is required that instils a sense of purpose and consequently runs over into a productive fit between the physical opportunities of the building and how it is used. These are the ingredients for successful buildings.

Gabriel Aeppli's opinion piece on briefing and construction reflects on the importance of shared understanding, mutual respect and defined responsibilities to achieve ambitious goals. The description of the London Centre for Nanotechnolgy is included here, rather than as a case study at the end of the book, as it raises so many issues pertinent to Parts 3 and 4, and will hopefully help the reader reflect on the interrelationships

and importance of each stage of the process.

Fiona Duggan describes methodologies to ask the right questions of the right people to determine the brief.

Andy Ford describes the challenges facing the university sector to achieve improved environmental performance, in order to lead the way towards living within the means of our planet.

Optimising good outcomes through the design and construction process is discussed by Ian Taylor, highlighting the importance of continuity in the project team, commitment to ambitious outcomes, and proactive contracting to achieve quality.

3.1 BRIEFING TO OCCUPATION: LONDON CENTRE FOR NANOTECHNOLOGY OVERVIEW

Gabriel Aeppli

OPINION and CASE STUDY

Science and engineering research is essential for human culture as well as for finding the solutions to today's social, technical, environmental and medical problems. With classroom education at large state universities under competitive pressure (e.g. from lower cost private providers taking advantage of modern information technology and from online learning) for the first time since its development in the 19th century, the importance of student participation in research for their university education has become much greater. What distinguishes successful institutions is experience in dealing with new problems based on prior knowledge, requiring moderation and interpretation by expert colleagues, followed by creative calculation and experimentation. There is a demand for buildings which makes it possible to assemble the interdisciplinary and inter-generational teams needed to invent theories and perform experiments that are important both intellectually and practically.

In the example I discuss below, I will show how the development of such a building itself benefits immensely from an interdisciplinary approach involving the design team and end users.

I also believe that university buildings perform better when the academic users are engaged in their design and management, and are allowed to take some responsibility for ensuring their optimum operation and performance. Rather than a building project being run centrally by an estates department or a third-party developer, I believe projects benefit from direct relationships established between the design team and academic users, with facilitating project management. The end users, together with the design and construction team, should be given control, as long as the initial cost envelope is not breached.

The project below owes its unique success, including value for money, to an exceptional trust on the part of the University College London (UCL) administration at the time. In today's

English-speaking countries where public university administrators are much more anxious to exert central control than a decade-and-a-half ago, it is very unlikely that a similar project would be achieved with the same cost and performance.

If a substantial proportion of the earnings of academic departments is automatically diverted to university estates divisions, there needs to be accountability to deliver good building performance, and in a highly technical research building, maintenance of technical performance. Decisions taken on the development of the estate should take account of the potential development and expansion needs of academic departments.

The obvious solution is for the user clients themselves to be given more control over the funds they are earning (via overheads on research grants) for the occupation, maintenance and expansion of their laboratories. This means that if the estates divisions do not deliver cost-effective solutions, the funds can be used for external service providers. This will align estate management and development much more with the interests of the front-line workers of the universities. Such an approach is demonstrated by the success of the design and build phase of the London Centre for Nanotechnology (LCN), which was due to the full engagement of the prospective residents with the project whose costs they fully understood and over which they shared control.

LEARNING FROM THE LONDON CENTRE FOR NANOTECHNOLOGY

Scheme designs for London Centre for Nanotechnology (LCN, completed 2006; Figures 3.1, 3.4, 3.5, 3.6), an interdisciplinary academic research facility at the heart of the UCL campus in London, and PARK INNOVAARE (PiA, design 2016; Figures 3.2 and 3.3), a public/private partnership near Zürich, Switzerland. The Swiss scheme will provide space for government and corporate research laboratories operating at the interfaces between technical fields. It employs a similar strategy to that developed at LCN: maximum cost-effectiveness and flexibility are achieved by a simple box-design with the highest value laboratories closest to ground level, a standard lab core/office perimeter layout for above-grade floors, and exploitation of stairwells(rendering for PiA in Figure 3.2, photograph of LCN in Figure 3.4) as social spaces. Figure 3.6 shows finished nanobiotechnology laboratory at LCN.

▶ Figures 3.2 and 3.3: *PARK INNOVAARE (PiA) Villigen: Staircase visualisation and cross section - Erne AG Holzbau / Hornberger Architekten AG 2016*

▶▶ Figures 3.4 and 3.5: *London Centre for Nanotechology - staircase and cross section - Feilden Clegg Bradley Studios*

▶ Figure 3.1 *The London Centre for Nanotechnology*

▶ Figure 3.6 *LCN typical laboratory*

THE LONDON CENTRE FOR NANOTECHNOLOGY

The LCN was a small project at a rapidly growing university. It is an interdisciplinary research institute held jointly between UCL and Imperial College London. Nanotechnology is defined by the ability to design, measure and manipulate matter on the nanometre scale (0.000000001 metres, or roughly the amount that human fingernails grow in one second). The formation of the LCN entailed construction of an entirely new building on the Bloomsbury site of UCL, and renovation of space at the Imperial College campus in South Kensington. The first occupants of the new building would be existing staff from several UCL departments in the engineering, biomedical and physical science faculties.

The budget was provided by the Strategic Research Infrastructure Fund of the Wellcome Trust and the UK government, which was designed to revitalise UK university facilities largely during the first part of the last decade. By international standards, the monies (£13.9 million) and site size (400 sqm) for the UCL project were decidedly modest – peer research centres in Europe, Asia and the USA were being constructed with budgets typically in the US$ 50–150 million range.

The dense urban site is very close to the major and busy Euston Road and below- and above-ground rail lines, including stations characterised by strongly accelerating and decelerating trains. Therefore, the site seemed decidedly sub-optimal (especially given the modest funding) for a nanotechnology research institute which, by its nature, demands laboratories well-isolated from vibrations, electromagnetic noise and temperature fluctuations. However, the site also had positive features, deriving most notably from the embedding of the LCN in the fabric of a large urban university with particular excellence in biomedicine, which is a key application area for nanotechnology, and the unique multicultural metropolis that is London. On the strength of the latter, the then Provost and President, Sir Chris Llewellyn-Smith, decided to proceed in spite of the significant technical risks.

The site and building envelope itself had been selected previously for a centre devoted to instrumentation for optical astronomy, with a planned occupancy of perhaps 40 people. It had only a single basement, and six levels at or above ground, encompassing considerable atrium space. When this project was rejected UCL, at the behest of academic staff, decided in 2000 to create a nanotechnology building with the same envelope and footprint. In the interests of efficiency, they employed the design team of the optics centre. Because of the radically different and more diverse scope of activities characteristic of nanotechnology, a complete redesign of the building was required. Given the need for laboratories with low levels of acoustic and electronmagnetic noise, Feilden Clegg Bradley Architects, who had visited a number of similar projects in the USA, and the Director-designate of the new centre made a case for a second basement. This was the most important decision in the early design phase, as the second basement is where the high-value LCN experiments are performed, notwithstanding the dense urban location.

THE BRIEF

The design brief was simple – to house and promote the solution of important problems in fields from information technology to biomedicine using interdisciplinary teams from UCL working especially with partners from Imperial College. This brief encompassed both technical and social requirements. The former accounted for the demands of housing sophisticated nanofabrication and nanocharacterisation tools, while the latter arose from the need to create meaningful interactions between scientists from different disciplinary silos, generations and institutions.

THE PROCESS

The design process had to take into account the budget constraints as well as the interdisciplinary nature of the project. Key features were::

1. Design team appreciation of what the end users (scientists) wish to achieve using the new building.
2. End user appreciation of the challenges facing the design team.
3. Dedication to finding off-the-shelf solutions to all problems, ranging from the sourcing of staircases to the electrical shielding of laboratories.
4. Realisation that good designers share much common ground, as creative professionals, with scientists; a research institute is a professional partnership with many similarities to a good architecture practice.
5. Simply structured procedures for accommodating the different needs of disciplines under a single roof.

6. Direct discussions between end users and building designers, engineers and contractors, with minimal overheads in the form of intermediation by others.

7. A collegial and timely approach to value engineering between the project team responsible for delivery and the end users, focusing on practical solutions to deliver features necessary for building performance, even if costs seem to have escaped control.

8. Clear awareness on the part of both the design/construction team and the end users of costs, performance, schedule and the associated trade-offs, allowing, among other benefits, the maintenance of change order discipline.

9. Tracking of realised value and contingency spend (this project followed the USA pattern – not common for projects of this type in the UK – of including a substantial contingency budget) as simple project health metrics understandable by all stakeholders.

Execution consistent with points 1–9 implied a single point of contact on the client side, with dual reporting to the scientists and the UCL estates division, who worked together with a partner at FCB (who had the overall coordination as well as the design role) to arrange meetings and workshops, initially for identifying the project vision, and as the project evolved into ever more detail on technical specifications and execution.

The process of close engagement between the design/build team and the clients extended to the construction phase, during which joint value engineering kept the costs within budget on completion. It also allowed the timely detection of, and a well-calibrated response to, a major under-specification of the cooling needs in the building. It is difficult to imagine how any conventional approach relying on intermediaries would have outperformed our partnership among creative professionals in solving this major problem, identified only after construction was well under way.

Friday afternoons were generally reserved for visits to the construction site by the client, and permitted in-course inspections as well as the establishment of shared objectives between contractors and scientists.

SCHEME DESIGN

The key feature of the building is its division into two vibrationally isolated blocks: a stairwell and lab-office complex. The stairwell block also includes the lift serving all floors, restrooms, kitchen areas and furnished landings and functions, as the social spine of a building with a large height-to-width ratio. In addition to encouraging social interactions, its inviting nature, provided partially by its scale, light and specific items of visual interest, including alternating hardwood (furnished landings) and resin flooring, and a semi-transparent lift enclosure, also encourages preference for stair climbing over lift use, with associated health and energy benefits.

The lab-office block contains high value laboratories and service areas in the two basement levels and ground floor, a 200 sqm clean room on level 1, standardised laboratory core/ office perimeter layouts for levels 2, 3 and 4, and level 5 accommodating a server room and small cluster for supercomputing and a large open-plan office area uniting scientists and LCN administrative staff.

LCN: the clean room and associated service corridors occupies all available space on its level, and contains three fingers, with ascending levels of cleanliness and occupied by surface-processing apparatus, wet benches and characterisation tools. Between the latter two fingers, there is an electron beam 'write room' for the top-down creation of ultra small structures. A smaller clean room for an electron/ion beam microscope/fabrication tool was installed on level–2; this laboratory was later modified to host additional machines, including an electron/ion tool with a cryogenic stage for nanoneuroscience, and a scanning tunneling microscope for writing individual (dopant) atoms into silicon wafers, with the eventual purpose of building quantum computers.

For the specialist facilities, most notably the clean rooms, the chief client representative was strongly assisted by a clean room specialist, hired by UCL during the design/construction phase; the presence of this specialist on the client side was crucial for the success of the construction project.

Gas, water and compressed air lines and associated machinery, cabinets and scrubbers (gas reaction columns), as well as data lines and other utilities were all designed and delivered as part of the project. Considerable effort also went into the design of electrical distribution systems with appropriate reliability for their intended clients, and separate earths were provided for some laboratories. The clean rooms were also within the original project scope. Costs were controlled by insisting on a downward progression of laboratory performance specifications from high to low, ascending from level –2 to 4.

OPERATIONS

Once a building has been designed and constructed, it must be maintained and modified for safe and efficient use. Accordingly, the project team, including the architects, engineers and end users, held extensive meetings with the relevant members of the UCL estates division during the design and construction phase. The need for scheduled maintenance, rather than relying on the principle of 'fix it after it breaks' was emphasised. After project completion, the chief client representative (the single point of contact described in 'The Process', above) during the design and construction phase became the LCN facilities manager, whose remit was to ensure proper functioning and evolution of the project for the end users. A role subsequently added was that of chief safety officer for the LCN. A particularly important duty for the facilities manager was to form the interface between the scientists and the UCL estates division concerning both maintenance and modifications. On his retirement, however, he was replaced by others who did not have his prior experience in the estates division or his deep understanding of the building. Preventive maintenance was not prioritised by UCL– a lapse which did not affect operations

immediately, when the LCN and its components were still new and under warranty – but has more recently led to needless downtime. Furthermore, notwithstanding large overheads paid to UCL from LCN research income, an adversarial culture, with lost productivity, evolved from debates about liabilities due to inadequate maintenance, loss of documentation, and a lack of intellectual ownership of the sophisticated building.

THE OUTCOME – SCIENCE, TECHNOLOGY AND TRAINING

Over the years since project completion in 2006, the building has a played an important role as a technical and social enabler for nanotechnology in London by providing state-of-the-art facilities in a setting optimised for the social interactions which are a prerequisite for interdisciplinary problem solving. The building – alongside the high calibre staff recruitment which it enabled – was a key tool for introducing to the non-biomedical faculties at UCL a culture of performing difficult, high-impact experiments at home. As desired, the net outcome has been high-impact science and engineering, and numerous successful alumni holding positions worldwide.

The underlying design philosophy of isolating noise at the source, the high-to-low floor hierarchy of lab specification and the use of simple off-the-shelf products for noise mitigation paid off in the form of scientific results fully competitive with those from more bespoke, expensive laboratories in more isolated locations. In addition, the building design, including open-plan

offices on levels 2–5, has been flexible enough to allow the accommodation of approximately 50–60% more researchers than originally planned. Research laboratories have also been successfully modified, and the major problems are now overcrowding and inadequate maintenance (cleaning and cosmetic upkeep have been adequate) of what remains the most sophisticated building associated with the non-medical faculties of UCL.

Recently, a decision was made to construct an outdoor terrace platform in the vacant lot behind the LCN, which forecloses further expansion.

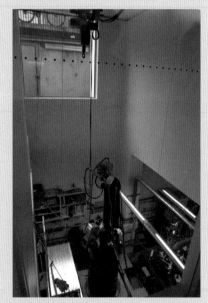

▲ **Figure 3.7** *The London Centre for Nanotechnology : double height basement laboratory - with subsurface daylight window and built-in crane - for single atom manipulation and imaging*

3.2 RETHINKING THE BRIEFING PROCESS

Fiona Duggan

THE CHANGING LANDSCAPE OF HIGHER EDUCATION

In a world where access to information can increasingly take place anytime and anywhere, learning environments that provide compelling here-and-now learning experiences are becoming ever more important. Such environments are about encouraging students, staff and others to come together in memorable settings – to engage in a lively programme of events, gain access to a wide range of resources, take advantage of places to work collaboratively, find quiet spots to pause and reflect, and make time to relax and socialise. At the same time, as blended-learning approaches combining face-to-face and online activities become more common, and research/enterprise/innovation activities become more diverse in their partnerships and locations, it is increasingly difficult for higher education institutions to accurately identify the types and amounts of space required to meet their needs. Current requirements are constantly changing, while programme change and/or growth are no longer a robust guide for future requirements. We need to find new ways to help institutions articulate and validate their space requirements.

SEEKING THE MOST FEASIBLE WAY FORWARD

The primary purpose of any briefing process is to plot the most feasible way forward, a best-fit approach that seeks to align the following key project parameters:

- vision
- needs
- space
- budget
- time.

This process relies on understanding and appreciating the different ways of thinking and doing that each participant brings, with the most innovative briefs being those where project parameters are woven together in unexpected ways. A compelling project *vision* sometimes grows out of grappling with very particular circumstances rather than engaging in unconstrained, blue-sky thinking. User *needs* tend to be better met by asking people *what they do* rather than *what they want*, as this opens up the potential to explore with users a whole range of settings (existing and yet-to-be-defined) that might effectively meet their needs. Types and quantities of *space* can be arrived at in a variety of ways, including change-the-rules (e.g. using existing space differently, calculating new space differently), rationalise, remodel, extend, new-build and relocate. Funding strategies where *budget* seeks to balance capital, operating and life-cycle costs, might result in a portfolio of owned, shared and borrowed space. Deciding factors around *time* might include the degree of organisational/academic change desired, procurement route options and funding availability.

In short, the specific characteristics of each parameter will largely shape the client brief. The role of the leader of the briefing process is to articulate and guide the process, focusing on value-for-money decision-making and opportunities for desired change. Radical academic or organisational change can sometimes be achieved at little cost, such as reassigning under-used departmentally owned space for shared faculty use, which can generate an increase in cross-disciplinary collaboration. On the other hand, high expenditure can sometimes have minimal impact; for example, a relocation project based on a user brief that reinforces the status quo may limit opportunities for academic or organisational change.

WORKING MORE EFFECTIVELY WITH UNCERTAINTY

As future requirements become more difficult to articulate with confidence, developing the client brief takes on a more collaborative process requiring multi-disciplinary input from the outset. This process tends to work with typical requirements initially, actual requirements gradually coming into focus as project parameters become better understood. The merit of this, *typical needs first, actual needs later* approach is that it allows the client brief to develop in more detail as more information becomes available. It is also an inherently sustainable approach whose loose-fit character supports organisational and spatial change over time.

In defining initial user requirements, a framework is sought that will accommodate a range of typical group sizes and needs, to build in sufficient flexibility for change over time. While each project is different, general patterns around group sizes and basic requirements can be ascertained.

Learning programmes tend to address particular pedagogies and staff-to-student ratios via group sizes of, say, 5–7 students, 10–12, 20–30, 40, 80, 120+. Timetabled hours vary with the institution but are typically 10–12 contact hours a week, depending on the subject area, with independent peer group learning becoming an increasingly important component of programme delivery. With this kind of information, hypothetical scenarios can be shaped, thereby deepening discussions around possibilities, early on in the briefing process.

In defining initial space requirements, working with existing information, generic space norms, precedent studies and hypothetical space models, actual space needs start to become clearer through user engagement. Trends in recent years include an increase in the amount of space devoted to commons, initially in teach+learn spaces, but increasingly appearing in workspace too. Workspace is shifting to include a more diverse mix of individual and collaborative settings, in open and enclosed configurations, for both live-in and drop-in users. Support space is becoming more sophisticated as it expands to meet the needs of ever more diverse activities and users throughout day and evening. Circulation space is no longer solely seen as balance space to be kept as efficient as possible, but as playing a key role in way-finding strategies that seek to enhance general awareness, provide opportunities for informal interaction and create a sense of identity and belonging.

The space provided/required by most buildings tends to follow a similar pattern:

- 50–60% core activities
- 10% supporting amenities
- 15–30% circulation
- 20% core.

The space provided/required by most campuses also tends to follow a similar pattern:

- 30–50% learn space, which we subdivide into commons (social, library, general purpose ICT), general (lecture theatres, classrooms, project spaces) and specialist (teaching labs, workshops, studios, performance, etc.).
- 15–30% work space, which we also subdivide into commons (social, meetings, tea points, admin hubs), general (staff work-stations, enclosed/open) and specialist (research labs and workshops).
- 10–15% support space, including catering, student services, amenities, facilities management (stores, security, maintenance).
- 20–30% connect space, i.e. gathering places (such as atria), all horizontal circulation (entrance lobbies, corridors, fire routes through open-plan areas).
- 15–20% balance space, i.e. vertical circulation (stairs, lifts), toilets, building services (ducts, equipment, plant, loading bays).

In defining place-making principles, campuses are increasingly responding to the needs of learning programmes with a variety of attendance options. For those on traditional full-time programmes, contact time varies considerably between 10 and 30 hours a week. Block-mode programmes take a variety of formats, such as 3 days (Thursday–Saturday), 5 days (Wednesday–Sunday) or 3+2 days. Full-time programmes will increasingly become a fast-track option, while block-mode programmes will provide pace-of-choice options. Online options are currently seen as a work-in-progress, with the evidence to date suggesting that online works best alongside face-to-face activities (e.g. flip-teaching, where material is studied online in advance of contact time, which focuses on discourse). Institutions are increasingly partnering with businesses to meet the employment demands of students (full-time students who want work placement opportunities, part-time students who often need their employer's support to pursue academic qualifications), as well as providing opportunities for students to develop and showcase work skills through volunteer programmes, exchanges and participation in research and enterprise initiatives. As programmes become less fixed in time and space, campus place-making focuses on creating environments in which learners will want to linger.

Place-making principles commonly in use vary considerably in scale, from application within a single building through to multi-campus estates:

- Routes that facilitate way-finding, build general awareness, showcase activities, create opportunities to meet and linger.
- Hubs that cluster resources together in primary locations, to create centres of activity that can be efficiently and effectively supported, with provision for extended-hours access where appropriate.
- Neighbourhoods that provide diversity via the particular characteristics of both users and space.
- Thresholds that provide clear, intuitively understood, transitions between public, invited and private space.

FINDING A WAY FORWARD

The request: we want a corporate leadership centre (vision) to deliver executive learning programmes to our most senior staff (needs). We think we need about 2,000 sqm (space). We don't have any money (budget). We want to open the centre within the next 12 months and deliver programmes for the next 5 years (time).

The resulting brief: a collaboration project with a hotel group for a weekday leadership centre and a weekend hotel. 3,000 sqm refurbished space. Financed by hotel group with leadership centre renting 2,000 sqm for 180 days/year over a 5-year period. Refurbishment of an existing building to minimise construction time. Separate identities maintained by signage that flips over from corporate to hotel use to suit weekday and weekend activities.

LISTENING TO USERS, LISTENING TO BUILDINGS

The briefing process should encourage users and buildings to 'listen to each other', so that each set of requirements is informed by the other, in pragmatic and creative ways. The goal is sustainable place-making – environments that will effectively accommodate the evolving needs of users, estates, institution and environment for as long as it is economically viable to do so.

In listening to users, the aim is to understand their existing activities and their aspirations for the future. Together, there can be an exploration of the kinds of role space might play in supporting both continuity and change. As a project moves into construction, the focus should shift to preparing users for the changes ahead and providing assistance throughout the settling-in period.

Conversations with users will generally include the following topics:

- People: numbers/types of users involved – students, staff, partners, others
- Programmes: full-time, part-time, work-based, online
- Pedagogies: traditional, emerging
- Processes: support systems
- Place: time spent on campus, online, elsewhere
- Personality: brand and identity
- Priorities: must have, nice to have
- Precedents: national and international exemplars.

'Listening to buildings' seeks to understand existing conditions, including spatial characteristics and the potential opportunities or constraints involved. It is then possible to explore opportunities for enhanced efficiency (net to gross, sqm/user, £/sqm, etc.) and enhanced effectiveness (flexibility, adaptability, etc.). There can be a focus on the kinds of uses that existing space or sites might be suitable for, some of which may challenge user requirements already under discussion.

'Conversations with buildings' could include the following topics:

- Site: location, presence, access (permanent)
- Structure: structural grid, loading capacity (60+ years lifespan)
- Shape: floor-plate configuration, heights (60+ years)
- Skin: building envelope (30+ years)
- Services: environmental systems, easy to maintain, upgrade, replace (20–30 years)
- Services: technology systems, easy to maintain, upgrade, replace (5–10 years)
- Scenery: layouts that are reconfigurable (year-by-year)
- Settings: user-friendly, plug+play, flexible (day-to-day).

To enable users and buildings to listen to each other more effectively, institutions should establish a project governance model that includes representation across a wide spectrum of interests and responsibilities – the everyday needs of users to carry out their work effectively and enjoyably, the long-term needs of buildings and campuses to accommodate change in affordable ways. A key feature of this approach is to make explicit the roles, responsibilities and decision-making powers of all involved, so that each participant's attention is focused on those issues that they are best placed to address.

A typical project governance model might include the following roles:

- Project leader: providing project vision and leadership
- Project sponsor: setting project parameters, ensuring value for money

- Steering group: keeping the project on message, on time and on budget
- Project champion: engaging all stakeholders, coordinating activities, managing communication
- User groups: articulating needs, testing what-if scenarios, providing feedback
- Technical groups: ensuring specific requirements are met (services, ICT, catering, etc.).

Different priorities will come into focus as a project develops:

- Site decisions are about the intended long-term future of building/s and their surroundings. Conversations will focus on location and presence.
- Base-build decisions are about long-term flexibility and adaptability (responding to changing needs over time). Conversations will focus on structure, shape, skin and services.
- Fit-out decisions are about medium-term flexibility and

adjustability (allowing for regular reconfiguration). Conversations will focus on services and scenery

- Furniture decisions are about short-term flexibility and agility (supporting day-to-day needs). Conversations will focus on settings.

Setting out the briefing and design process in this way clarifies what conversations need to be had when and who needs to be involved. The goal is to balance the desire of those who will be using the space to keep options open for as long as possible, alongside the concern of those providing the space to freeze requirements as early as possible in order to progress design and stabilise costs. This involves timely decision-making – not too late, which increases the risks of incurring additional costs and/or delays, but also not too early, when decisions are more likely to be based on existing ways of doing things, insufficient information and/or little awareness of possibilities that may be potentially well within reach.

▼ **Figure 3.8** *Articulating project values*

SPACE CRITERIA	EFFICIENT	EFFECTIVE	EXPRESSIVE
For student	meets my requirements	supports my learning	makes me feel proud
For faculty	supports our programme	encourages creativity	reflects our identity
For estates	affordable operating costs	facilitates change	demonstrates values

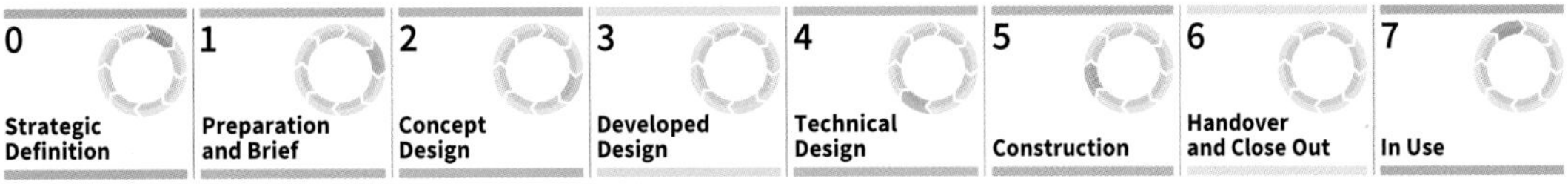

▶ Figure 3.9
RIBA PoW stages

0	1	2	3	4	5	6	7
Strategic Definition	**Preparation and Brief**	**Concept Design**	**Developed Design**	**Technical Design**	**Construction**	**Handover and Close Out**	**In Use**

HAVING TIMELY CONVERSATIONS

Developing the client brief is first and foremost a social process in collaborative sense-making. It is about knowing who needs to talk to who, what needs to be talked about when, what is important to who and why.

BRIEFING

Conversations around the RIBA Plan of Work Stages 0–1 aim to understand the key project parameters. This involves some uncertainty and it is important to maintain openness and curiosity about possible directions to pursue. The focus is on establishing a clear *statement of intent* where none of the big questions are left unanswered. Topics to be addressed include client aspirations, academic vision, business case, image and identity, approximate building size, principal spatial components, site/location issues, funding characteristics, anticipated timescale, phasing strategy (if required), decision-making processes and potential risks. The information provided should be comprehensive enough to guide and inspire, not so detailed that it cannot continue to evolve through design dialogue. Client involvement is primarily focused on key decision-makers. Activities include:

- reflecting on the existing situation (aspirations, attitudes, work processes, space use, client perceptions, etc.)
- learning from others (site visits, case study reviews, etc.)
- exploring possible scenarios (a very effective way of opening up thinking)
- focusing on aspirations.

> **The strategic brief** provides an overview of the client's requirements regarding users, space requirements and operational systems.
>
> **The concept brief** develops these requirements alongside emerging design ideas.
>
> **The project brief** tests developing requirements against developing design ideas, in order to establish requirements in more detail.

DESIGN

Conversations around the RIBA Plan of Work Stages 2–3 work towards mutual understanding. This involves appreciating diversity and normalising conflict as project hopes and concerns are revealed. The focus is on establishing a series of client briefs at progressive layers of detail. The process is iterative, where project priorities are elaborated, tested and refined (or changed) in response to information becoming available.

Activities throughout include articulating, testing and adjusting requirements to meet the objectives of both users and providers/managers of space, understanding the different priorities that may be involved and developing the design scenario that best fits the complexity of needs involved.

TECHNICAL DESIGN

Conversations around RIBA Plan of Work Stage 4 are about commitment and appreciating what is and is not negotiable. The focus is on checking that the brief and design are fully aligned. For the client team, it is about all stakeholder needs converging into a cohesive whole. For the project team, it is about all professional input converging into a coordinated whole. The knowledge that both client and project teams now have provides an excellent opportunity to pause and touch base with project priorities. The process used to achieve this is known as value-management. This stage is the last major opportunity to ensure the best possible alignment between brief and design, and should include the possibility of radical changes. Unfortunately, most value-management processes do not allow for this level of openness around change, perhaps because of the time, energy, resources and emotion that have already been invested in the project. This underestimates the power of the knowledge now available to make brave decisions where one can be fully aware of the benefits and costs likely to be involved. Not testing the brief as part of the value-management process can make for a less successful outcome.

CONSTRUCTION

At RIBA Plan of Work Stage 5, there is a major shift in attitude – all the big decisions have now been made and it is full steam ahead. Client conversations are about managing expectations and the anxieties some users may have as the project becomes more real. User engagement moves from *preparing the building for its people* to *preparing people for their building*. The focus is on ensuring as smooth a transition as possible, while generating enthusiasm and confidence among all users for the opportunities and challenges ahead. Activities include keeping everyone informed and involved, preparing a countdown programme, allocating tasks and responsibilities, familiarising users with new space and technology, and saying goodbye.

HANDOVER

At RIBA Plan of Work Stage 6, the team discusses working through transition. Conversations focus on organising good endings and new beginnings; providing settling-in support. For users, the real project is just starting – learning how to work in their new space. Activities may include preparing welcome packs, providing on-hand support for glitches, implementing new workplace protocols and celebrating arrival.

BUILDING-IN-USE

RIBA Plan of Work Stage 7 develops an ongoing culture of reflection-in-action – what works well, what could be better, what action can we take? It is also about appreciating the pace of change an organisation can tolerate. Conversations focus on aftercare – helping users settle in and addressing any issues arising. It is an opportunity for everyone (client, design and construction teams) to capture key lessons for future projects. It is about continual monitoring and fine-tuning. Activities include follow-up action team meetings, user group feedback sessions, post occupancy evaluation and widespread sharing of experience.

IN SUMMARY

The role of the briefer is to create and protect an evolving conversational space that brings the requirements of users and buildings into clear focus, and to do so while being mindful of building programmes, budgets and the need for timely decision-making. The most rewarding projects are those that find their voice in ways which surprise and delight everyone involved. In the words of one client, *'We didn't expect to end up here, but what a great place to be'.*

▼ **Figure 3.10** *Conversations that develop over time*

IMAGINE	ELABORATE	ACCEPT	PREPARE	SETTLE-IN
what if …?	typical requirements	specific requirements	first-users' requirements	in-use requirements
what are the big questions?	make timely decisions – not too early, not too late	maintain priorities and long-term view	commence handover process	fine-tune as necessary
who needs to be involved?	tolerate uncertainty while striving towards specificity	clarify what is and is not negotiable	communicate and involve everyone	support users through transition

3.3 BRIEFING AND DESIGN FOR SUSTAINABILITY

Andy Ford

When approaching the design for a new campus one should begin by considering the input from the educators. This is their show and, as designers, we need to enable, understand and then push the envelope.

When asked about the future of higher education, these are the points educators raise:

Democratisation of knowledge and access: the internet and digital technologies are reshaping the way we share information and deliver education. Knowledge is now often accessible outside the university environment and even some courses are becoming accessible to all.

Globalisation: mobility increases, competition intensifies and the global marketplace of ideas means broader access to student and academic talent. Universities are franchising and setting up campuses away from their home location.

Funding paradigms: in the UK tuition costs have tripled. The idea of higher education as a public good, and the financial viability of the university as either a research centre or teaching institution is threatened. Students are much more demanding, feeling they are more consumers than ever before.

Bridges with industry: these may drive innovation but at a loss of control of the curriculum. Influencing the curriculum by external top-down pressure is a very sensitive area easily viewed as intruding onto academic freedoms.

So what does the changing nature of higher education mean for campus design within the context of a sustainability agenda that is becoming increasingly urgent for society and universities in the future?

THE ROLE OF THE UNIVERSITY

The campuses of the future must be highly connected, flexible and sustainable. Accomplishing the first two design objectives while delivering the third will be a tremendous challenge. These days campuses (as with nearly all buildings) must approach a near zero carbon standard of performance.

A zero carbon built environment is a challenge faced by the whole of society. However, universities do not just provide courses for practical policy and industry driven outputs but also uphold society's ideals, vision and potential. Higher education provides the opportunity for people to meet and interact with the brightest minds to form long-term links and ambitions in environments that value knowledge and its use for the greater good.

Society values them for this and should provide universities with the best access to technology and the research environments needed to make progress. The reality of climate change makes such progress all the more urgent.

For low carbon sustainable communities the university campus must become the laboratory for this future. Many exemplar buildings are constructed on campuses and the universities rightly pride themselves on them. It is time to go beyond this. Individual buildings are not a community; a campus is.

Universities must be live laboratories for the transition to a low carbon sustainable future. They need not only to educate, but to demonstrate the changes needed along the entire building supply chain. Higher education creates and trains the industry's decision

makers and practitioners. What they learn shapes the built environment for the decades that follow. This means that university ambitions must precede the country's ambitions. The timelines to low carbon are clear to 2050 and guidance is available to help demonstrate how this might be achieved[1] but our view is that those for universities should be a decade shorter to allow time for two to three cycles of graduates to leave and enter the world of work and 'life'.

In 2011, Royal Academy of Engineering research proposed a programme for university centres of excellence in sustainable building. This suggested that £30 million seed funding over five years would deliver cumulative savings in excess of £1 billion by 2030.[2]

WHAT ARE THE CARBON REQUIREMENTS FOR CAMPUSES?

The carbon footprint for universities is massive and projected to increase. Student populations have increased by a factor of five over the past 30 years and this number is likely to continue growing. UK university estates' annual turnover is £27 billion, equivalent to the fourth largest FTSE company. Universities occupy 26 million sqm of space (more than 2.5 times the government's estate), with annual energy costs of ~£200 million.[3] Recent trends in academic buildings have concentrated on improving facilities rather increasing built area, through a combination of infilling, replacement and refurbishment. All of these offer a tremendous opportunity to improve energy performance, sometimes at little additional capital cost.

UNIVERSITIES AT THE VANGUARD

The future campus will need to be progressively more low energy and low carbon. The UK government, in response to the Committee on Climate Change (CCC), has required that universities achieve carbon reduction targets for their campuses of 43% below 2005 (equivalent to 34% below 1990) by 2020 and 83% below 2005 figures by 2050 (equivalent to 80% below 1990).

Some suggest these are too slow for the sector, which must lead the way and demonstrate knowledge about how to deliver such results across the nation by the 2050 deadline. This view is supported by the Higher Education Funding Council for England (HEFCE) in the carbon reduction target and the 2008 strategy for higher education in England.[4]

These are large steps and in line with the whole built environment targets. Key is the need for universities to present and guide the rest of society towards how such figures might be achieved – so universities should consider higher targets.

Recent performance is not greatly encouraging – electricity use on on a per sqm basis has stayed largely constant since 2008, although the corresponding carbon per sqm dropped, owing to a reduction in the grid carbon intensity. Heating (non-electrical) use per sqm has dropped in the period and the corresponding carbon has reduced too. However, overall, most of the carbon reduction appears to be associated with the grid carbon intensity reduction. This analysis suggests that any actual electrical load reduction through improved management and lower energy systems is being offset by

▼ **Figure 3.11** *Carbon emissions in English higher education institutions (HEIs), 2008–2013 compared with carbon targets to 2050*

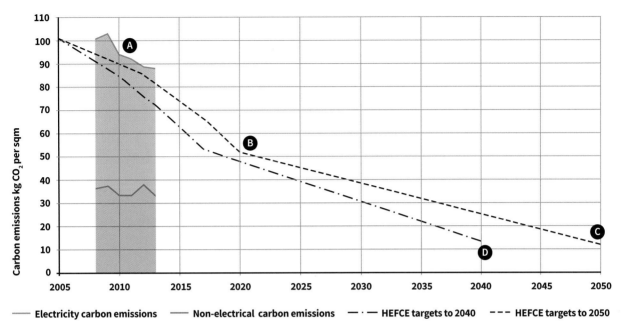

A Current energy usage in HEIs

B HEFCE 2020 target for 34% reduction in carbon emissions over 1990

C HEFCE 2050 target for 80% reduction in carbon emissions over 1990

D HEFCE 2050 target for carbon emissions brought forward to 2040

This shows the estate carbon pre square metre against the projected HEFCE targets from 2005 to 2050, and the HEFCE targets if they are brought forward by 10 years as suggested. The targets allow for estate growth, estimated from growth in the period 2008 to 2013. This shows how significant improvements in carbon intensity would need to be made to achieve the targets, likely including electricity and heating demand reduction as well as gid decarbonisation. The overall reduction in carbon of the current HE building stock is caused by the reducing grid carbon density.

increased energy demand per sqm. Refer to Part 4 for further discussion on building performance in use.

DISPLAY ENERGY CERTIFICATE TARGETS

Display energy certificate (DEC) targets provide a neat illustration of this. It is that the 2013 average university DEC rating (using the CIBSE University Campus benchmark) is 97 (or a high 'D')

Only 30% of DECs are currently C or better, and under 1% of DECs are currently A. Target average DEC scores to achieve the 2050 trajectory would be:

- 2017 – 73 (high 'C')
- 2020 – 58 (mid 'C')
- 2050 – 14 (mid 'A')

Current sector performance in DECs is discussed further in Part 4.

We identify three approaches to achieving these new targets:

1. Reduce local and distributed energy supply carbon impacts.
2. Establish ways to fix carbon reductions once established through good management and cultures.
3. Follow progressive initiatives to drive down loads from small power devices, particularly relating to research (which could be challenging).

INNOVATION

As research institutions, many universities are keen to explore how they can embrace innovation in their estate. This can include novel environmental approaches – in some instances in collaboration with academic departments, as illustrated in the following examples.

Centre for Efficient and Renewable Energy in Buildings
London South Bank University [6]

CEREB is a partnership between London South Bank, City and Kingston Universities. Each has related courses and other ventures which link to CEREB. The partnerships provide CEREB with a more diverse skills base and allow more projects to be delivered.

Centre of Excellence in Sustainable Building Design
Heriot-Watt University, Edinburgh [7]

This is one of four such Centres established at UK universities in collaboration with the Royal Academy of Engineering which, together, form a national network to demonstrate and exchange best practice in teaching and research for the sustainable built environment.

EXAMPLE
SUSTAINABILITY HUB
HOME FARM, KEELE UNIVERSITY [5]

The Hub supports the development of sustainability both within and beyond the higher education sector. It is home to the MSc Environmental Sustainability and Green Technology, and provides consultancy work to industrial partners, puts on continuous professional development (CPD) activities and lectures, welcomes hundreds through the doors every year for training and conferences, and to find out about new developments in sustainability research.

▼ **Figure 3.12** *Sustainability Hub, Home Farm, Keele University*

EXAMPLE
CREATIVE ENERGY HOMES
UNIVERSITY OF NOTTINGHAM ARCHITECTURE DEPARTMENT [9]

Green Close is a street of ecohouses, constructed in partnership with industry, and run by the University's Department of Architecture and Built Environment (see Figure 3.8). The Department has built a series of houses which investigate different technologies including micro smart grids, energy storage and demand site management – the 'Creative Energy Homes'.

EXAMPLE
ENERGY TECHNOLOGIES BUILDING UNIVERSITY OF NOTTINGHAM [8]

This building is home to research into: renewable energy using a biofuel combined heat and power (CHP); low energy lighting and intelligent controls; heat recovery ventilation with earth tube supply; responsible material selection including recycled materials to the concrete frame; and hydrogen production and filling stations with electric car charging points.

▲ **Figure 3.13** *Energy Technologies Building, University of Nottingham*

▲ **Figure 3.14** *Creative Energy Homes, University of Nottingham Architecture Department*

EXAMPLE
URBAN SCIENCES BUILDING
UNIVERSITY OF NEWCASTLE

This is a new building incorporating test bed strategies, including energy scavenging and storage technologies, building micro-metering and direct current test beds linked to PV panels avoiding losses incurred by DC-AC inverters. All of these can be integrated into research programmes and key items can be easily replaced as technologies evolve.

▶ **Figure 3.15** *Urban Sciences Building, University of Newcastle*

For energy-focused design teams the possibilities inherent in working with a professional and engaged client such as a university are rewarding. Items key to developing successful and ever-improving environmental performance from projects are listed below:

1. Agree the environmental aspirations at the outset.
2. Develop achievable targets through the design process.
3. Measure results in use.
4. Form an ongoing design partnership/work with the same design team over multiple buildings.
5. Demand every building to be better than the last.
6. Be consistent and persistent in the demands.
7. Do not add too many innovations at once – it confuses results.
8. Utilise controlled innovation – if something works do it again – but better.

99

CONTINUOUS CONTROLLED INNOVATION

A prime UK example of this approach is at the University of East Anglia (UEA), which has worked steadily for 20 years towards energy and carbon reduction.

The building services engineers Fulcrum worked on five buildings on the expanding campus in the 1990s culminating in the Elizabeth Fry building, which achieved building performance unsurpassed over the following decade. The designers learned that it was important to take clients to visit exemplars which pushed the boundaries, both in the UK and Europe, allowing the client to question and probe the users unhindered. This way the clients learned what was possible and could understand what to ask for and why design features were being suggested. They condensed these key lessons into a brief against which the buildings could be judged. In this way, both designers and client could agree what was possible.

A visit to Scandinavia was used to explore the appropriate appointment of consultants. As a result, responsibility for delivering detailed advice on fabric thermal performance was uniquely placed within the building services engineers' fee agreement. The decision to eliminate distributed heating and cooling systems to increase simplicity within Elizabeth Fry also came from this visit. It was possible to convince the engineers, and it allowed the client to give their informed consent to a design focusing on a fabric thermal store solution and high levels of fresh air ventilation and heat recovery.

Product manufacturers were engaged as part of the early stages, with meetings focused entirely on low energy and high comfort in a holistic way. The designers insisted on a process of leaving things out rather than adding new systems in, covering everything from orientation, window size and performance to structural integration of services.

As a result, the fabric was designed first, with specialist assistance on thermal detailing delivered to near PassivHaus standards and comfort through a ventilated concrete slab. The building was visited by the PROBE[10] (see page 124) team after two years of operation to explore its performance in detail, both from the perception of the occupants' professional support and energy consumption figures. It was revisited 12 years later to compare these results. In both cases, results were publically published – a step that should be required nationally of all buildings that claim exemplar status. These results showed that energy use had increased 20% following refurbishment with increased lighting and open-plan occupancy. Basic airtightness issues that were identified a decade earlier remained.

Buildings such as Elizabeth Fry demonstrate why universities emphasise performance as well as efficient design. As owner-occupiers, the client had a vested interest not only in the sustainable design and construction but in the reduced costs that came with it. The Manchester School of Art, later in this section, is another good example of this approach.

ENGINEER-OUT THE ENGINEERS

The Elizabeth Fry building offers a caution against the tendency to over-design. Sustainability must be simple. Building services often act as a risk-mitigation exercise, designing for the worst case plus a safety margin rather than for the averages and designing the building to even out the peaks. It is extremely easy for design to tend towards complexity and it should be the role of a nominated member of the team to actively challenge decisions.

Natural ventilation solutions are particular culprits here and all those involved need proper consultation; simple conflicts such as windows being closed because of noise, clashing with window blinds or security concerns can destroy an apparently simple strategy. The response of motorising and adding sensors can appear logical but simply adds complexity and further frustrations for users and issues for maintenance. Challenging such ideas must be done early in the design process and a vigilant eye kept, ensuring such ideas do not creep in later under the guise of cost-saving.

PASSIVE DESIGN

Well-designed buildings that rely on passive measures for environmental control are generally more popular with their occupants and in many instances use less energy than their mechanically conditioned counterparts. In particular, the academic cellular office model and the low occupancy often found in the sector are well suited to the demand control offered by natural ventilation. Control of building form, careful façade design, use of thermal mass and control

▲◄ **Figures 3.16 and 3.17** *The Forum, University of Exeter, WilkinsonEyre*

of internal gains are all key to ensuring good passive performance; it must not be forgotten that ventilation is required in winter as well as in summer, and the façade design must ensure that draughts are not an issue.

Passive buildings – with appropriate user training where necessary – can also be more resilient to changes in use, and are generally easier and cheaper to operate.

Where passive performance alone is not adequate – for instance in the centre of a city or where the building form or use make it impractical – mixed mode operation is often a good solution, with mechanical assistance required when it is particularly warm or cold, or in selected areas only.

Large atria and streets – popular in universities such as Exeter and Nottingham Trent – can be designed to capture passive solar gain in winter, particularly if the energy can be stored in surfaces during the season; whereas atria and streets can help to cool spaces in summertime when they are in shade. It should be noted that the challenge in many modern buildings is the avoidance of overheating rather than dealing with issues of heat loss in winter.

University buildings present particular challenges with regard to environmental performance which require particular attention during the design stage:

- Low utilisation and unusual occupancy patterns: how can we avoid wasting energy by conditioning unoccupied spaces yet ensure that they are comfortable when required?
- Seasonal use: buildings are principally designed for students, academics and researchers, yet conference and summer courses provide significant income and there are obvious differences in the requirements of students through the academic year. How can facilities cater equally for these different uses without simply over-providing?
- Rapid turnover of occupants: whether viewed on an annual, weekly, daily or hourly basis, buildings and spaces often have transient occupancies. It is often not clear who has ownership of spaces and their control. How can universities avoid the 'default to on' and engage such a wide range of occupants in environmentally sensitive operation of their spaces?
- Continually evolving funding sources and methods of teaching, learning, living and research: how can estates accommodate future demands that are unknown?

RENEWABLES AND OCCUPANCY

Solar low carbon sources of energy must be collected and the area required for this purpose must be protected from shade. Wind energy requires safe exposure to wind and all are challenging when the scale of energy need is considered in the context of individual buildings.

This makes energy efficiency and accurate prediction of energy demand a top priority in correct briefing. The question of how many people will be where, when and doing what must be answered clearly and accurately.

Renewables in the form of biomass (in whatever form) requires knowledgeable design and operation, which is generally outside the scope of typical facilities manager experience and requires specialist input and maintenance. Biomass also requires storage and delivery, and a reliable source of fuel, or commonly they are provided with duplicate gas as back-up. Sadly, in many cases the back-up takes over as the primary source due to its relative simplicity and reliability. This totally undermines the purpose and it is vital that client buy-in is achieved and the cost of operation includes skilled operation and maintenance.

To avoid such overdesign the whole team should be involved with the brief preparation. Occupancy in particular should be discussed openly with the implications recorded and incorporated. It is perhaps worth emphasising that occupancy when designing for low energy should be the form of an occupancy profile over time, ideally for each room.

These should also indicate anticipated fluctuations over the year. This is of particular importance on university buildings, as their occupancy can vary enormously and running for maximum occupancy in a holiday will lead to much waste.

LONGEVITY

For a building to be truly sustainable, it must have a long life. In rapidly changing times, this means that it should be easily adaptable to cater for future uses, many of which may not exist at this time. Who could have foreseen the impact that mobile IT devices would have on the lives of students today – and how this has affected the way in which our buildings function? The IT revolution is in turn triggering new ways of accessing information – while MOOCs have not had the impact which some expected, there is no doubt that there is a slow move towards blended learning – whether this is formalised or not. Student expectations are higher than ever, and in an increasingly global market this change is likely to take place at an increasing rate.

Buildings – and the spaces between them – must be designed to allow for future developments; in the absence of a crystal ball to predict future subject matter and curriculum delivery methods, it is vital that many buildings will need to avoid being bespoke to a particular department or group, and that a 'loose fit' strategy must be followed, with the ability to change layouts and uses, spare capacity in services installations and additional space for future plant enhancements.

One key aspect of building longevity is to ensure resilience to the effects of climate change. Setting aside the cooling effects of possible changes to the Atlantic Jetstream and Gulf Stream, climate change is of course expected to result in a general increase in global temperatures combined with more extreme weather events. If buildings are designed appropriately – including attention to façades, use of natural ventilation and other passive measures such as thermal mass – then there is no reason why this should not be achievable in most cases.

In some cases, for instance in Central London or in buildings with high heat gains, this resilience may not be achievable, and in this case the mechanical systems should be designed to allow simple upgrading to respond to changes in use or climate.

ESTATES AND BUILDINGS

In many universities, the buildings form part of campus developments. These offer great opportunities to ensure that the relationships between buildings are optimised, providing useful external spaces and appropriate connectivity. Buildings with similar functions can be grouped together to encourage collaboration and, if suitably designed, can allow departments to 'flex' and promote interdisciplinary working. Centralised timetabling of spaces – which is often used to improve space utilisation – can also increase the chance of interaction between academics and students, particularly from different subject areas; the 'water cooler moments' that often generate the most stimulating ideas. Connectivity for future campuses does not only apply to people and information: an additional benefit of grouping buildings together is that they provide opportunities to reduce energy use and carbon emissions through enhanced plant efficiency.

There has been a move in recent years towards more centralised energy systems, reversing the trend of the previous two or three decades. New and improved technologies in energy production and distribution, combined with increased energy costs and environmental awareness, have made such installations commonplace. For instance, there was an increase in the number of CHP installations in UK universities of over 120% between 2009 and 2014, now they now account for over 13% of total energy consumption.

District energy systems are at their most powerful when a variety of buildings are located in close proximity to each other, and where different load profiles and characteristics can enable total plant capacity to be reduced; in some instances, waste heat from buildings – such as IT server rooms and load-intensive areas – can be reused in other spaces. Ground source heat pumps can enhance performance further by storing energy in the ground on a seasonal basis. Lastly, centralised systems offer great opportunities to improve resilience, as well as the ability to upgrade and change plant as technologies change, evolve and improve, rather than having to deal with each building on a piecemeal basis.

WHAT ABOUT THE ROLE OF HEATING AND COOLING NETWORKS?

There is tremendous potential for improved efficiency through heat networks and long-term heat storage. It has also been noted that factors such as climate change, increases in IT loads and highly glazed designs are all increasing the need for cooling solutions. We must rethink how we can maximise the efficiency of our networks to deliver both heating and cooling.

Consider that heating and cooling are both essentially energy management. You move heat away from places that need cooling towards places that need heating. Treating heat as a resource across a campus can lead to tremendous energy savings overall.

A good example of this working in practice is Eindhoven University of Technology (TU/e) in the Netherlands. It has a heat and cold storage (Aquifer Thermal Energy Storage – or ATES) installation, which is one of the biggest of its kind in Europe. The ATES has been executed with two central rings: a cold ring and a warm ring. 70% of the TU/e campus is connected to the ATES network, which allows buildings to exchange heating and cooling with the ground as needed throughout the year.

The buildings forming part of the Campus 2020 projects are fully heated by means of the ATES in combination with a heat pump and low-temperature heating (in these buildings no natural gas is used for the heating). Likewise, the cooling of the buildings (high-temperature

▼ **Figure 3.18** *Central university library and the Faculty of Mathematics & Computer Science (W&I) by Ector Hoogstad Acthitecten - part of the Compact Campus 2020 masterplan for Eindhoven University of Technology, Netherlands*

cooling) is realised by the ATES. There are currently 32 boreholes serving the network, soon to be extended to 48 (24 cold and 24 hot wells). Water flow is 2000 m³/h now extending to 3000 m³/h in final format with a design heating/cooling capacity of 25MW.

By storing heat and cold in the soil, TU/e annually saves some two million kWh of electricity and more than 300,000 cubic metres of gas.

Both research and practice (e.g. TU/e) have shown that Cold Water Heat Networks (CWHN) offer significant benefits. University campuses are well suited to demonstrate these benefits,

such as the forthcoming Balanced Energy Network (BEN) project at London South Bank University (LSBU). We are working to demonstrate this heat-sharing technology here in the UK, further linking in demand management of electricity and carbon capture and storage from high temperature fuel cells.

This would be a paradigm shift for how universities manage their heating, cooling and electrical loads. The very nature of estates management stands to change. The role becomes a constant monitoring of need and shuffling of temperature into and out of energy stores. Campus planning could be

shaped around a CWHN. This is highly appealing to universities, which have a large mixture of old and new stock. By careful planning, matching new build with appropriate refurbishment, they can begin to balance the future heating and cooling demands and reduce the total need. Buildings could be strategically located to share heating and cooling demand, using borehole storage and waste heat recovery.

▼ **Figure 3.19** *Higher education estate carbon management*

A Existing estate

Understand the performance of the existing estate

B Classify buildings

Identify categories review: age, servicing strategy, building type (science, engineering, general academic, non-academic, residential).

C Grade energy performance

Record annual energy use (electricity, gas, other) and floor areas. Compare across the estate and benchmark eg. CarbonBuzz. Identify high-energy users which may be suitable targets for intervention.

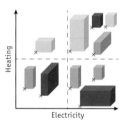

D Assess energy savings and compare with targets

Consider scope for operational carbon savings / reasons for high-energy use and interaction with occupants. Identify suitable interventions such as operational change, refurbishment and new-build options.

E Compare operational and embdied carbon

For each intervention, compare potential operational carbon savings with additional embodied carbon impact. A sense of scale is important: for HE typical lifetime embodied carbon impacts are in the range of 0.5 to 1 tonnes CO2e per sqm, whereas lifetime operational carbon emissions can range from 2 to 15 tonnes CO2e per sqm. As buildings become more efficient, the embodied carbon becomes far more dominant.

F Contextual factors

Consider contextual factors: heritage, future accommodation, changes in academic focus, wider society out-reach/integration, and construction disruption. Estate management and the institution's future plans influence these factors.

G Redevelopment brief

Using the contextual factors and the interventions identified in stages D and E, create the redevelopment brief. Capture the embodied and operational carbon performance expected for each building, using its unique characteristics.

H Design and delivery

Evaluate design against the expected performance set out in the redevelopment brief. Ensure energy use of the scheme is measured appropriately. Review design calculation methods to reflect operational characteristics and predicted usage. Methods such as CIBSE's TM54 can provide a robust framework for accurate energy use prediction. Use Soft Landings processes.

I Operational performance

Carefully manage to ensure savings materialise in use. Carry out detailed monitoring, seasonal commissioning, and post-occupancy evaluation to help identify changes in use, highlight opportunities for improved efficiency and make suggestions for future buildings.

3.4 DESIGN, CONSTRUCTION AND HANDOVER

Ian Taylor

This section summarises important issues which affect project outcomes during the life of a development project with reference to Feilden Clegg Bradley Studios' Manchester School of Art as an example project at each stage.

PEOPLE: DEVELOPING TRUST AND A SHARED VISION

Post-occupancy studies of new buildings are demonstrating clear links between positive client engagement in the briefing and the design process, and subsequent good user satisfaction and building performance in use. When the user client group has been closely involved in the visioning and detailed briefing process, an engaged operation of the building develops which brings out the best in the use of the facilities. This should not come as any surprise. What is surprising, however, is that so little effort is put into ensuring that client project teams and their counterpart design teams and contractor teams retain consistency through the different stages of the project process, losing so many opportunities for better understanding of the context of decisions at each stage.

Continuity in these processes is a critical factor for success. Once a clear overall strategy defines the parameters for an individual project, so that priorities in the context of the university's ambitions are established, the success of any project is dependent upon the understanding, skills and drive of the individuals and teams involved.

- A strong project champion – a senior client figurehead – should remain involved throughout to hold onto the vision to help steer decision-making through the opportunities and challenges of the process.
- Continuity of the client team members, so that ideas can develop through each phase of the project, this should include the early involvement of both users and the facilities management (FM) team so that decisions on operation and maintenance are made within a common understanding of the aspirations for the project.
- A clear strategy for choosing the project team, identifying the skills and attributes that are sought from the construction industry in terms of design, management, cost control and construction will

influence how and when the university chooses to appoint the design team. This selection process should be used to provide clear parameters for the priorities of the project, so that the skills of the team are suited to the ambitions of the client body. A design competition may be inappropriate for choosing skills in dialogue and briefing, while a developed, construction tender could elicit strengths in programming and process.

These factors create the context for the project and set the stage for the development of the brief through a creative dialogue with the client: prioritising where design effort and money is best spent to the overall benefit of the project. A building design project is, by its very nature, a vehicle that enables us to imagine a better future, and the process of that journey should in itself be an enjoyable and stimulating one. The best projects are those where a synergy develops between client and design team without too much intermediary project management, and where the solutions that arise through the process exceed the expectations of the client.

PEOPLE: THE MANCHESTER SCHOOL OF ART

This project established, and subsequently benefited from, strong working relationships between client, users, design team and contractors.

The architects had previously completed a successful project for the university, and a trusting relationship had developed with the estates office as a result of the approach and success of the earlier building.

There was a visionary and proactive Vice Chancellor, strongly advocating the benefits of good design and championing the importance of the physical estate.

The Dean of the Manchester School of Art wanted to engage in the design process in the pursuit of a transformational building for the school. Professor David Crow led a team who were interested to explore how the new environment could respond to their teaching ideas, and help shape a new collaborative culture. He wrote:

The chance to redesign the school for the 21st century was a dream job. We have a fantastic team of staff in the school who all recognise that this is an important moment for the school and the city. It is a moment that marks a change in art school education and it reflects the wider cultural shifts in our society.

It is also a chance to break down old divisions and reactionary attitudes that frustrated me as a student many years ago. There has always been a sense of hierarchy between the various disciplines in art schools. For some reason the terminology and the names often get in the way of a fully integrated practice.

We were able to use the estate project as a chance to help remove these attitudes and reveal the common ground. It has also enabled us to help bridge the gap between education and professional life.

Our new building is a chance to design a space with our architects that celebrates the inter relation of our various fuzzy edged disciplines and encourage our 21st century students to work alongside each other and enjoy the crossover rather than concentrating always on the differences. It is also a building that is proud of its product and shows the work to everyone who passes by.

Professor Crow's observations on the relationships between disciplines in the Art School working in the completed building resonate for me with the process of creating architecture – and the relationships which I feel are so important for the creation of successful buildings:

I have a very healthy respect for all our disciplines and have grown to realise that we learn from each other all the time, that the past informs the future, that theory informs practice, and practice informs theory. Our processes are neither linear nor predictable. Our subject areas are not defined by our tools and job titles are often misleading. It sounds like a confusing picture, but to us, to artists, designers, craftspeople, whatever we are called, it's a hugely exciting arena where anything is possible and everything is relevant.

THE DESIGN PROCESS

It is important to develop a good understanding of the expected quality, cost and time parameters for the project, and to highlight the critical features of the development. Benchmarking against other buildings and spaces within the same client's estate, as well as visiting precedent buildings and exemplar schemes is useful. The design team should establish how the building will be operated and maintained, and encourage serious debate about whole-life value to inform decision-making affecting capital cost by consideration of in use costs, performance, adaptability and sustainability targets.

The design team should take care to understand the levels of experience of the university client body – some of whom may never have been involved in commissioning a building and may not readily understand two-dimensional drawings and building jargon. The designers and client team should agree on appropriate presentation methods (using models, drawings and other presentation techniques) to ensure that ideas can be explained in order to enable the client group to engage in the briefing and design dialogue. At all stages, the use of models and mock-ups to demonstrate scale, design ideas and to establish quality standards is invaluable.

It is useful to set out a clear programme for design development, to help the client understand when different decisions need to be made. It is important that this ties into a consultation programme so that separate internal client engagement and stakeholder consultation can genuinely feed into the design process

▲ **Figures 3.20 and 3.21** *Manchester School of Art, Feilden Clegg Bradley Studios*

at the most suitable times to benefit the outcomes in a timely manner.

The design team response to the academic briefing, estates priorities and sustainability targets builds up through the work stages (as described earlier on page 93) and is usefully captured in design stage reports which should become ever-more detailed reference documents describing the project as it develops. Complex projects which require detailed coordination are well served by a design programme which allows for a comprehensive design team report at RIBA Plan of Work Stage 3 Developed Design, which should ideally be in advance of submission of a planning application, and before

commencement of detailed design (RIBA Plan of Work Stage 4 Technical Design) There is often time pressure to submit both an early planning application and to commence technical design without a period to enable a strong 1:50 and 1:20 scale coordination process to be completed – both of which can add risk into the project, and could have adverse impacts on out-turn cost, quality and programme. Complex building briefs require careful thought, and time is needed to coordinate holistic solutions incorporating timely client input and review

A well-integrated and strongly led design team is key to successful outcomes in projects which generally

set demanding targets and have highly aspirational agendas. University clients deserve exceptional design and professionalism.

THE DESIGN PROCESS: MANCHESTER SCHOOL OF ART

The design team need to capture the essence of the building brief, reflecting that back to the client so that the base functional data can be verified as correct, and so that interpretations of the brief can be explored in order to help prioritise issues and highlight the most critical features desired in new environment.

User consultation needs to be understood and categorised.

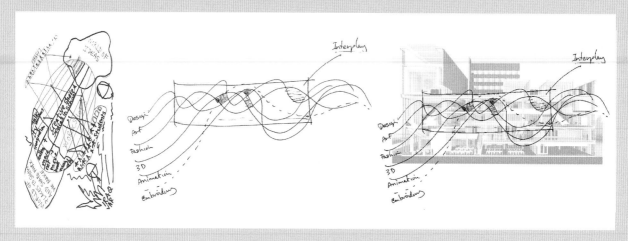

▲ ▲ **Figures 3.22, 3.23 and 3.24 (top row)**
Existing and anticipated uses need to be understood and represented in the brief

▲ **Figures 3.25 and 3.26 (middle row left and centre)** *Ideas need to be well communicated*

▲ ▼ **Figures 3.27 and 3.28 (above and below)**
Different drawing styles and models are useful communication tools to represent design intent

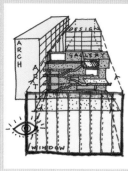

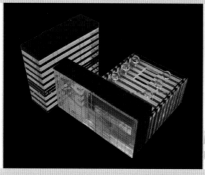

CONSTRUCTION

The positive impacts arising from continuity of staff experience and mutual understanding discussed at the start of this section equally apply to the individuals in the contracting building teams, and this has led many universities to develop framework arrangements with contactors (and design teams), which operate with varying degrees of success. The large scale of development that some universities are now engaged in can make frameworks attractive as long as cost issues are dealt with in a transparent and controlled process.

On the other hand, the specialist nature of certain projects is better served by one-off procurement in order to obtain very tailored services from specialist contractors and designers.

Highly constrained sites, either through their geography, urban context or building adjacencies sometimes create conditions which require significant construction advice early in the design process. Appointing contractors to give early advice, through framework arrangements or separate appointments to review access and building impacts is often critical for development decision-making. Mitigating construction impacts on the life and productivity of the existing estate – especially when a building project might run for the full length of a student's attendance on their course – become business critical issues.

The increasing use of less adversarial construction contracts, such as the NEC New Engineering Contracts, forms used in the UK is improving the building process and reflecting the idea of the more joined-up complete project team, where the contractor is seeking a similar set of successful outcomes as the client. Better integration between the client and contracting team is particularly relevant to the commissioning and handover process, where there can be genuinely improved outcomes by facilitating the early engagement of the client's building management team into witnessing commissioning and understanding the building systems on site, and then subsequently retaining the same client team to operate the building in use, alongside members of the contractor team to help optimise performance in the first years of operation. Any stand-off between contractor and building operator during the first year ('defects period') of operation resulting from apparent problems, can cause enormous damage to users' attitudes to their new environment. Contract terms must be established to enable more proactive responses.

Once the building is handed over, much can be done to review and improve the performance of that building is in use, informing decision-making on the design of better spaces in the future, and influencing building design and strategic planning of the estate. Value and Performance are discussed in Part 4.

CONSTRUCTION: MANCHESTER SCHOOL OF ART

The design team needed to communicate design intent clearly for the contractor – providing clarity on the required quality of the completed building, and wherever possible engaging individuals in the contracting team to input ideas into construction methodology and best practice. On this project, the contractor was appointed before all the details for construction were complete, allowing for detailed development to incorporate contractor input.

▼ **Figure 3.29** *The detailed design of the façade was fine-tuned using tested mock-ups*

▼▼ **Figure 3.30** *Sustainable design features were prioritised with the contractor*

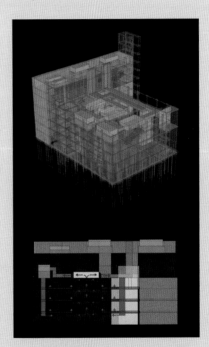

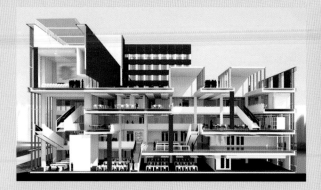

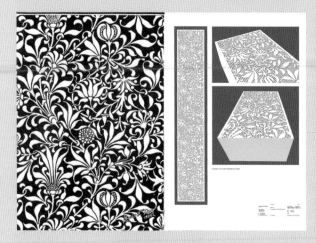

▲ ▶ **Figures 3.31**
*Development of
the patterned
feature concrete
columns was a joint
enterprise between
mould casting
manufacturers, the
concrete contractor,
the main contractor,
architect and client*

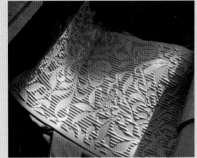

value and performance

4

The success of a university building should be assessed by its overall contribution to the aims of the institution: the educational, research, social, cultural and economic outcomes that it facilitates. Some of these outcomes might be considered absolute, but many are either subjective or highly influenced by the context in which the project was framed, spatial requirements and project processes already described.

In the Opinion introduction, Julian Robinson reflects on the issue of 'value', discussing the importance of the physical estate on the character of the institution.

Joanna Eley reviews the importance of post occupancy evaluation (POE), and give guidance on the timing, tools and approaches available to help understand how well a building is performing in use.

Mike Entwisle sets out technical issues which impact on the gap between design intentions and operational performance, both in terms of comfort and carbon.

The academic performance of the building is more difficult to assess. Kenn Fisher describes his current research in this field, investigating the fit between spatial configurations and the teaching and learning they are facilitating.

Four case studies conclude this section, reflecting on factors which have contributed to successful outcomes.

4.1 VALUE

Julian Robinson

OPINION

What do we mean by value? Oscar Wilde quipped 'nowadays people know the price of everything and the value of nothing' but I would contend that most universities do know this difference. In terms of their built environments many have conducted research to ascertain the value of high-quality buildings and estates.

Put simply, and to quote Warren Buffet, 'Price is what you pay and value is what you get'. Additionally, as Karl Marx said, 'nothing can have value without being an object of utility', which of course well-designed buildings have in abundance. However, quantifiying this value and utility is not a straightforward exercise.

UNIVERSITIES AND THEIR ESTATES

Between 1996 and 2011, universities in the UK invested a massive £27.5 billion in their buildings and estates and between 2012 and 2013 spent £2 billion on non-residential capital development.[1] Looking ahead, the University of Manchester is transforming its campus and surrounding area, with a total of £1.75 billion to be invested by 2022 – the largest-ever estates investment by a UK university.

WHY DO UNIVERSITIES INVEST?

The main driver is competition. Directors of Estates are aware that inspiring buildings and high-quality facilities play an important role in attracting students to a particular university. As the cap on student numbers is lifted and a free market emerges, having well-designed and maintained buildings is going to be a key driver for all universities; but how much value should be given to these aspects, in relation to the other contributors of a positive student experience?

RESEARCH AND EVIDENCE

There is, in fact, scant evidence that higher education buildings of significant architectural merit produce better degree results, improve staff retention or increase student satisfaction. Research in this area has been relatively sparse. The Commission for Architecture and the Built Environment (CABE) attempted to address this issue in its 2005 publication *Design with Distinction*.[2] It found that 90% of students identified teaching facilities and 75% of staff identified support facilities as influencing their performance, with 81% and 64% respectively saying the same about the campus. However, it is difficult to discern from this research whether there is a direct link between high-quality design and academic excellence.

The Russell Group, which comprises the UK's leading research universities, acknowledges that 'The buildings are often stunning – not just in their aesthetics but in how space can be used imaginatively and how they actively promote problem solving entrepreneurialism in their design.'[3] Their report provides some interesting examples, but again solid metrics are harder to come by.

At the LSE, it was decided we had insufficient empirical evidence to support investment in new buildings and campus improvements, so we commissioned ZZA Responsive User Environments to survey our students' views.[4] The reasons for this were fourfold:

1. students had just become the main funders of higher education
2. we wanted to survey their opinions on what was good and bad about the campus
3. to gauge the importance of buildings and facilities to their overall experience
4. to provide evidence to support funding applications to the School for more expenditure on estate development and renewal.

Interestingly, only 25% of LSE students considered the quality of the campus and buildings as a factor in their decision. However, once they had arrived, 75% said it had become important to their experience as a student.

Due to the absence of sector wide research, the HEDQF published *Estates Matter!*,[5] which presented a quantitative survey of students' opinions on the importance of buildings and estates. The findings were staggering – 36% of students said they had rejected certain institutions because of the quality of their buildings, facilities or physical environment. Once students had chosen a university, estate quality remained an important factor, with 83% of respondents saying it was very or quite important.

Building on the HEDQF research, in July 2015 the Association of University Directors of Estates (AUDE) published additional data[6] from a survey of 2,000 students which showed that facilities are key for 67% of UK students when choosing university. As expected, course (79%) and location (69%) were marginally more important, with reputation (47%) and the Students' Union (18%).

While every university will have an estates strategy containing ambitions for new buildings, the results sometimes leave a lot to be desired. Some see any new building as good in itself, and for many staff and students who have been accommodated in poor quality accommodation anything which is shiny and new is well received. Many create poor connectivity with adjacent buildings, unsatisfactory public spaces and little consideration to an overall masterplan. How many of the buildings which have been thrown up in the past two decades will stand the test of time? Or will they, like many of their predecessors from the 1960s, be regarded as sub-optimal and be demolished and/or redeveloped? Only ongoing research and time will tell.

CONCLUSION

The UK higher education sector should not be regarded as a homogenous entity. Universities are self-governing institutions much less reliant on central government funding than in the past. However, what they have in common is they all compete for students – both nationally and internationally – and all (even the Open University) have physical estates.

The evidence shows that over the last two decades universities have invested heavily in their estates. While there was a slow-down during the last recession, this investment has steadily continued. The university estates of today, save for historic buildings, are unrecognisable from 30 years ago.

Directors of Estates and their representative organisations, keen to justify capital expenditure, have begun to appreciate that the need for investment in the physical estate is not necessarily self-evident and that empirical research is required to demonstrate value both to students, their higher education Institutions (HEIs) and the wider UK economy. These range from POEs of individual buildings, to student opinion surveys, through to macro studies of the entire higher education sector. An example of the former is explored in case study 4.

4.2 BUILDING PERFORMANCE

Joanna Eley

University activity globally is growing rapidly as our economies depend ever more on an educated, knowledge-based workforce. University estates and campuses are growing to accommodate the expansion in this long-established form of education. The earliest UK universities had similar origins to eleventh-century Bologna, where the first university was created as a community of scholars and students. Today, university communities exist in widely varied physical environments with virtual layers being increasingly overlaid.

Universities within the UK are a large and growing sector of real estate investment, as are student residences for the two million university students. Investment in university buildings is growing in the UK. Regions such as Asia and the Middle East are looking to the UK and USA for expertise in education, research, and building and campus design.

This chapter summarises how 21st-century universities can meet what they aspire to be now and to become in the future, through ensuring that their buildings perform well – and as intended. It looks at what current university clients and their designers are, can and should be doing, to judge the success of university buildings and learn from this for future projects to support the success of each institution.

GOOD DESIGN STARTS WITH UNIVERSITY PERFORMANCE

Universities depend for their long-term survival in part on how well the buildings and campuses *perform* to meet their current needs and future aspirations.

University clients need designers who can create buildings that help to them to deliver their core business while inspiring the staff and students. They need buildings that communicate their future vision of an environment for enquiry, knowledge and learning. They may need campuses and buildings that create environments only for the academic community, or they may instead seek to create permeable places that welcome local communities and enterprise to co-create the future. Architects and designers therefore need to understand what matters to universities and how their professional expertise can help in its delivery, and clients need to learn how the design professions can help them to achieve their goals.

Universities are regularly judged and ranked on different activities and by different parties. They have two main purposes: research and teaching. In many countries, including the UK, the research excellence of each university, academic department and of each academic member of staff is subjected periodically to scrutiny. Research excellence scores lead to rankings of each university and each department. These form the basis for governments to decide where future research funds from the public purse should best be directed, and for researchers to decide where their interests will best be supported. Architects and design teams able to create buildings in which research activity can be improved will win university projects, but must be prepared to provide irrefutable evidence of the link between research outcomes and building design. Their clients are

likely to be cautious about believing claims that cannot be backed up by hard data, some of which will need to come from building performance evaluation.

To help future students decide their preferred university, teaching excellence is assessed by student surveys or other data, such as the average grades for acceptance into a programme of study, and the results are widely publicised and readily accessed. Students are commonly asked to rank aspects of the student experience, such as teaching quality, feedback and assessment, contact hours, organisation and management, facilities and infrastructure.

Architects and designers who can help to improve teaching through the spaces and places they shape are greatly in demand. Not only can they improve the environment for current staff and students but their designs may be able to attract more students of higher academic ability that in turn will create the virtuous circle central to the needs of each university, by setting the stage for standards to continue to improve.[7] Evaluation of building performance supports this process.

EVIDENCE OF GOOD PERFORMANCE

Imagine that, as an architect or client, the design phase of a new project – a refurbishment or a new building – is complete, the construction phase is over, handover has taken place, people have moved in. Is now the time to look back at what has been achieved? Or should everyone have been measuring performance, or value, much earlier in the building process? Would that improve the chance of meeting goals?

Common university goals are to:

- create campuses and buildings that provide spaces to serve today's users, and that endure by adapting over time to new expectations and needs
- be spatially efficient, cost effective to run, easy to maintain, comfortable to use, delightful to be in and observe
- attract the right staff and students.

To deliver designs that meet those needs, designers need to understand what users need now, what matters to them, how they behave, what servicing systems are needed and how these really do perform. In addition, they must understand emerging trends, such as how changes in pedagogy may alter space requirements.

Some of this essential information should be in the brief, and additional understanding comes though participating in its development. To strengthen future designs, architects should learn from evidence of what has worked well in the past, how conflicting agendas have been resolved and unforeseen requirements met. They can learn to identify and emulate good practice from the early stages of briefing, through to design development, construction and handover. In terms of the RIBA Plan of Work, lessons can be learned from Stage 7 – completed university buildings in use – that can then inform Stages 0 and 1, the early stages of briefing for the next project. Learning from experience, creating a virtuous circle where hindsight creates insight and allows effective foresight, will lead to better buildings. This is the virtuous circle that will ensure that the

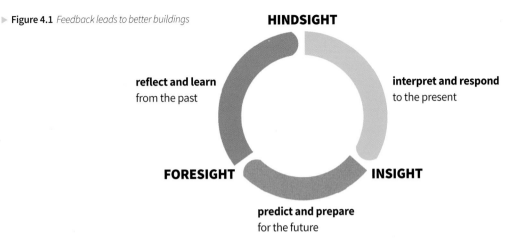

▶ **Figure 4.1** *Feedback leads to better buildings*

HINDSIGHT

reflect and learn
from the past

interpret and respond
to the present

FORESIGHT

INSIGHT

predict and prepare
for the future

built environment of a future campus community meets the needs of the future university.

Despite wide recognition of the benefits of learning from an evaluation of past projects, their processes and outcomes, POE happens far less often than it should. Many clients are reluctant to reveal any failings after large amounts of capital have been spent and years of effort have been expended. They are not motivated to spend even the relatively tiny amount of money a POE may cost after the building is complete; their concern is now to get on and use it. Professional teams may be reluctant to expose any inadvertent errors and be fearful of any implications for their professional indemnity insurance. The cost of doing a POE was not built into the original project cost – that might have made them less competitive than their rivals. In any case, they have moved onto the next project.

However, experienced clients and their expert design teams recognise the need to define and communicate

desired outcomes and test if they have been achieved. Fortunately, university estates' clients are among the most experienced around. They are serial clients, who commission many large and small projects to maintain, adapt and renew their sizeable estates. In the UK university sector, carrying out POEs has been encouraged by university estate directors, with the intention that the university community will thereby be able to share experience and learn from one another. Techniques such as the Design Quality Indicator (DQI)[8] and the HEDQF post-occupancy review have been used to excellent effect.

More evaluative research is needed to pin down important outcomes. Satisfying the core mission – delivering a place that supports high-quality teaching, learning and research over time – is what design must aim for. All the basic, as well as statutory, requirements must be met that any competently designed building should achieve. Challenging sites and demanding and specialised functions

must be understood and provided for. Suitable evidence for such issues must be agreed in advance and monitored in execution by all those involved. In addition, designers and clients who are developing new space types to meet new pedagogical needs, as described in earlier sections in this book, need more evidence of what works. Research into innovative spaces for new pedagogy is under way and their use will spread if the evidence proves that they perform well, as discussed by Kenn Fisher on page 127.

UNIVERSITY CLIENTS NEED TO ARTICULATE THEIR GOALS

For successful projects, therefore, all those involved must be able to discuss and agree what they are seeking to achieve. Estate clients, architects and other project team members working in conjunction with the academic staff should provide statements of desired outcomes and planned targets. Usually this will require building up a shared understanding and a common vocabulary by spending time together,

119

reviewing papers, visiting related buildings elsewhere and inviting experts to share their ideas.

Open discussion of the aims of the various stakeholders is essential, as is resolution of conflicting agendas, such as the need to be economical with finances and space and the desire to give academic staff individual offices. Or there may be a conflict between keeping capital costs low with later consequences for increased revenue expenditure over the longer term.

This process is first undertaken at the vision development and briefing stages, and must itself be based on good evidence for the desirability of any conflicting goals, in order to resolve them into a single vision. It must continue throughout the process, maintain a record of the primary objectives, the 'must have' results, as well as the 'nice-to-haves' in order, after completion, to establish if the objectives have been met and if the project performs well.

BUILD QUALITY, FUNCTION AND IMPACT

As has been mentioned, university performance is measured by methods such as the results of student and staff surveys and periodic peer assessment of research quality. Such ratings provide little information to help understand how the campus and buildings support universities in their primary objectives. Better questions about the impact and importance of buildings in providing students with the environment they need and academics with good places to teach and do their research would help universities target their investment in the built environment wisely.

The estate, the landscape, buildings and interiors, must also work in their own right. Each can be judged by how well it satisfies the trio of 'firmness, commoditie and delight', as Sir Henry Wooton translated Vitruvius's three characteristics essential to buildings: *firmitas, utilitas* and *venustas*.[9] The DQI – launched in the UK in 2003 and in the USA in 2006 – reinterpreted these as build quality, function and impact.[10]

BUILD QUALITY

- At present (2016) building performance measurement often concentrates on build quality ('firmness') particularly energy efficiency, reduction of carbon dioxide (CO_2) emissions or other quantifiable and thus measurable aspects of environmental 'sustainability', such as waste and pollution or water use.[11]
- More fundamental aspects of build quality – such as structural soundness or weather enclosure – are usually taken for granted by a client.

FUNCTION

- Whether any specific user group is satisfied and has the spaces it needs, can be investigated using the various POE methods discussed below.

IMPACT

- If a building is liked and is praised for its qualities, it may signify that it provides delight or has a positive impact.
- Whether a building meets stakeholder expectations may be measured against desired outcomes.

Designers and clients are proud to receive design awards signifying public praise; however, subjective criteria sometimes creep in, so an award may not guarantee quality or appropriateness.

CREATING A FEEDBACK LOOP

Universities are in a good position to establish feedback loops. Estates departments in universities share experience through various groups, so they can learn from each other. Despite considerable differences between individual universities, they face similar challenges: estates that are continuously changing to meet evolving needs, new pedagogies, changes in IT and shifting expectations of their users, as well as a generally similar annual timetable where much work is done over the summer when main teaching sessions are not taking place. With support from the AUDE and the HEDQF, the POE culture could – and indeed should – be stimulated so that students and academics benefit from better places to learn and conduct research created by a more intelligent and informed construction industry, providing higher-quality buildings. The need to learn and to pass on lessons gets more acute as change accelerates and as competition for the best students and academics becomes more intense.

Feedback supports better future performance and helps to create a 'learning organisation'. Evaluation can highlight 'quick wins', immediate, low-cost improvements for the benefit of current users.

Despite the increased acceptance of the concept of POEs, even when these are conducted, the results are not well publicised. Some comparative information is available from the websites of the Usable Building Trust[12] and of the HEDQF.[13] However, as mentioned, neither clients nor professionals yet share such information freely as a matter of good practice. The RIBA and other professional institutes, and AUDE on behalf of the client body, should be encouraged to put more emphasis on the importance of shared information and feedback to increase the value provided by design. Designers could be rewarded for publicising POE results, while clients should be encouraged to invest in sharing such information.

LOOK BACK AND FORWARD

Projects can take several years from the first vision though a briefing, design and construction process to completion. Are there obvious times to check performance? Should one wait until after completion to review what has been built? How long after handover is a building really finished? Can it be evaluated during the design process?

A 'wash-up' session – a post-construction review – does not measure performance or quality. It happens too soon to do more than start to evaluate the process. Awards and prizes are commonly judged too early if based on visits when a project has just been completed and may still have snags. A POE done six months to a year after the building occupants move in is more realistic. A good time to start is after a full teaching year and with experience of the annual weather pattern. A building about to be replaced or extensively renovated should be evaluated before work starts, so that the brief can be systematically informed by current experience.

Visits to other buildings before finalising a brief, data about their performance and the views of estates, facilities managers and students will help crystallise specific outcomes to be met by the new project, identifying some of the post-occupancy issues that they illustrate.

Many processes emphasise the importance of evaluation as a regular rather than a one-off activity:

- Building performance evaluation (BPE) methods stress the importance of evaluation and review at all stages during the procurement cycle: planning, briefing, design, post-construction stages and during occupation.
- Soft Landings, adopted for UK public buildings, monitors some aspects to agreed targets throughout the project and may continue for years afterwards.
- Annual estate measurement statistics (EMS data) have to be provided to the Higher Education Funding Council of England (HEFCE), including teaching space utilisation, functional suitability and other building-based measures.

One can also ask how well a building has 'stood the test of time', perhaps many years after the building is completed and occupied, after many modifications in its form and function, renewals of short-life elements, changes of fashion in aesthetic or other design areas. This is in itself a measure of quality, and ways to measure this are needed.

EXAMPLES OF CHARACTERISTICS TO MEASURE

Build quality

- Internal environmental quality, energy efficiency, CO_2 emissions, water consumption etc. testing actual use against predictions
- Health and wellbeing data
- Cost in use – whole-life value

Function

- Accessibility and ease of wayfinding
- Amounts of space, adjacencies and the extent to which they match the brief
- Appropriate levels of utilisation of spaces for general and specialist teaching, learning, offices and other uses – a potentially wider range than required by HEFCE
- Productivity – perceived or actual
- Use of flexibility and adaptability features
- Ease of management

Impact

- User satisfaction with comfort – air quality, temperature, visual, noise, etc.
- Client satisfaction – meeting desired outcomes
- Improvements/changes desired by users
- Awards – immediate and over time
- Image /brand recognition, recruitment/retention of staff and students

WHAT AND HOW TO MEASURE

If you can't measure it you can't improve it. Lord Kelvin

The box (left) suggests targets to consider. Some exist in regulation or guidance, others may need to be agreed between the client and the design team. As the project evolves, adjustments may be needed which must be agreed and recorded.

Measuring success in meeting these targets can be done in a range of ways.

William Bordass, in *Designing Better Buildings*,[14] describes four techniques for collecting the necessary information:

1. observation: of exemplars and then the project in use
2. facilitated discussions
3. questionnaires/interviews
4. physical monitoring and analysis of performance statistics.

This matches closely to the well-established WorkWare[LEARN] toolkit[15] (by Alexi Marmot Associates) used for HEI buildings, allowing relevant data to be systematically collected and reviewed against agreed targets, and benchmarked against other projects and places.

The BRE Design Quality Matrices described for buildings generally in *The Design Quality Manual: Improving Building Performance*[16] suggest five broad categories of information to be collected:

1. Architecture: a subjective measure
2. Environmental engineering: against objective figures
3. User comfort: against measureable conditions
4. Whole-life costs: overall occupancy costs
5. Detailed design: as poor details or bad execution often lead to 'failures'.

The University of Sunderland (see box below) suggested desired outcomes for their refurbished labs.[17] These are expressed in terms specific to their needs and framed their own project, though many, slightly reworded, would apply to other buildings. Some of them

UNIVERSITY OF SUNDERLAND OBJECTIVES FOR THEIR SCIENCES COMPLEX REFURBISHMENTS

- Reinvigoration of existing buildings to provide upgraded laboratory teaching and office facilities .
- Transition from department-owned to cross-faculty facilities.
- New work environments for staff, supporting interaction and collaborative working.
- Provision of flexible and effective laboratory research facilities.
- Accommodating larger group sizes in laboratories and increasing space utilisation.
- Efficient spacial use of shared facilities supported by good practice in timetabling.
- Positive impact on student experience.
- Vacating poor quality space as a result of efficiencies in space use through consolidation and shared facilities.

will be easier to 'measure' than others but for each a way to measure could be defined and many could be measured before the project starts to create a benchmark for success. A POE can also be conducted for a whole campus (see box below, right).

EVALUATION TOOL KITS

There are many available measurement 'tools', often grouping several different methods as 'kits'. Several stress the need to precede a project with an assessment to establish goals and targets so that later it is possible to monitor progress in achieving them.

Some tools in regular use include:

- The HEDQF 'no shame, no blame' assessment method.[18] A day of workshops covers briefing, design, construction and use, attended by relevant stakeholders including the staff and student users. Positive and negative lessons for each stage of the process are reported to improve subsequent projects.
- AUDE and HEFCE sponsored a guide to POE,[19] a comprehensive document explaining the purpose of POE and incorporating templates and checklists for those wishing to measure against very full checklists and numerical targets.
- Alexi Marmot Associates' WorkWare[LEARN] toolkit has been used for over 200 university buildings and provides information from over 15,000 staff and students, allowing universities to evaluate and benchmark their building and estate performance against others.

- Leesman developed their office index to create 'Leesman Education'[20] to collect self-reported subjective views: 'My-Uni' covers 11 aspects of how students feel the university buildings impact on their educational experience. The Leesman Campus Survey focuses on employee assessments of the buildings' ability to support them and how it affects their sense of pride and productivity, as well as satisfaction with specific features and services.
- Space utilisation surveys (SUS) provide observed data on how often teaching rooms are used (frequency in relation to number of opportunities during an observation period), and by how many students (occupancy in relation to capacity). This provides a proxy for efficient use of space.[21] Similar techniques were originally developed for office space and are sometimes used by universities to review the way their academic and support offices are used.
- Building Use Studies created a survey tool that collects the views of building users – generally in offices, though now used under licence in a wide range of building types.[22] Its focus is on comfort and building services as well as users' perceptions of the support for their activities provided by the building.

Tools to help make decisions must be used with care. In a questionnaire seeking people's opinions, the number of respondents matters. When a prize is awarded, the qualifications of the judges

are relevant. When key performance indicators (KPIs) are measured, the way data is collected should be known to understand its value. Realising that people learn in different ways is leading to pedagogical changes, using new space types and new furniture arrangements.

Now the challenge is to spread the information more widely.

BUILDING PERFORMANCE

POE COULD TAKE PLACE AT CAMPUS LEVEL

Build quality

The Dublin Institute of Technology estate at Grangegorman has started with a clear fix for its brand new campus layout in particular the ground-level treatment and landscaping to provide the opportunity for an entire campus to rise gradually but coherently from a blank canvas. A POE in say 2020, will be able to ask whether the detailed campus planning rules, enshrined in an immutable planning permission, have succeeded in creating what they wanted: a lively pedestrian place, well connected to the local area, attracting top quality students and staff and allowing collaboration between hitherto separate disciplines.

LESSONS FROM EVALUATION

The same mistakes are still made time and again. Some findings from POEs appear regularly. Openness about both success and failure is essential.

Results from 16 PROBE POEs on office buildings carried out between 1995 and 2002, looking primarily at building services and user comfort, found some recurrent problems even though the buildings were generally good.[23] These included, among others:

- interface issues between work packages and for users
- shortcomings with handover processes
- user dissatisfaction with environmental comfort
- higher than anticipated energy use.

HEDQF workshops regularly find communication problems, loss of continuity of team members and the difficulty of providing academic staff with time to participate effectively in all stages. If the client – the university – cannot find suitably motivated individuals and provide them with space and time in their schedules to act as true client representatives, it should be no surprise if a building project is in some respects disappointing to the users.

Questionnaires frequently show users to be least satisfied with heating, cooling, air quality and noise. University staff and students regularly criticise inadequate WiFi and mobile phone coverage and strength. Uncomfortable furniture – especially chairs with attached writing surfaces – and inflexibility are regular targets for dissatisfaction.

Reviews of finished buildings show that energy use models, prepared early in a project to guide services design, have not accurately predicted the final built situation. For example, Carbon Buzz data,[24] provided by a selection of HEIs, shows that on average CO_2 emissions are almost twice that targeted: 39.9 kg CO_2/sqm/yr at the design stage versus 77.8 kg CO_2/sqm/yr when actual energy data in use are reviewed. The detail behind this finding indicates a wide spread between those that performed well and those that were much worse than predictions. The latter can learn from the former.

There is, however, a note of caution in relation to energy use here: one major issue is that the building models are generally compiled for building regulation compliance. They usually contain unrealistic usage patterns and exclude unregulated energy (equipment), which can be significant. A successful building may be more intensively used and have longer operational hours, both factors likely to push up energy consumption, sometimes reflecting a popular and well used building and excellent use of resources. Perhaps carbon emissions should be measured against financial turnover, teaching outcomes or research outcomes/income?

Acting on all these regular and disappointing findings must be built into project governance, be explicit in briefs and be costed and allowed for in the monitoring and management of the design and construction process. It is unacceptable to keep making the same mistakes.

RESEARCH TO ANSWER QUESTIONS

Some questions remain at least partially unanswered and occasionally unasked. More research is needed, though it must avoid the type of bias illustrated.

STUDENTS' INTEREST IN THE PHYSICAL ENVIRONMENT

The HEDQF and AUDE have carried out some research to show that students feel that 'Place Matters'.[25] It can be hard to survey students and academics about this, but more work is needed to make it happen. The views of the users need to be systematically sought by whatever means. The case study from the LSE on pages 162-167 is an example of the value of seeking this feedback.

SOLO OFFICES FOR ACADEMICS

UK universities have wrestled with whether academics can be asked to work in open-plan areas without destroying their ability to meet students and do great research. Questions fly around the university estates network asking where open plan for academics has worked. There seem to be few answers, although newer buildings are getting bolder about the use of open plan than historic campuses. There is an urgent need for careful evaluation and communication with the users on this subject.

The Australian perspective on

AN OFFICE OF ONE'S OWN IS OVERWHELMINGLY DESIRED BY ACADEMICS

This type of communication and 'research' will confirm the existing bias.

One English faculty faced with the ruling that they would have to share larger offices in an old building, where room sizes could not be altered, created badges for all staff and room door stickers saying ' Virginia Woof – A Room of One's Own.'

In August 2015 the Guardian Higher Education Network circulated the following: 'Calling all senior academics: has your office been turned into an open-plan space? We're looking to hear from those who hate working in a shared office to talk about how it's impacted on their work. Email me if that's you.'

Some university departments have accepted much smaller offices, but one of the key issues is that the nature of academic work which is the most highly rewarded – scholarly writing for peer reviewed journals and research grants – is, for various reasons, best carried out in an office.[26] This was tested most recently at TEFMA in Wollongong,[27] where an audience of primarily Directors of Estates noted that there was very little uptake of activity-based workplaces by academics.

From Kenn Fisher's literature review and several academic office consultant reports, it appears that the key issues needing to be understood are:

- cross-disciplinarity
- status/hierarchy
- power relations
- academic work practices
- the economics of offices
- temporal issues
- environmental systems
- psycho-social factors
- acoustics
- labour relations
- surveillance.

Until these issues have been examined and analysed across all academic disciplines in significant depth, it is unlikely that open-plan or activity-based workspaces will be accepted by the academic community, at least in Australian universities where this research is taking place.

academic office mirrors UK experience. Questions into changing space use and capacity issues there have suggested investigations into how often spaces are changed to meet needs, and what features of design make the alterations easy or cause problems. Follow-up could be integrated into POE studies, to understand what changes have been implemented and why, and how long after the initial creation of the space.

Utilisation of specialist and innovative teaching and learning spaces needs to be rethought. Pedagogical changes, shifts in electronic interaction, new emphasis on shared learning, project-based science teaching and new student expectations make room capacities fluid and changes how space-use efficiency and effectiveness in meeting university goals should be judged.

ALIGNING PEDAGOGY WITH SPACE

In concluding this book with a section on 'performance', the fitness for purpose of learning environments must focus on pedagogical and curriculum issues. In the next section, Kenn Fisher, at the University of Melbourne, Australia, discusses his experience of research taking place.

4.3 ACADEMIC PERFORMANCE

Kenn Fisher

ACTIVITY-BASED WORKSPACE

As yet there is little information on how far new pedagogical approaches are really supported by spatial/design concepts aimed at doing so. There is a research grant application in progress in Australia addressing this question. An initial literature review has indicated that a number of key driving factors are evident and also points out the lack of scholarly research on this topic. It appears that open plan – or rather 'activity-based workplace' design – has really only been significantly taken up by academics in the creative disciplines such as design, architecture and the creative arts, as well as in commercial offices.

Since around 2007 there has been significant interest in the evaluation of what are collectively known as new generation learning environments (NGLEs). Under this generic name fall active learning classrooms (ALCs), scale up active learning classrooms, the flipped classroom, technology enabled active learning classrooms (TEALs) and conceive, design, implement and operate (CDIO).[28]

The principal extant hubs of legitimate NGLE research activity – that is, where scholarly evidence-based research aligning space, pedagogy, technology and learning outcomes – are sited at the Universities of Minnesota and Melbourne. At the former, the Office of Classroom Management has undertaken an ongoing evaluation of ALCs with findings showing improved student learning outcomes.[29] Additional related work in ALCs in the USA has been carried out at the Central Michigan University[30] and at Educause (2015).

Concurrently, at the University of Melbourne, the Learning Environments Applied Research Network (LEaRN, 2015) is embarking on a number of new research projects in this area and the outcome will start to throw more light on this complex subject.

A key outcome of these studies is the need to provide academic professional development for teachers to shift their practice from a teacher-centred model towards a learner-centred technology/online assisted, blended and active learning model working within an NGLE framework.[31] In developing such NGLEs on a scaled-up basis, Educause has also been active in developing a new 'learning spaces rating tool'.[32]

While Educause is largely focused on the use of technology in teaching and learning, this focus has meant that it has also had to address the need for re-engineering learning spaces to reform the teacher-centred model associated with the predominant model of students in rows all facing the front. This passive form of learning no longer makes the best use of synchronous online learning capabilities offered by new and emerging technologies. Students can and will learn where they have the most active and engaging experience. Now we need to understand how student learning behaviours are evolving in such blended and flipped learning spaces, through the mapping of the digital with the physical.

To achieve this understanding, a study 'Mapping Complex Learning Spaces'[33] is in its first phase of a five-year project. This study will seek to map student face-to-face interactions in NGLEs, and at the same time map their synchronous virtual activities in using online learning tools. We want to understand what settings students prefer to work in when they are working online, using a variety of tools. These days, student have access to CDIO concept spaces, which adds to the complexity of options, and hence the need for such an evaluation.

Academics are urged by university administration to focus on the cost of delivery of programmes, and this inevitably means there is still a strong retention of the large lecture theatre. The staff:student ratio of 1:300 or 1:500 – or 1:800 in the case of one university in the UK – is at face value a very compelling argument for the retention of lecture theatre pedagogy. But statistics are consistently showing across all universities that, unless student attendance is compulsory, and where the lecture is podcast later on, due to the lack of an active and engaging learning experience student attendance rates drop at an alarming pace, especially in the first three weeks.

Research is showing that this form of passive learning is inadequate and universities will ultimately have to 'bite the bullet' and encourage their academic staff to take up synchronous blended face-to-face online pedagogical practice. Evidence is now emerging that this form of learning is superior.[34] The question of space is uppermost in both student and academic minds at an early stage in the procurement process, but unless there is a willingness by the university in question to explore large 60–100 student blended active learning spaces, then student learning outcomes in passive learning environments will continue to be sub-optimal.[35]

THE STUDENT EXPERIENCE

There is now a gradual transformation of spaces towards the aforementioned NGLE, ALC, TEAL, flipped, blended and CDIO spaces. This is being reinforced by the message of student experience surveys[36] and especially the statistical results of student course survey data, where students are demanding more informal and social space on campus.[37]

Furthermore, many university subject guidelines, which mandate a framework of one or two hours per week of lectures, one or two hours of tutorials and – in the case of laboratory practice subjects – two or three hours of lab attendance, are now slowly changing in their ratios. The class contact hours allocated to lectures are now in some instances being swapped for 24/7 tutor-assisted online learning programmes where students view podcast lectures online in their own time. When they attend class it is in a flipped classroom mode where workshops, collaboration, team-based

and synchronous online learning and other interactive forms take place in a much more active and engaged practice.[38] For further notes on the flipped classroom model refer to page 41 and figures 2.26, 2.27 and 2.28

Fisher and Newton[39] reviewed a wide range of NGLE research papers leading up to 2012 and selected four sufficiently scholarly studies with significant positive findings around ALCs. Subsequently, Fisher and Ellis[40] reviewed additional NGLE research papers from 2012 to mid-2015 and selected five which were scholarly enough to be useful in this debate. The core idea of these evaluations is to provide irrefutable evidence to teachers that these NGLE do, in fact, produce better student learning outcomes. It is hoped that this proof will convince teachers and universities alike to move away from the passive lecture theatre model. Another key strategy is to produce NGLE teacher professional development programmes so that teachers have sufficient 'scaffolding' to perform in these spaces adequately.

This is work in progress, but the research will – due to the rapid onset of online learning – be growing at an equally fast rate.[41] In terms of space utilisation, it is already irrefutable that the frequency and occupancy rates of ALCs far exceed those of lecture theatres, although it is acknowledged that the ALCs use more area per student station. But if learning outcomes are also included in these measures, and additional informal and social spaces are provided in slightly enlarged circulation spaces, then space efficiency can be – and is – fully optimised.

4.4 TECHNICAL PERFORMANCE

Mike Entwisle

With increasing emphasis on the quality and performance of university estates, buildings must provide environments which are comfortable, adaptable, easy to operate and maintain, but above all must delight their occupants. The technical aspects of building design and performance are critical in achieving these ambitions, whether through extensive use of daylight, effective and controllable ventilation, or simply ensuring that a building is used as much as possible – 'sweating the assets'. The technical performance of a building – or group of buildings – involves more than just energy data, in the same way that sustainability is a more complex issue than LEED and BREEAM can capture.

University estates and buildings must respond to changes in use, the effects of climate change and ever-tightening requirements to reduce the use of natural resources, and can reduce carbon impacts. The onerous 2050 carbon emissions targets (mentioned on page 97) can only be met by a multi-pronged attack, including replacing or refitting existing buildings, increased attention to energy efficiency in new projects, extensive use of renewable energy and district systems and – critically – improved operation of buildings, whether by occupants or estates teams.

Reducing energy use and carbon emissions should not be an isolated goal. One sign of a successful building is intensive use, for instance either with increased occupancy or longer hours of operation; both of which are likely to result in increased energy use. Any assessment of energy use must therefore be related to the activities taking place in a building and the resultant outputs.

Successful buildings can introduce undesirable side effects; if one building on a campus is more intensively used than expected, this may be balanced by other buildings being less well utilised but still requiring a base level of environmental performance.

In addition, many successful and internationally renowned universities have significant science and engineering research activities, which often require energy-intensive equipment and extended hours of operation; chasing low energy use at all costs can risk killing the goose that lays the research golden egg.

As an example, the carbon emissions from a world leading university based in the UK increased by around 17% from 2005–06 to 2012–13, principally as a result of increased electricity use; however, when normalised by area the increase is only around 6%. When measured in relation to the (inflation adjusted) total income of the university, the emissions fell steadily over this period with an overall reduction of around 10%. While there is no doubt that more can be done, this example shows that absolute carbon reductions may be difficult – and in some instances undesirable – to achieve in institutions which are growing and providing increasing economic contributions.

Organisations that are downsizing may find it easier to demonstrate absolute carbon emission savings, but this should be viewed with caution and perhaps normalised according to area, student numbers or income.

TRENDS

Current trends in the HE sector in the UK show that overall greenhouse gas emissions principally from energy use in buildings and from its generation (scope 1 and 2 emissions) have gradually been reducing from the university estate as a whole over the last six years (see Figure 4.2). This is principally as a result of greater use of renewable and low-carbon technologies and a focus on increased efficiency, and is despite an increase in floor area of around 5%. This is mirrored by the general improvement in Display Energy Certificate (DEC) ratings; while these are a crude measure of energy performance, this is additionally encouraging (see Figure 4.3).

There is evidence to suggest that while plug loads (e.g. for PCs and other non-fixed equipment) have increased over the last 15–20 years, the increasing reliance on IT for curriculum delivery has been partly offset by the move to lower power mobile devices.

IMPROVING ENERGY EFFICIENCY

It is clear that despite all attempts to create buildings that are energy efficient, this still remains a goal that is not always met. Little seems to be known at present about what is being done to remedy poor results in the buildings that 'fail' to meet their targets. Better sharing of information about why the buildings did or did not meet targets, including what remedial measures work or mitigate the situation, would go some way to combating the impact that the built environment has on overall carbon emissions.

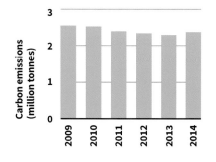

▲ **Figure 4.2** *Carbon emissions in tonnes for HE institutions (based on HESA Data)*

▶ **Figure 4.3**

	DEC category (% of buildings by category)							
	A	B	C	D	E	F	G	UNCLASSIFIED
2009	0.1	4.5	9.9	18.4	14.5	7.5	11.1	34
2010	0.2	4.1	12.0	16.9	15.5	7.2	9.2	35
2011	0.3	5.4	14.1	20.2	12.2	6.7	9.0	32
2012	0.3	6.1	15.5	20.6	11.2	5.5	8.4	32
2013	0.6	6.2	18.9	20.5	13.6	6.4	7.5	26
2014	0.8	7.5	18.8	19.4	12.8	5.8	6.6	28

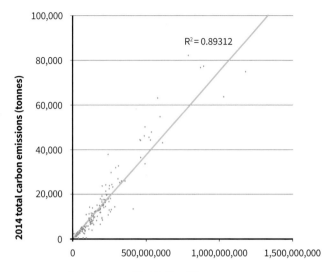

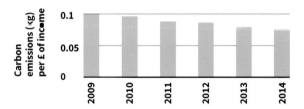

HEALTH AND WELLBEING

There is increasing interest in providing facilities that promote health and wellbeing. The WELL building standard[42] is increasingly viewed as an authoritative assessment methodology for a broad range of issues associated with how a building affects health and wellbeing. The standard starts from a physiological standpoint and looks at seven key factors or 'concepts', based on medical research:

1. Air: particularly indoor air quality (IAQ).
2. Water: availability of high-quality purified water.
3. Nourishment: encourage healthy eating habits by providing better quality food and nutritional information.
4. Light: minimise disruption to the circadian rhythm by using daylight, and provide task-appropriate light levels.
5. Fitness: encourage physical activity and allow it to be integrated into 'normal' daily operations.
6. Comfort: create an environment that is distraction-free, productive and soothing, with appropriate internal thermal and acoustic conditions.
7. Mind: support mental and emotional health by providing the occupant with regular feedback and knowledge about their environment.

Use of this technique requires clients not only to engage with the design process but also to ensure that other operations – particularly human resources and facilities management – are integrated into the design, construction and operation of a building. This in turn can

▲▲ Figure 4.4 and 4.5

Ouput-based metrics produced by Buro Happold from HESA data (see Figures 4.4 and 4.5) shows a good correlation between emissions and income across UK universities – and very strong carbon reduction performance on an income basis.

In contrast with many other building types, universities are in an enviable position with regard to taking a long-term view. As (generally) long standing institutions and owner-occupiers of most of their estates and buildings, they can accept longer paybacks than many commercial organisations from strategic investments to reduce energy consumption in both new and existing buildings. Most universities also have effective estates management teams and energy officers who can be exceptionally proactive in ensuring that buildings are designed, upgraded and operated efficiently; however, many suffer from issues such as inadequate metering, which can hinder accurate measurement of energy consumption and accurate identification of any problems.

131

improve building performance, both in terms of occupant experience and environmental impact.

BUILDING AND UNIVERSITY TYPES

Universities, like cities, include many different building types. From student accommodation, arts venues and leisure centres through to teaching and research facilities, each has its own specific requirements and challenges. Some lend themselves to passive environmental strategies; others – for instance research laboratories – by their function require extensive mechanical treatment and generally have energy consumption much higher than 'generic' academic buildings.

This is explored in more detail in the Higher Education Environmental Performance Improvement (HEEPI) Energy Performance Benchmarking exercise[43] from 2003–04; note in particular the difference in electricity consumption between chemical and medical labs and other types (see Table 4.1). This difference is still relevant today. This is one possible cause for the higher carbon emissions from the research-intensive Russell Group universities than other university types (see Figure 4.6).

It is important to recognise that there are opportunities in all building types for the environmental strategy to provide high-quality internal conditions while minimising environmental impact. A key approach in all instances is to focus on demand-led strategies, ensuring that systems respond effectively to their users. This not only increases user satisfaction but also ensures that

BUILDING TYPE	TYPICAL ENERGY PERFORMANCE (kWh/m²)	
	Fossil fuel	Electricity
Admin/support	166	90
Sports Centres	325	199
Libraries	176	186
Residences (fossil fuel heated)	240	57
Teaching	240	118
Laboratories (medical/bioscience)	256	325
Laboratories (physical/engineering)	148	130
Laboratories (chemical sciences)	175	264
Computing – maths	105	106

▲ Table 4.1

▼ Figure 4.6 *Russell Group universities tend to have higher carbon emissions per £ income than non-Russell Group universities*

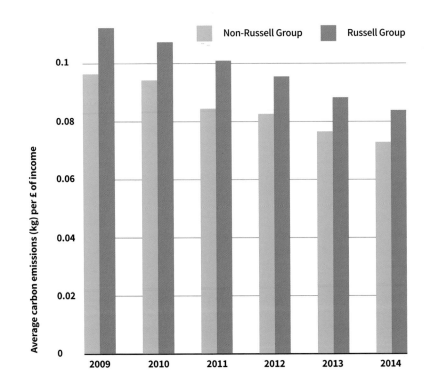

systems are not used unnecessarily. One of the more important examples of this is in laboratory buildings, where there is huge potential for reductions in energy consumption through efficient control of ventilation by responding to demand. In traditional academic buildings, a demand-led strategy can ensure that low-occupancy spaces are only conditioned when occupied, and that equipment defaults to off or a setback condition. In many instances, there is much greater scope for energy saving by focusing on operation of a building outside core occupied hours. This is where 'default to off' becomes a critical strategy, particularly in buildings used predominantly by undergraduates and teaching academics.

EXISTING BUILDINGS

It is tempting to focus on new building stock as a way to deliver significant carbon savings; while these opportunities should be embraced, there is greater potential to make savings by attending to the existing building stock. The AUDE 2015 Higher Education Estates Statistics report[44] shows how the ages of non-residential buildings in UK universities has changed since 2009; despite the large investments in new buildings in recent years, over 60% of building area is over 35 years old; with 25% being over 55 years old. Given that these are likely to be the less energy efficient buildings, it becomes clear where most effort should be made in reducing energy use.

Buildings of different ages typically present different environmental challenges (see Table 4.2).

Typical period	Characteristics	Potential environmental upgrades (other than updating of services systems and energy sources)
Up to 1920	• Generally thermally heavy, little insulation and often large areas of single glazing. • Often have high ceilings. • Often well daylit but have high winter heat losses. • Generally resilient to summertime overheating but adapting their layouts can be difficult, as load bearing walls are commonplace.	• Demand-led and occupancy-controlled environmental control. • Daylit and occupancy linked lighting control. • Insulation of roof spaces and floor voids. • Double glazing and improved draughtproofing. • Improved efficiency of heat sources (note that low temperature sources such as heat pumps are often not well matched).
1920–59	• Widely differing – often thermally heavyweight with lower ceilings and variable glazed areas. Pitched and flat roofs both common. • Summertime and wintertime conditions can both be problematical. • Some use of structural frames enabling layout flexibility.	• Demand-led and occupancy-controlled environmental control. • Insulation of building envelope. • Improved window performance – double glazing and improved draughtproofing but also ensuring secure night ventilation to engage the thermal mass. • Improved efficiency of heat sources.
1960–79	• Large single-glazed areas, lower ceilings, little insulation. • Flat roofs very common. Often cold in winter, hot in summer and over daylit. • Thermal mass in some cases; use of structural frames the norm, enabling simple reconfiguration.	• Reduced glazing areas and improved envelope performance, including insulation. Solar-treated glazing may be worthwhile. • Daylit and occupancy-linked lighting control.
1979 to date	• Widely variable, but many buildings have small windows and are thermally lightweight. Suspended ceilings often used and can be quite low. Insulation levels can be reasonable, depending upon building age. • Summertime overheating often a problem.	• Increase size of windows if possible to improve daylighting and ventilation. • Remove suspended ceilings to improve ceiling height and expose thermal mass. • Demand-led and occupancy-controlled environmental control. • Improved efficiency of heat sources.

▲ Table 4.2

EXAMPLE

THE DAVID ATTENBOROUGH BUILDING
UNIVERSITY OF CAMBRIDGE, NICHOLAS HARE ARCHITECTS

The rehabilitation of a 1960s Brutalist concrete building originally housing a variety of departments as well as a museum, a large lecture theatre and computer lab. The main occupant now is the Cambridge Conservation Initiative, which brings together a range of conservation-focused organisations into a single location. The building has had an environmental makeover including a new atrium to bring daylight and natural ventilation into the centre of the deep plan building, as well as replacement of the failed glazing and enhancement of general thermal performance; concrete repairs and replacement of services systems were also included. A key element for the project was the compilation and implementation of a bespoke sustainability framework, recognising the singular nature of the building and its occupants.

▲ ◥ Figures 4.7, 4.8 and 4.9

▶ Figure 4.10

EXAMPLE
THE MUIRHEAD TOWER
UNIVERSITY OF BIRMINGHAM, ASSOCIATED ARCHITECTS

This is a large 1960s Brutalist building, with all the usual problems of poor thermal comfort and energy performance, disabled access, and circulation which are common in buildings of that era. However, the distinctive nature of this listed building (the tallest on the campus), as well as the space it provides for the University, made retention and rehabilitation preferable to demolition and replacement. The scheme involved a complete replacement of the façade to reduce heat loss and summertime solar gain, replacement and enhancement of lifts, renewal of services systems and concrete repairs to bring the building up to date and provide space appropriate for a leading UK university.

135

EXAMPLE
THE EARLE M. JORGENSEN LABORATORY
CALTECH, JOHN FRIEDMAN ALICE KIM

The rehabilitation of a 1970s deep plan computer lab provides an inspirational centre for energy research. Renewal of the façade along with oversized sunshades has been accompanied by the introduction of an atrium to improve daylighting and the quality of the spaces. Introducing research labs for the first time into an existing building was always going to be challenging – the most intensive areas are located on the top floor to be close to roof-mounted plant, the size of which has been minimised by using demand-led techniques, and write-up areas (where researchers typically spend most of their time) are located around the building's daylit perimeter spaces.

Sustainable refurbishment of an environmentally failing building.

▶ Figures 4.11 and 4.12

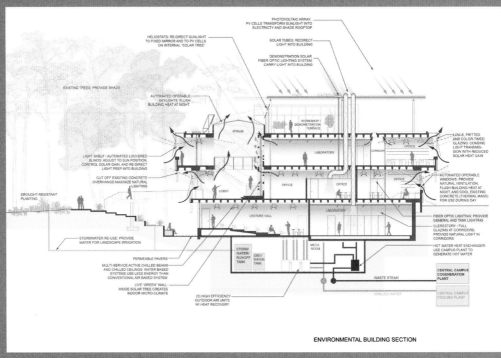

ENVIRONMENTAL BUILDING SECTION

▲ Figure 4.13

EXAMPLE
THE RICHMOND BUILDING
UNIVERSITY OF BRISTOL,
FEILDEN CLEGG BRADLEY STUDIOS

The combination of re-using the existing building and radically
improving how it operates has resulted in the achievement of
a BREEAM `Excellent' rating. The new glazing design combined
with new layouts also allows a shift from mechanical to natural
ventilation for many of the spaces, helping further for the project
to meet the University's exacting sustainability targets.

NEW BUILDINGS

There are many excellent examples of new buildings designed for sustainable operation; some incorporate innovation which is self-evident in their appearance, whereas others embed the sustainability in a more subtle way.

Particular examples include:

- A series of projects at the University of Nottingham, where there has been significant innovation centred on the Jubilee Campus, including the use of windcatchers, lake water for heating and cooling, and earth tubes. The University is a big proponent of POE, and makes review reports publicly available in a drive to improve design, procurement, handover and operation.

EXAMPLE
THE URBAN SCIENCES BUILDING UNIVERSITY OF NEWCASTLE, WILKINSONEYRE

The Urban Sciences Building at the University of Newcastle, where sustainable and energy-related innovation is embedded within the scheme, with the aim of using the building and its systems for research. Innovations include smart grids and enhanced building performance monitoring, fuel cell energy storage to provide demand side management, and enhanced visibility of building performance to its users, all integrated into the context of the new Science Central development. This approach has been integrated into a bespoke sustainability framework, which is more specifically aimed at the needs of the occupants than other methods such as BREEAM or LEED.

EXAMPLE
THE FORUM UNIVERSITY OF EXETER, HAWKINS\BROWN

The Forum, University of Exeter unifies a series of buildings to provide a sustainable heart for the university. Centred around a daylit and naturally ventilated street, the Forum project has reinvigorated campus life. A new mini district energy centre has been provided: serving a building area which has increased by over 130%, energy consumption only rose by 40% despite extended opening hours of many existing buildings. The freeform timber gridshell roof (the largest in Europe) locks in over 65 tonnes of CO_2 and has become part of the branding of the University. Earth tubes are used to temper incoming air and reduce heating and cooling demands.

▼▼ Figures 4.14 and 4.15

▶ Figure 4.16

MANAGEMENT, MAINTENANCE AND OPERATION

University estates teams often have large portfolios of buildings of widely varying ages and functions. Some will be simple to manage and maintain; others will require more intensive attention, particularly those which are heavily serviced or where refurbishment or replacement of services is overdue.

Whatever the building type, age and occupancy, there is much that can be done to improve environmental performance. For new buildings, Soft Landings processes help to ensure that estates teams and occupants are aware of how best to operate buildings. A key element is ensuring that systems and controls are kept simple, particularly where occupants – many of whom may be transient – are required to interface with them. Bill Bordass, a renowned expert in building operation, has a few powerful catchphrases:

Keep it Simple – Do it Well – and only then be clever.

The excellent is often the enemy of the good.

Avoid unmanageable complexity.

POEs have an important part to play in understanding how buildings and estates are being used, and can then allow dialogue with users to better equip them in how to get the best from their facilities.

Where possible, both Soft Landings and POEs should involve members of the original design team and specialist contractors, such as controls and general services systems providers.

Where users and managers are suitably equipped with information and skills in how best to operate their facilities, significant gains in performance can be made. A particularly effective method of enabling this is to provide a 'flash card' in each room, outlining to non-technical users how they can get the most from the space.

Other techniques include encouraging competition between different areas or zones in a building; one common example of this is in student residences where comparisons can be simple to make and energy performance can be incentivised. This has even been extended to be part of a Europe-wide project called SAVES.[40]

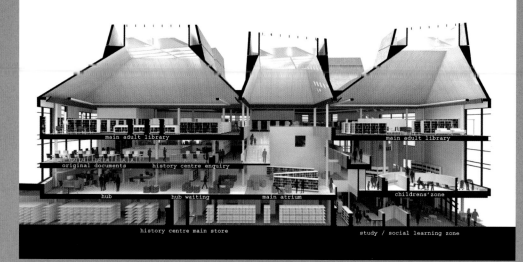

main adult library
original documents   history centre enquiry
hub   hub waiting   main atrium
history centre main store
main adult library
childrens' zone
study / social learning zone

▲▼ Figures 4.17 and 4.18

FEATURE

THE HIVE, UNIVERSITY OF WORCESTER

FEILDEN CLEGG BRADLEY

The Hive is a groundbreaking partnership between Worcester County Council and the University of Worcester to create a fully integrated public and university library. This is an idea completely new to the UK and highly innovative internationally.

- Parametric modelling was used to remove 250 tonnes of steel in the roof by replacing it with laminated timber. This saved 2,000 tonnes of CO2 compared with a concrete or steel alternative.
- Cooling using water from the nearby River Severn.
- Biomass heating boiler uses locally sourced woodchip
- Natural ventilation
- 'A' rating in EPC
- BREEAM 'Outstanding'

◀▲ Figures 4.19, 4.20 and 4.21

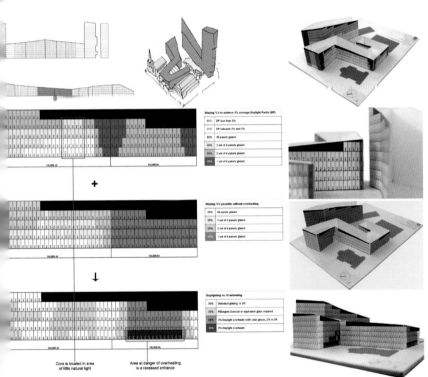

Facade Models - showing computational daylighting analysis

FEATURE
**BROADCASTING PLACE,
LEEDS BECKETT UNIVERSITY**
FEILDEN CLEGG BRADLEY

- Student housing and academic buildings designed around retained listed buildings

- Careful glazing design to maximise daylighting, reduce solar gain and optimise the thermal performance of the building façades

FRY BUILDING, UNIVERSITY OF BRISTOL
WILKINSONEYRE

Refurbishment of this 100-year old listed laboratory to house the maths faculty, will include a new atrium to capture solar gain and improve connectivity and circulation within the building, as well as extensive investigations into the thermal performance of the existing building fabric. The metal-framed single-glazed windows are due to be refurbished, and a demand-led heating system will provide comfortable conditions for out-of-hours occupants without the need to heat an entire building zone.

Due to be completed spring 2017.

ARKWRIGHT AND NEWTON BUILDINGS, NOTTINGHAM TRENT UNIVERSITY
HOPKINS ARCHITECTS PARTNERSHIP

Incorporation of 1930s Art Deco office into new 'mini campus' in central Nottingham. The renovation, and infill between, two historically significant Grade II* listed buildings has created a new main entrance, additional social and teaching spaces, link building and external quadrangle. The large central forum space is designed to promote continuous informal academic interaction and study that flows into the space at all levels.

▼ Figures 4.24 and 4.25

▶▼ Figures 4.22 and 4.23

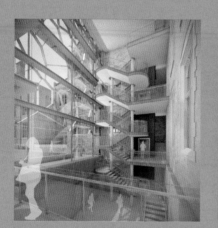

◀▼ Figures 4.26 and 4.27

FEATURE
AMRC, UNIVERSITY OF SHEFFIELD BOND BRYAN

Carbon neutral in operation; manufacturing facility for research.

This cutting edge research centre was developed by the University of Sheffield in partnership with Boeing and Rolls Royce, and has a strong sustainability theme running throughout. From the beginning of the project the team applied a clear road map to deliver a low-energy sustainability programme. The building envelope ensures that 97% of the internal space is lit naturally during daylight hours. As well as the obvious energy saving associated with this, the daylight provides an exciting and stimulating environment which was praised by users and management alike in a post occupancy evaluation process. To further help the AMRC to reduce emissions, two 250 kW wind turbines were installed to generate the bulk of the site's energy.

CASE STUDIES

Melbourne School of Design
Tom Kvan

New Learning Spaces at Karolinska Institutet and the Karolinska University Hospital in Sweden
Jonas Nordquist

Interfaces and Territories: Blurring the boundaries, ownership, management and inclusion
Eleanor Magennis

Saw Swee Hock Student Centre, LSE
Julian Robinson

Learning from experiences of the building process and the impacts of new development informs decision-making on future projects. These case studies demonstrate examples of how the approaches described through the sections of this book can influence outcomes.

Good value and performance are hard won. These examples give insights on the value of responding to context, creating appropriate spaces for university life, focusing on a consistent design process and improving performance through focus on building operation. All these considerations contribute to the outcomes in the examples described.

The Melbourne School of Design responds to the contextual masterplanning principles described by Tom Kvan in Part 1, in an exemplary design process concentrating on spaces and environment.

The Karolinska Institute and Hospital demonstrate outcomes from the learning-focused spatial approach described by Jonas Nordquist in Part 2.

The role of the University of Strathcylde's estates department in brokering a better understanding of the needs of the University's spaces is described by Eleanor Magennis, echoing guidance in Part 3.

The Saw Swee Hock Student Centre is reviewed to understand how well it performs and adds value to the LSE in the terms explained by Julian Robinson in Part 4.

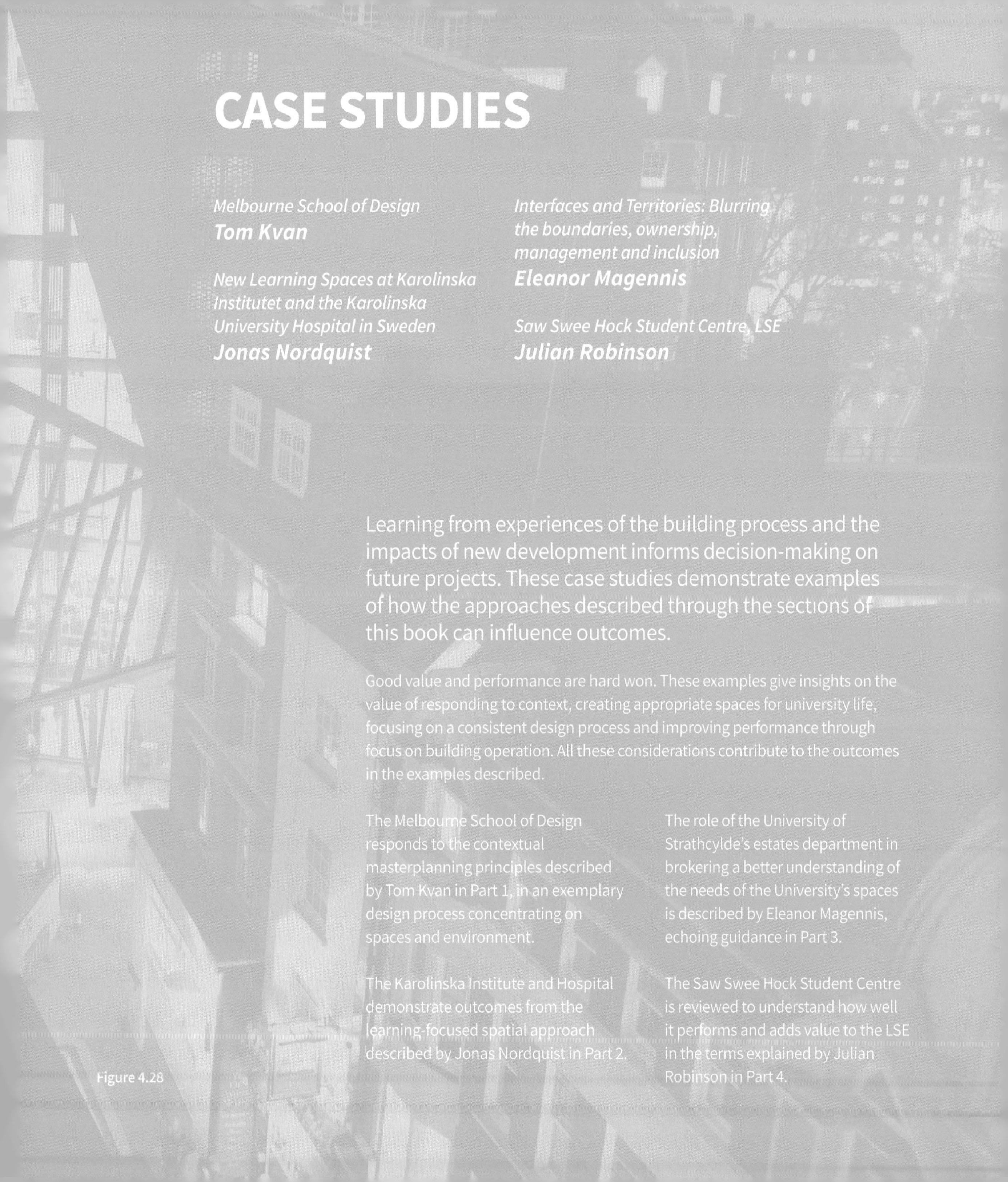

Figure 4.28

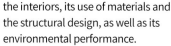

CASE STUDY 1

MELBOURNE SCHOOL OF DESIGN

Tom Kvan

CONTEXT

This case study describes the Melbourne School of Design (MSD) at the University of Melbourne campus in Parkville, Melbourne, Australia.

The building provides approximately 16,000 sqm of useable area. It was handed over by the builders, Brookfield Multiplex, to the university in August 2014, completed in 15 months – four months early – and for an average construction cost that is 5% below the average cost of 26 comparable buildings in Australia constructed in the previous three years. The project has been published extensively[46] and readers who wish to view plans and details are referred in particular to the journal *The Plan*.[47] Within 18 months of its completion, the building had been recognised by over 15 awards for architecture and campus context,

the interiors, its use of materials and the structural design, as well as its environmental performance.

A replacement building had been an aspiration of the faculty for many years. It had been accommodated primarily in two adjacent structures, a custom-built concrete frame structure from 1964 and a smaller load-bearing brick building erected to support a neoclassical Bank of New South Wales façade built in 1856 that had been relocated from the city in 1936. Since moving into the custom facility at that time, the academic users had grown from 350 students in a single academic programme to over 3,000 students, comprising over 1,000 in six streams of a graduate school, including a doctoral programme and over 2,000 in a broad undergraduate programme that prepared students for four different graduate schools on campus.

Academic staff numbers had also increased, though not commensurately, as had professional (administrative) staff reflecting the operating model at Melbourne in which faculties and graduate schools are responsible for successful delivery of their operations.

The capital funding context in which the building was delivered was challenging. As is the case in many countries, the funding model for higher education in Australia no longer provides capital explicitly for campus infrastructure, including buildings. These costs must be met from the general income stream, of which approximately 20% is provided directly by the national government based on

◀ **Figure 4.29** *Exterior north*

domestic student numbers and the balance from competitive sources, fee income or other sources. As the building stock ages and, in particular, the inventory constructed in a time of lesser construction quality needs to be replaced (for us, that is the period of the 1960s), a case must be made for a broader value of construction investment than simply providing academic offices and teaching spaces.

BRIEFING (A CASE FOR CONSTRUCTION)

The case for the Melbourne School of Design building was written to frame the project as a research opportunity for many disciplines, both in the delivery phase and onwards into occupation and use. The opportunity was there, too, to recast the role of an academic building to work not only for its occupants but also to contribute to the academic vision of the University in promoting multidisciplinary collaborations and to provide campus users, students, staff and visitors the opportunity for insights into other bodies of knowledge.

The faculty had been accommodated primarily in a purpose-built structure completed in 1964, originally designed for some 600 students but accommodating over 1,300 by early 2007. Constructed with an inadequate budget, the structure was failing. Metal cladding had been added in the 1980s to enclose the external concrete that was spalling; other extreme failures were experienced in servicing and fittings. An adjacent 1936 building provided additional office space. Overall, the site was serving the campus poorly.

Planning for the building gained focus in late 2007. The faculty embarked on the preparation of the project brief; this coincided with the introduction of the Melbourne Curriculum (popularly known as the Melbourne Model), entailing a thorough reworking of all teaching and the establishment of a graduate school in which six professional degree programmes are taught, together with changing expectations in research and engagement performance. These academic aspirations underpinned the brief and guided development of the design and construction through the protracted period it took to secure financing to deliver the building.

The brief was written after an extensive analysis of needs that included engaging the users in exploring changed modes of working and learning. Space was approved to accommodate over 1,800 students and 130 staff; by the time the building was completed, the population being served had risen to over 2,600 students and 140 staff, illustrating further how difficult it is in a dynamic academic context to plan with certainty.

When completed, the brief comprised over 800 pages of aspirations, detailed space requirements and performance expectations. These pages were summarised in four statements that the project should explore:

1. Research into the future of academic workplace.
2. A study in the future of studio learning.
3. A living building.
4. A pedagogical building.

The site is in the centre of the main campus for the university, located adjacent to the principal administrative

building (and location of the Vice Chancellor's office) and opposite the Student Union, with the hard surface Student Union Lawn an active centre of campus life. With this central location not directly approached by a main road, site access posed challenges and it was strongly suggested that the new accommodation could be better provided on a site off the main campus. The MSD argued for remaining on the more difficult site as the building offered an opportunity to reinvigorate the centre of campus and demonstrate therefore the new academic vision. The decision further challenged the budget but provided considerable campus value.

DESIGN

An open competition was run in 2008 in which architecture practices were asked to submit responses to the four statements – that is, not to provide a design proposition as a singular response to a schedule of needs – and 134 entries were received.[48] In a two-stage process, the selection was made of a design consultant team that had demonstrated an ability to engage in the project as a research exploration on these four questions. While most submissions repeated the usual architectural positioning ('I studied architecture so I know exactly how to design a school of architecture'), the shortlisted teams all demonstrated an understanding of the potential for exploring the four questions posed. This first appointment set the precedent of bringing to the project those firms, consultants and the main contractor who could engage with the research potential of the project.

A central ambition for this project was to reinvigorate the core of the campus and provide a place of community for all students and staff. An audacious goal for a single building, this demanded that the design rejected the closed nature of the typical campus building. Instead, the strategy was to provide ready access from the primary transport hub to the Student Union building and to invite everyone to walk through.

CONSTRUCTION

The building is characterised by its careful and close detailing throughout. All vertical concrete elements (columns, walls, stairs and lift towers) were manufactured off-site as were the timber roof elements, steel stairs and other fittings. This enabled the building to be constructed in 15 months after a five-month contract for site clearance and remediation.

Some elements of the building were made on site, in particular the wishbone beams that cover the basement bookstack of the library, above which is the south-facing sloped lawn and the curvaceous glazed wall. The careful formwork, taking six weeks to prepare, was possible as the basement level stacks lay outside the critical path. As an example of construction reference material, the level of finish achieved here reflects the care of cabinetry rather than typical formwork.

In demonstrating the process of design, the building highlights the opportunity for an academic project to be undertaken as a research project. In this case, the project team set aside approximately 1% of the construction budget (that is, AU$1 million) for innovation at the start of design. This sum was to be allocated to building elements with the agreement of all of the consultant team to support innovative features that would further the goals of the project. As the project passed through its several budget reviews and value management exercises, this budget provision ensured that key aspects of the design survived. One example of this was the use of structural timber for the atrium roof, important in extending the pedagogical purposes of the building, achieving a 6 Star outcome and creating a visually engaging workspace.

A PLATFORM FOR RESEARCH AND TEACHING

Throughout the design and construction period, students and academic staff participated in the process of delivery. Consultants worked with students in classes to examine aspects of the design, explaining decisions made and exploring options. Several research projects were framed to examine aspects of the delivery.

The construction team not only delivered the building four months early but conducted over 100 site tours to enable students to observe progress regularly. The team also taught regularly scheduled classes in which they shared decisions they were making, as well as having students work through challenges.

SPACES IN USE

The result is a building that welcomes all visitors, demonstrates the outcomes of good design and construction in a legible manner, with materials used in multiple and innovative ways and provides a variety of workplace formats to support the different user communities.

A building in the round conceptualised with four primary façades, the building creates places for casual gathering on all sides. A generous passage runs across the ground floor, inviting all to flow from the city access on the east through to the Student Union and centre of campus on the west. Organised along this axis are three primary activities: the library, extensive workshops and two exhibition galleries. Visitors to the building enter to observe readily the two primary modes of working in the faculty – a scholarly one of publication and study that is complemented by the active use of models and assembly through which materials and performance are experienced. These visually lively (and often messy) spaces convey a sense of how design is engaged and encourages students from other disciplines to linger and viscerally experience the knowledge explored in the faculty.

Complementing this is a large atrium one floor up, itself a public plaza though protected from the weather, surrounded with workplaces for research and teaching. An opening in the floor above near the entry-level workshop offers a glimpse of the atrium above and extends the invitation to explore the building.

Modelling their future professional experience, students in the graduate programmes in the Melbourne School of Design are expected to engage substantively across the six professional streams, both formally by taking elective subjects in the other streams but also casually by working alongside and with students enrolled in those streams. The building reflects this expectation.

Academic workspaces are provided in a variety of configurations. While approximately 40% of academics are provided with cellular offices with glazed walls, the Dean's workplace sets the tone for the rest – the faculty executive works together without walls and doors. The best views across campus and the city beyond are to be seen from the lounge and kitchen area accessible to staff and doctoral students, a generous space on the top level adjacent to a large and generously planted roof terrace.

Recognising that circulation routes are a purposeful transit, as well as an opportunity for serendipitous encounters, they ring the atrium void with a timber-lined staircase to the west

end, encouraging occupants to walk rather than use the lifts. The landings on these Y-shaped stairs or glimpses of colleagues walking along the balconies often lead to impromptu conversations. The configuration enables staff and students to see one another.

The atrium level is a primary teaching space as well as the location of the Dean's office. The atrium floor is flanked to the south by five studios that are enclosed by two doors and a centrally pivoted wall, thus able to open up completely. This enables us to celebrate one of the distinctive aspects of design teaching, the review or 'crit', inviting students across the programmes to drop in and participate in this essential experience, and it creates a very large exhibition space to be used for end-of-year shows. To the north of the atrium are digital support facilities – computer

labs for casual use when not timetabled for teaching, and printing facilities and additional classrooms.

In the atrium, a long fixed table runs east to west across most of the 60m length, providing a workspace with power and network sockets, as well as a robust wireless signal. Moveable furniture fills the rest of the floor, with tables small and large. The variety of work areas allows for a breadth of function, from sole study through private meetings to more casual collaborations. The space responds to commentary that tertiary study can be an isolating experience, even though much of it takes place with large audiences. For many, the campus experience is limited to timetabled and programmed spaces that do not facilitate more casual encounters and discussions.

An unexpected feature is the timber-finished atrium space with three levels of classrooms suspended from exposed laminated veneer timber beams. This large (20m x 60m x 15m) volume is filled with workplaces and ringed upper levels with more diverse workplaces. The atrium is enclosed by a 1500 sqm stainless steel mesh surface that is tensioned across steel tube fixing restraints. These tubes pull the mesh into a faceted and sculptured surface that provides appropriate safety barriers while allowing the atrium to be experienced without visual, acoustic and airflow separation.

On busy days, there can be over 200 people working in this open volume across four levels. The acoustics are remarkable and the many conversations

◀ **Figure 4.30** *Interior atrium*

▲ **Figure 4.31** *Interior staircase and timber coffered roof*

▲ **Figure 4.32** *West-facing heritage façade*

make for a quiet hum (rather like a cathedral experience) that encourages conversation while supporting quiet working. The acoustic outcomes have been achieved by deploying sound-absorbent wall linings that also act as presentation and pin-up spaces along the passageways, and have been used behind perforated timber linings of doors and the suspended structure.

The building reveals itself in unexpected places throughout. A glazed wall in the library bookstacks reveals the machine room, positioning building operations as reference material. Likewise, the foundations are revealed in the lobby area outside the basement lecture halls. The undersides of the primary Y-stairs have not been clad, showing off the large steel trusses which support stairs that are experienced when walking up them as delicate and finely finished. Thus, both the informed and casual visitor can read the building and interpret their experience of the spaces.

CULTURAL VALUE

Universities play a role in maintaining cultural patrimony and engaging heritage in future purposes. This building does so in several ways. The open and collaborative mode of working is central to the culture of peer learning, variously called studio, problem-based or project-based learning. The generous distribution and variety of informal workplaces throughout the structure demonstrates the culture to all visitors. The 1856 façade has been transformed from an item of urban wallpaper, oddly adhered to a poorly proportioned brick backdrop, into an engaged and vital theatre piece that now frames the Student Union Lawn and can be studied at close hand in the student lounge, an immediate teaching aid. A third cultural element is the restoration of a Japanese room, first installed in 1965 in the previous building to mark for the first time a cultural reengagement with Japan after the traumatic Pacific War. It was designed by Professor Shirgeru Yura, who also sourced all the construction materials and finishes from Japan.

ENVIRONMENTAL PERFORMANCE

Parametrically designed perforated zinc solar shading systems are wrapped around the north, east and western façades, moderating insolation while allowing for open sightlines and operable windows. To the south, where direct sun seldom shines, the window and ventilation elements are playfully disposed with honed concrete panels to create greatly varied interior experiences in the teaching studios, demonstrating how a fixed vocabulary can be deployed to change user experience.

Used daily by a wide community from all disciplines, the building seeks to demonstrate to all users the benefits of design through the configurations of spaces, choice of materials and their construction. In creating a comfortable and pleasurable workplace, the building is primarily naturally ventilated and illuminated. All exterior rooms have operable windows – the few that do not are internal computer labs and basement theatres, but these are mechanically provided with fresh air. Even on the hottest summer days, nights are usually cool so a night-time flushing system is activated to provide passive cooling through operating hours, supplemented by high-efficiency water-cooled chillers that use captured rainwater, which is also deployed for toilet flushing and landscape irrigation.

A large counterbalanced window (essentially a 5-tonne sash window) on the east façade and high-level vents on the west façade transform the atrium into an outdoor plaza on clement days, thus cross-ventilating all classrooms. Natural light is maximised with clear glazing on all windows; insolation is managed by the perforated zinc screens on the three façades exposed to the sun. The atrium is sealed by a 300 sqm double-glazed roof with an offset frit that, in combination with the canted timber roof coffers, ensure ample refracted sky lighting while blocking direct solar penetration.

The perimeter office spaces are mixed mode, operating when weather permits, to allow natural ventilation through the use of automated louvres that can also be used in the central atrium to draw air through the building. The counterbalanced glazed wall that can be opened to open the space to the external climate.

As part of the water efficiency strategy, a 750,000 litre underground rainwater storage tank has been installed to collect harvested rainwater to provide recycled water for the toilets throughout the five-level building, for the external gardens and for use within the high efficiency water-based heat rejection system on the roof. Throughout the building, sensors collect data on the use of energy and water, as well as rates of CO_2, humidity, temperature and flux. This data is displayed on screens in public areas of the building to provide an operating profile to users, but it is also archived to provide teaching and research materials.

In addition to the recognition awarded for the design of the building, several awards have been given for environmental performance. Although the building was originally being targeted in line with the University of Melbourne's threshold expectation for all projects of 5 Stars, the design and construction processes led a 6 Star rating under the education rating tool of the Australian Green Star system operated by the Green Building Council of Australia[49] in which the maximum rating is six. As the Green Star website notes, the building '… proves that sustainable design can be achieved without the need for technological bells and whistles. The foundation of this 6 Star Green Star building is simply, good design.'[50] This is the first project in Australia to be awarded all ten innovation points; in this instance these were awarded for a full life-cycle assessment that addressed carbon and water impacts of the construction, the integration of heritage, the research undertaken in cross-laminated timber construction, the market research carried out to inform the design process and points for exceeding threshold Green Star benchmarks.

CONCLUSION

On a campus in which cross-disciplinary research and learning is a central tenet, this building offers a workplace to students and staff that speaks to these ambitions. Used extensively by all, the building not only manifests the activity within but creates a variety of workplace experiences for students and staff, from intimate and quiet to collaborative and open, in support of both individual scholarship and co-working. In a school that presents design as spanning from policy writing through form making to budget allocations and operating decisions, the building illustrates all aspects of designing from briefing through budget-making to operations. While demonstrably presenting contemporary academic ambition of engagement and openness, the building supports the many facets of deep scholarship.

John Wardle Architects
in collaboration with NADAA

NEW LEARNING SPACES AT KAROLINSKA INSTITUTET AND THE KAROLINSKA UNIVERSITY HOSPITAL IN SWEDEN

Jonas Nordquist

CHALLENGE

The overall aim of the Karolinska projects was to align all physical learning spaces with the emerging curricula in health professions education.

In 2009 it was established that physical learning spaces at Karolinska Institutet (KI) and the Karolinska University Hospital (KUH) were not aligned with current and emerging curricula for education of health professionals. There was a clear case for realignment of physical learning spaces in clinical and non-clinical settings. It was further noted that physical learning spaces in new buildings did not reflect contemporary curricular theory based on active learning and the use of new learning technologies. Instead, many new buildings still reflected ideas about teaching from the first half of the 20th century, with an emphasis on teaching as 'transfer of information', discipline isolation and lack of informal learning spaces.

All physical learning spaces at KI and KUH were assessed on the metrics of their suitability for enabling active learning approaches in formal and informal (social) learning environments.

CONTEXT

KI is a leading bio-medical research university founded in 1810, providing world-class research. It is the home of the Nobel Prize in physiology of medicine, and offers approximately 25 different education programmes for the health professions. KUH is a 1,400-bed tertiary academic health centre dedicated to comprehensive patient care, clinical research and education. Many of the KI students do significant parts of their clinical training at KUH. KI and KUH have two sites: Solna and Huddinge. The Solna site was planned in the 1930s and opened in the period 1940–45. The Huddinge site first opened in the early 1970s and has been extended with many new buildings during the 1980 and 1990s.

A new programme for aligning physical learning spaces with the emerging curricula was developed, intended for redevelopment/repurposing of existing learning spaces and for the construction of physical learning spaces in new buildings.

APPROACH

One hypothesis was that the lack of alignment between curricula and physical learning spaces was caused by the design of the actual briefing process. It was hypothesised that both the 'software and hardware problem' and the 'museum problem' (see 'Teaching and Learning Spaces' in Part 2, pages 25-28) had the same root; briefing, in particular the early stages of the briefing process, when the wrong group of people were in charge of the visionary and strategic brief. *Hardware developers* – such as real estate or property developers and architects – were involved too early in the process and too few, if any, software developers were involved in the early parts of the briefing.

A new approach to briefing was developed, led by educational experts, with three phases:

1. The development of the educational vision and the corresponding performance requirements of physical learning spaces on various scales (see below).
2. The translation of these performance requirements into a conceptual programme.
3. This conceptual programme (for formal and informal learning spaces) was then applied to specific building projects, both redevelopment and new construction.

Phase 1 and 2 (vision and concept) were both seen as framing stages and Phase 3 as application and solution focused on specific and concrete projects.

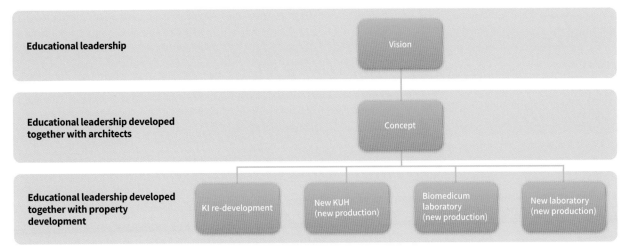

Educational leadership				Vision
Educational leadership developed together with architects				Concept
Educational leadership developed together with property development	KI re-development	New KUH (new production)	Biomedicum laboratory (new production)	New laboratory (new production)

THE NETWORKED LEARNING LANDSCAPE

▲ **Figure 4.33** *Future learning environment concept 2009–2015*

Nordquist and Laing[51] operationalised the networked learning landscape into four scales: classroom, building, campus and city. Each scale provides a distinctive milieu within which particular kinds of learning activities can be organised or provided. The distinction of these four scales by no means suggests that other settings for learning do not exist. They do, nevertheless, represent significantly different kinds of venues for learning experiences that are worth highlighting for the purposes of designing learning spaces in order to align with the needs of the curriculum. The networked learning landscape is an organising conceptual framework and makes it possible to see the integration of physical learning spaces on various scales.

The visionary (Phase 1) brief was based on a theory-driven curriculum approach. Three major guiding principles for the performance of learning spaces

on all scales were extrapolated from contemporary learning theories (such as guided discovery learning, experiential learning, social constructivism, collaborative learning and adult learning principles): dialogue; visualisation of previous experience and knowledge; and peer-to-peer learning. TEAL was also added to the visionary conversation (see page 127).

Two conceptual programmes (one for formal and one for informal learning environments) were developed by the architects during Phase 2 in close collaboration with educational experts and property developers.

PREFERRED PARTNER

It is important to keep in mind that students have quite some power to determine what physical learning environments to use in the networked learning landscape. Scheduled activities on the classroom scale, or scheduled

clinical activities, are normally located to pre-determined physical learning spaces with limited room for individual student choice. However, what learning spaces to use outside of scheduled time are left to the discretion of the individual students and their preference. There are several options available: staying at home; using the university library (or a library); or informal learning spaces provided by the university. In addition, there are of course other spaces available in the connecting urban landscape, such as cafés, bars or restaurants. A worst-case scenario would be an empty campus after class hours due to lack of attractive, inviting and inspiring informal learning spaces.

Private providers of informal learning spaces, outside the control of the university domain, need to take their physical environments into serious consideration. Such spaces are normally an expression of the brand and carefully thought through. This is unfortunately not always the case with informal spaces within the domain of universities or university hospitals.

The design of the in-between learning environments at all the Karolinska projects – and making them as inviting and unique as possible – has been a key strategy to keep students within the Karolinska facilities outside scheduled classroom hours. The overall goal has been to become the preferred partner (or provider) of all physical learning spaces, even when students have a choice, and to create a unique Karolinska experience expressed through formal (classroom scale) and informal (building scale) learning environments intended ultimately to create a sense of a community of learners and to foster peer to peer learning.

RESULTS

The conceptual programmes were then applied to four major projects: one redevelopment project of all current physical learning spaces at KI and three major new development projects (among them the largest hospital project in northern Europe for the last 50 years).

INFORMAL LEARNING ENVIRONMENTS (IN-BETWEEN SPACES)

An initial POE was conducted in the autumn of 2014 by a group of anthropologists using an ethnographic approach. This study focused on the redevelopment of the first large informal learning environment that was opened in early 2012, which had, at the time of the study, been in use for almost two years. The overall question was: how were students using the new informal learning spaces?

The space where the new learning environment had been developed used to be empty corridors connecting different parts of a building containing classrooms and lecture theatres, a library and a restaurant. The redeveloped spaces had previously only been used for circulation and not for any stationary

Project	Redevelopment / re-purposing of physical learning spaces	New learning spaces
Karolinska Institutet (campus Solna and Huddinge)	115 classrooms 15 informal learning spaces	
New Karolinska University Hospital		All bookable classrooms and conference rooms Specific physical learning spaces in the clinical environments, wards, procedural rooms and in outpatient settings
Biomedicum laboratory		One 220-seat learning hall Three 40- to 60-person classrooms All designed informal learning spaces in the building All conference rooms
Neo laboratory		One 200-seat learning hall One 80-seat learning hall All designed informal learning spaces in the building One multipurpose room (combined exams, exhibition hall and multimedia studio)

◄ **Table 4.3** *Scope of the initial POE carried out on the first phase of development at the Karolinska Institutet*

▶ ▲ **Figures 4.34 and 4.35** *Future learning*

▶ **Figure 4.36** *Informal learning environments*

activities. The educational idea with the redevelopment had been to foster peer-to-peer learning and create a space where students could collaborate outside scheduled class hours.

The study showed that the new learning spaces were used throughout the day and over the week, starting before 8.00am in the morning and lasting well after 7.00pm. Students were using the space both to study individually and to study in small groups of three to four people. Some students used the space also for formal group assignments. A few complaints were made that the space was cold during the winter but it was still used intensively despite these caveats. Many of the students told the anthropologist that they had previously been studying at home or outside Karolinska Institutet (KI) but the new environments had provided them with space to study and meet their fellow students.

A number of new informal learning environments have been opened since then and the same phenomenon can be observed: students are using them from early morning to late evening to work individually and to study together.

Figure 4.37 *A large and more comprehensive study will be initiated during 2016*

What is interesting to observe is how tremendously popular all whiteboards have become in almost all informal learning spaces.

A large and more comprehensive study will be initiated during 2016 where all informal learning environments will be analysed in terms of when specific spaces are being used, by whom and for what purpose. The results will be analysed in relation to the educational intentions with the redevelopment, which were primarily to foster peer-to-peer learning and secondly to get students from different health professions programmes to come together.

FORMAL LEARNING ENVIRONMENTS

The first new classrooms opened in 2013 but the vast majority (>90%) opened after the summer holidays in 2014. Because it takes time for the faculty to get used to the spaces and find ways to relate to them, a formal POE has yet to be conducted on the educational impact of the redevelopment. Data has only been collected in relation to the actual physical qualities of the spaces: how whiteboard surfaces work, the quality of the swivel chairs and the new furniture, and how technology works. This has provided substantial feedback on what to consider when selecting appropriate materials and furniture.

Small introductory half-day workshops have been conducted on the ideas behind the new spaces and how they are intended to work with the faculty. This has also provided interesting insights in how spaces are being taken into occupancy by faculty. The horseshoe format of many redeveloped classrooms and the round tables seem to be popular among faculty.

A group of explorative studies will be initiated during 2016 to more carefully analyse how faculty and students use the redeveloped spaces. Studies trying to 'measure effects' and causality between space and learning are methodological, very difficult to design and there will always be a problem with Hawthorne effects and lack of rigid controls. With this taken into account, the approach at KI will be to address the overall POEs from, and educational perspective by a series of explorative studies mainly using qualitative research methods with students and faculty in both formal and informal learning environments..

For further project descriptions see http://ki.se/en/medh/future-learning-environments

LESSONS LEARNED

1. It is important to develop an educational vision and to extrapolate performance requirements of physical learning spaces from this vision in order to achieve curriculum alignment.

2. It is important to base the educational vision on underlying curriculum theory and theories of learning in higher education.

3. The networked learning landscape conceptual framework enabled a holistic view of physical learning spaces and integration of different kinds of environments, formal and informal.

4. The important collaboration of educational academic experts, real estate developers and architects is key to both a successful project framing and the implementation of specific projects.

INTERFACES AND TERRITORIES: BLURRING THE BOUNDARIES, OWNERSHIP, MANAGEMENT AND INCLUSION

Eleanor J. Magennis

CONTEXT: THE ESTATES DEPARTMENT AS TRANSLATOR

In the 1980s the University of Strathclyde was typical of many universities in that it built walls around its edges to define its territory. However, less than 20 years later these walls were coming down and the boundary between city and university became intentionally blurred. This physical change was also symbolic of the government's agenda to widen access to universities to a broader range of students but also to enter into greater partnerships with the local community, businesses and neighbouring institutions. Another key change has been in technology.

This case study outlines the important contribution the estates department can play in translating between academics and design teams. The academics should lead and appoint a champion/sponsor for the project; however, there is much the estates team can do to support.

University staff may only be involved in one building project in their career and hence estates staff can guide them on the processes and best practice. Also, estates personnel will act as a translator of acronyms and terms used by university staff and design teams.

Estates personnel should collate key university documents and highlight appropriate inter-related projects. Although much of this will be on a university's website, it is helpful to point to the links and talk through the information.

OWNERSHIP OF SPACE

For example, when designing learning spaces and accommodating more space per student, this need not result in an absolute increase in area if parallel measures are being taken to increase space utilisation through timetable and policy review. The Universities of Sunderland and Liverpool are good examples of this, where laboratory classes were brought together to create excellent facilities which are well used. These are featured on the S-Labs website which is a good resource for laboratory design in higher education.[52]

This is just one of the many useful networks that exist in higher education that gather and share good practice in campus design and planning. Others examples are Society for College and University Planners, AUDE and the HEDQF.

Students do not think about who owns the space: what is important to them is that the space is fit for purpose, good quality and inspiring. It makes economic sense to share resources where possible. The senior estates personnel should be key in highlighting where there may be potential sharing opportunities. This can be difficult to facilitate for a number of factors; for example, an incompatible timetable or lack of knowledge of duplicate facilities. It also involves a culture change to see the benefits of sharing as a positive rather than as a nuisance or risk. A good example from the University of Strathclyde was when there was an immediate need for teaching space, due to a fire in one of the buildings. Time was booked in the local cinema for early morning classes. Some adjustments were required, such as additional task lighting, but overall it proved to be a cost-effective solution. The rental costs do need to be carefully weighed up and assessed but at various times the University of Strathclyde took advantage of its city centre location to use local exhibition, theatre and music venues, including recording studios.

Likewise, some university spaces may be used by the local community in the evenings and out of semester time to improve occupancy and gain income.

▲ **Figure 4.38** *Central atrium, University of Strathclyde Technology and Innovation Centre designed by BDP Architects*

◀ **Figure 4.39** *Technology and Innovation Centre, University of Strathclyde*

The University of Aberdeen has taken it a step further by being a key partner/funder with Aberdeen City Council and Sportscotland in the Aberdeen Sports Village, which collectively have enabled state-of-the-art facilities to be provided for both students and the local community. The University of Strathclyde has partnered with industry to develop the Technology and Innovation Centre based on research themes, which opened in 2015 and is estimated to have an annual economic impact of £64.5 million by 2021/22. In this building there is an intermingling of academic researchers and industrialists.[53]

Another aspect of ownership is having shared workspace. Although widely adopted in the commercial world, this has been rare in higher education, except for some part-time staff and post-graduate students. However, a couple of estates departments (the Universities of Newcastle and Glasgow) are piloting agile working by not providing a fixed desk for every staff member and acknowledging the high percentage of time staff spend at meetings or out on campus.

STAKEHOLDERS

Once a potential project is identified, it is important to assemble the best team. Again, the estates team has a role in making recommendations and securing the right personnel and the appropriate governance arrangements and structure. It is important to harness in-house expertise for projects where appropriate but it does also need to be carefully managed.

The success of any space on campus is dependent on people, so it is important to involve the key stakeholders at the correct time and keep in touch with them to pick up post-occupancy feedback for a virtuous loop of continuous improvement. It is often debated in universities who the stakeholders are: students, staff, industry partners, employers, parents, alumni, funding bodies and so on. In reality they all are, with slightly different expectations and requirements. Often the external demands drive a cultural change from within universities. Dealing with this can be one of the hardest issues to manage, but to ignore it could risk serious failings in the project. However, estates personnel must ensure they are supporting, rather than steering, the change. This is particularly true in terms of the academic workplace where academics may consider the individual office to be the only solution to support their scholarly work. It is important not to make assumptions on this and an academic workplace tool was created to try and help facilitate this.[54]

▲◀ **Figures 4.40 and 4.41** *Learning and Teaching Hub, University of Glasgow designed by HLM Architects*

With the advent of tuition fees and reduction in grants, the term 'student as customer' has come more to the fore. However, this is not always a useful way to describe the relationship, as students are more likely to consider themselves in a partnership rather than a simple business transaction. Hence, it is important within the client team to engage students. The University of Glasgow has successfully used student interns within their estates department on project work including student surveys to inform pilot learning spaces which in turn are informing a new Learning and Teaching Hub.

In thinking of stakeholders, we need to think of a diverse group of people with many different cultural backgrounds, beliefs and needs, and reflect these in a campus and buildings that support this rich mix of people and are inclusive to all. Within this mix, people need to feel empowered with an element of personalisation to suit different working styles. The same is true for students in learning spaces.

OUTCOME-BASED SPACES

Allowing this element of choice within boundaries has been shown to aid productivity. This is a key outcome in supporting any space. It is essential to focus on supporting outcomes when designing. Knowing the right questions to ask is critical to inform a compelling business case. Estates personnel must lend strong support, rather than attempt to lead. Examples could include:

- In a learning environment, it could be to accommodate greater numbers of students, support graduate attributes, achieve better engagement and attainment.

A learning spaces toolkit is available that is a useful resource.[55]

- In a research environment, it could be to raise research income.
- In the workplace, it could be accommodating more staff or changes in working practices and/or improving wellbeing by looking at biophillic design.[56]
- Reducing carbon footprint.

Cutting across all of the above could be knowledge exchange and increasing collaboration opportunities. The space and technology alone will not ensure successful collaborations but it can certainly aid. (The University of Michigan has carried out some interesting research on this,[57] which showed that when researchers share a building, especially a floor, the likelihood of forming new collaborations increases dramatically.)

NEW TYPES OF SPACE

Piloting and protoyping is best before wholesale change. Estates personnel have a role to play to ensure these opportunities are taken and proper feedback mechanisms are put in place. Many new technologies fail and do not become mainstream, so this needs to be built into a project. Innovation involves some risk of failing, so procedures need to establish manageable risks with fallback options. In the Loughborough Collaborative lecture theatre (see page 40) the fear of failure was such that full-scale mock-ups of the seating were created and even the final fit-out was designed in such a way that it could easily be removed
if unsuccessful. Thankfully that has not happened and the architects involved have continued to enhance and develop their ideas at various universities.

Another way to test ideas or respond to the seasonal needs of a campus is to consider pop-ups/plug-in structures. This was something the University of Strathclyde explored with temporary structures for open days, freshers' week, research week, graduation time, etc., to house information, projects and extra catering at these times when additional or concentrated numbers were expected on campus. Inspiration for this project was taken from the successful Merchant City festival in the year of the Commonwealth Games in Glasgow.

As well as the importance of individual spaces, the circulation that joins them is also important. This should be open and welcoming, particularly within accessible public areas to showcase the activities beyond. There have been an increasing number of atriums in higher education but these must be designed carefully to ensure they are useful rather than wasteful spaces.

Another issue to watch, which is frequently raised by users, is flexibility. Yes, it is important to future-proof spaces but not at the expense of making a space so flexible that it fails in its main purpose and is compromised too much.

LEARNING FROM OTHER SECTORS

In order to innovate, you often need to draw inspiration from other sectors, such as retail, hotels and museums. This seems to apply particularly at present to connecting the physical and virtual space. There was an interesting workshop at the Society for College and University Planners conference in July 2015. Some examples they highlighted were:

- While a new Kate Spade shop was being fitted out in New York, there was a window display of product images and a machine on which these products and others could be ordered. So not only did it build up excitement before the store was opened but allowed that to be translated into revenue.
- At a train station in Korea, a photographic touch screen display of supermarket products allowed passengers to order goods so that they arrived by the time they reached home.
- A British Airways advert changed to show where the plane flying overhead was travelling to or from.

What could universities learn and apply from these examples?

CONCLUSION

A final key question to bear in mind as a check on any university project is: 'What makes you want to come on campus and to this building?' The reasons may be changing as technology supports a more distributed work and learning community but we are still social beings and universities need to adapt and capture the best of an on-campus experience or they will fade away. There is a useful tool available for workshops with stakeholders at the early/warm-up stage of a project that looks at experience whether at campus, building or room level from the initial enticement stage through enter, engage, exit and extend in terms of toss, keep, improve and create. The right type of spaces/work should emerge from this process.

SAW SWEE HOCK STUDENT CENTRE, LSE

Julian Robinson

CONTEXT

It is fair to say that ten years ago the London School of Economics (LSE) was not recognised for the quality of its estate. In fact, while most people have heard of the LSE, not very many know where it is located or can visualise its public face. Accordingly, the two main tenets of the LSE Estates Strategy are:

1. The creation of a world class estate, commensurate with its international academic reputation.
2. The establishment of a 'University Quarter', with associated improvements to the ground plane and public realm.

Part of the response to this strategy was the LSE opening the doors of its Saw Swee Hock Student Centre in early 2014. It had been a long and sometimes painful journey (over 500 objections to the Planning Application and the entire £1million contingency spent in the ground!) but the School definitely thought it was worth it.

This unashamedly modern and unique building was constructed on a very constrained site, to a very challenging brief. In a departure from the norm, the School used a list of adjectives to illustrate how it wanted the building to be perceived and the messages it wanted it to convey. It said it wanted it to be: Adaptable/Ambitious/Award Winning/Beautiful /Distinctive/ Fun/ Innovative/Inspirational/International/ Original/Participatory/Recognisable/ Stimulating/Sustainable and Unique![58]

The questions for the School were:

- Did it achieve these ambitions?
- Was it well received by its users?
- Did it perform well?
- Did it add sufficient value to the LSE and its estate?

In terms of value, the building was not cheap to construct and the lofty ambitions of the brief resulted in a construction cost of over £4,000/sqm (including demolition). However, the new building at 6,000 sqm virtually doubled the floor space of the previous building on the site and it achieved a BREEAM 'Outstanding' rating. It generated unprecedented publicity for a university building, being featured in no fewer than 52 publications, it has so far won 15 design awards (with the LSE being named AJ 100 Client of the Year 2014), and was shortlisted for both the Stirling Prize and the Mies Van Der Rohe Award.

However, the point of designing and constructing buildings is not or should not be about PR and awards but about improving the experience and indeed utility of those who use, operate and enjoy them. But how can this be evidenced? The great modernist architect Louise Kahn opined:

A great building must begin with the immeasurable, must go through measurable means when it is being designed, and in the end must be unmeasured.

The Saw had something of this: John Tuomey's rudimentary cardboard model – all odd shapes and angles – and Sheila O'Donnell's soft and subtle watercolours were hard to measure, but measured they eventually were by our quantity surveyor and were then brought to reality by our builder. However, in a departure from Kahn, we did indeed measure the outcome and impact of the Saw and to do this the School commissioned a vox pop film[59] to capture users' initial reactions, together with a formal POE conducted by ZZA Responsive User Environments.[60]

The POE research is explored in depth in the book, *Saw Swee Hock – The Realisation of the London School of Economics Student Centre*[61] but the headline findings make for very interesting reading.

POE: NOTABLE ACHIEVEMENTS

Overall, the POE demonstrated that the Saw has been very well received by students and staff. Among the users' extensive positive evaluations for aspects of the Saw, some findings deserve particular comment.

The stairs, such a key architectural feature of this building are evaluated as a major success in terms of 'convenient location' (91% positive) and 'clarity of entrance' (100% positive). ZZA contend the positive response to the look and feel of the stairs is in notable contrast with frequent responses in other POEs that reflect the common condition of deprioritised stairs, hidden behind fire doors which have a paucity of natural light, quality finishes, external aspect and overall investment in design.

Thermal experience is widely recognised as an area of building performance that is susceptible to negative user feedback in POEs and to be fair this was also one of my main worries, given the Saw is essentially a naturally ventilated building. However, ZZA found that office users evaluated this mostly in terms of major successes, including 'air feels fresh', 'absence of draughts', 'humidity feels right'; and 'Temperature in the workspace areas and elsewhere in the building is at the right level now' and the 'temperature in the meeting booths' were likewise evaluated as successes.

The respondents sampled for the specialist spaces similarly evaluated all aspects of air quality in the index spaces as major successes. Against this atypically positive profile, the only issue, identified by office users, was insufficient user control.

One of the areas that gave me sleepless nights during the construction phase was the naturally ventilated gym. When one thinks of a London gym, they are normally packed full of heat-generating equipment, bodies and air-conditioning units! However, as a regular user of the new facility – which, by the way, has produced an exponential growth in gym membership – I am pleased to report that throughout the year the environmental conditions are fine. It is great to see the large wooden panels on the cool north side automatically opening via the building management system (BMS) to keep the space cool.

The Saw provides an environment for both work and play, and for those permanently based in the building the former is particularly important. ZZA found that office users identified most aspects of light as major successes, including:

- general ambience
- effective light level for work
- level of natural light
- level of artificial light
- lighting elsewhere in the building.

The users of the specialist spaces evaluate both aspects of lighting in these settings as major successes. Given the wide range of activities for which the Saw provides spaces and the associated variation in performance requirements, ZZA say this is an admirable result. Of the office users' two concerns recorded, one was in relation to user control, the other the lighting level in meeting booths based on inconsistent functioning and some excessive brightness. Both these issues can be

addressed by monitoring, adjustment and the introduction of minor tweaks such as baffles and filters if required.

LESSONS LEARNED

Commissioning a structured POE has enabled the LSE Estates Division to assess the value and impact of its new Student Centre. Although there were remarkably few issues arising from such a multi-functional building, it is correct to acknowledge that a small number were raised by the users. Some have already been addressed but one was not amenable to an easy fix – noise from people dropping weights in the fourth floor gym and disturbing others in the building. Unfortunately, the lowest floor where this use might have been ideally located is deployed for the Venue, with its more intensive usage for nightclub and gigs. However, this lesson has been learned and this facility will be re-located in the basement of our forthcoming building on Lincoln's Inn Fields. Most of the issues identified by the POE involve soft factors relating to facilities management and house services. ZZA quite rightly point out:

This is the most malleable domain for enhancing user satisfaction at low or nil cost. Examples of easy interventions indicated by the POE findings include provision of book storage for office-based users who require this, and secure laptop storage for students. Such measures highlight the rationale of post occupancy research as an activity, providing an actionable and productive steer on increasing effectiveness for users.

PROMOTING SOCIAL CAPITAL

This was perhaps the biggest and most positive finding of the POE. ZZA found a distinct potential benefit of both working in and using the Saw for any purpose, related to its range of facilities and amenities, as well as allowing the potential for users to engage in multiple activities. The School's aims articulated in the Saw's Design Competition Brief included:

- creating a hub for student activities
- to achieve cross promotion of Union services
- for the centre to be 'participatory'
- to employ an 'innovative design scheme which allows multi-use of space and maximizes the site's full potential'.

The goal in the design development stage was for the Saw 'to really contribute towards encouraging students to use it'.

The POE identifies considerable success in meeting this aspiration. Twenty-five per cent of all interviewees reported use of two or three spaces in the Saw, in addition to the space in which they were sampled, 18% reported using four to six other spaces, 20% used seven to eight other spaces, and 22% used nine to twelve other spaces. The most popular facilities in terms of reported use as places to eat, drink, and socialise and/or rest were, in descending order, The Three Tuns pub, the 6th floor café and roof terrace, and the Learning Café, all of which were reported as being used by 40% of respondents or more.

Specialist spaces, such as the Faith Centre (with reported use by 21% of interviewees), aimed at meeting

the specific needs of more defined users, provided value to them, as demonstrated by frequent usage – from multiple times a day to several times weekly. The research further showed the Saw's multi-use attributes were relevant to these users as well, with all reporting using other spaces in the Saw.

The ZZA surveyors found the multi-use and spatial contiguity contributed to enriching the users' experience and included these comments by students:

In general the building is a massive positive asset. I can pray, revise, and do Students' Union activities all in one building. For me, it's hugely beneficial and highly functional. I have nothing but praise for it.
Specialist space user, The Venue

My sister's doing a degree at UCL, and she wishes they had a Students' Union with both faith centre and gym.
Specialist space user, Faith Centre

◀ ▲ **Figure 4.42 - 4.44**

STUDENTS' VOX POP
- INITIAL REACTIONS

'Its not conventional.'

'Its not like anything I've seen before.'

'I love the natural look of it, the bricks and wood.'

'There are no right angles – that may be a myth.'

'It's great to have a new space different from all the other buildings at LSE.'

'Nothing else on the campus looks like this.'

'It's incredible.' 'I want more of this.'

'Brilliant architecture.' 'Artfully crafted.'

'It really grabs people's eyes when they pass by.'

◀▼ **Figure 4.45 - 4.49**

The respondents combined, evaluated 'the effectiveness of other spaces in the SAW' as a major success, and 82% of the combined sample reported that their use of other spaces in the building was not impeded because they did not know how to get involved or because the spaces were ineffective. Nevertheless, ZZA found the findings indicated scope for enhancement, in respect of the design giving an informative and welcoming sense of the activities on offer and the building's design and spaces promoting spontaneous interaction.

ZZA contend that *effects relate to the SAW's vertical stacking on a tight footprint, limiting direct sight of specific activities to the level users go to in the building, and confining spontaneous encounters to other people in the given setting and those they might meet on route. Whereas a full height atrium might have promoted sightlines, this would have been in tension with scarce usable space. Usefully, the evaluation indicates feasible supplementary action at the SAW, including spilling student activity onto the external apron across the front of the building, and providing dynamic digital displays of the interior activities menu outside and/or on lower levels.*

STRATEGIC VALUE TO THE LSE

In addition to the strong thumbs-up on the enhancement of both users' experience and the profile of the School, ZZA's evaluation also posited the question of whether 'the SAW's architecture respects and contributes to the local setting' and this was evaluated as a success. In respect of the building's impact on students' own perceptions of

the LSE, 69% say the SAW has changed these for the better; 31% say it makes no difference; no one said it changes it for the worse.

Reflecting on the value this building brings to the LSE, I asked a number of key individuals associated with the project what they thought about its value and was delighted to have my own judgements supported and extended.

Ziona Strelitz, founder of ZZA Responsive User Environments, who carried out the research commented:

'No student will think back on their time at LSE in terms of its heating and lux levels. For them, their overall sense of the School – as partly influenced and manifested by its physical estate – are what matter. And at this strategic level, their feedback on the SAW is highly affirmative, with a 94% positive rating for 'The building's facilities enhance student (and staff) experience', and a 92% positive rating for 'The building enhances the LSE's profile', and further successes for 'The centre serves as a hub bringing students together', 'The building's provides facilities that support learning', the SAW being 'A stimulating and inspiring place to work, learn and play', and 'of a standard to attract and impress world class students'.

LSE academic staff have also welcomed the value of Saw to the wider LSE experience, with Professor Ricky Burdett of the LSE Cities Programme observing:

A student centre needs to be at the heart of a university community. In a hard inner city site which the LSE occupies in central London this is even more important. The O'Donnell + Tuomey building adds real

urban value to the experience of being a student in London. Its design celebrates the special needs of high performing students for a place to relax and feel at home while engaging with global issues and exacting academic requirements. By enhancing the everyday human experience of the student, the building succeeds in intensifying and optimising the learning curve at the heart of an urban campus with spaces that feel comfortable, edgy, contemporary and dynamic.

For the School's Chaplain and Interfaith Advisor, Reverand Jim Walters:

Some of the value added to the LSE campus through the Faith Centre is quantifiable. We know, for example, that providing high-quality facilities for Islamic prayers meets a practical need of approximately 600 Muslim students. We know, also, that around 700 students of different faiths have regular meetings in the different spaces we provide. But to me, the LSE Faith Centre has added a qualitative value to the campus that is hard to measure. Who knows what encouragement and inspiration is provided to the student who sits for a few moments in quiet contemplation in front of our beautiful stained glass? Who knows how many students have found friendship and community life through the different cultural groups that now have a space to call their own? And in creating a space on campus for new conversations about faith, meaning and spirituality, we will never be able to measure what impact this Centre may have on the causes of justice and peace building to which students may be drawn.

The Acting Head of the LSE Careers Service, Shaun Harris feels:

The relaxed, informal quality of the building is particularly conducive for the careers service at LSE. It encourages students from a wide spectrum of the student body to use our services, some of whom might be intimidated by a more formal environment. It almost goes without saying that we are also helped considerably by being co-located with other student services such as the Faith Centre, Gym and Students' Union which again further encourages the flow of students to come and visit us.

CONCLUSION: VISION–DESIGN–CONSTRUCTION–POE

I suppose what you are thinking is, this all sounds too positive. Well the fact is, the LSE regards the Saw as a major success and thinks its investment in high-quality architecture has paid off. However, this did not come about by accident. Particular emphasis was put on the preparation of a project vision statement, the running of a fair and rigorous design competition (managed for us by the RIBA) and, most importantly, the involvement of the prospective users of the building. Naturally, as a student building, students were involved in all aspects of the project from initial briefing, including reference visits to other facilities, to being on the Jury Panel for the selection of the architects, to taking part in a general plebiscite on the six shortlisted designs (well, this is the LSE!) to sitting on the Project Board, attending site visits and of course being surveyed for their feedback on the completed building.

When I take people round the building I am quite often asked what I would do differently in terms of the design and my answer is absolutely nothing architecturally, but practically I would have made the BMS system less complicated and more intuitive for the staff who run it and in hindsight I would not have positioned the free weights area over the student accommodation office!

The structured POE and the more qualitative comments from built environment professionals, the students and staff operating in the building clearly suggest that the Student Centre has created significant value for the LSE and I would also contend it has achieved all of the original objectives set out in the brief, by being:

Adaptable/Ambitious/Award Winning/ Beautiful /Distinctive/Fun/Innovative/ Inspirational/International/ Original/Participatory/Recognisable/ Stimulating/Sustainable and Unique!

Don't just take my word for it, come and visit and decide for yourself! I think anyone would be hard pushed to claim these have not been met.

Moreover, the building has nailed both tenets of the School's Estates Strategy, by adding a piece of world-class architecture to the LSE estate and by enhancing the public realm and the concept of a 'university quarter' in this corner of London. How one places a value on this is hopefully explored in the above discourse, however, for the avoidance of doubt, if the question is: would we do it again and in the same way? The unequivocal answer is: YES absolutely!

REFERENCES

PART 1

CONTEXT

[1] R.G. Wilson, J.M. Lasala and P.C. Sherwood, *Thomas Jefferson's academical village: the creation of an architectural masterpiece*, University of Virginia Press, Charlottesville, VA, 2009.

[2] USP, *Prefeitura Quadrilátero*, 2015, retrieved from www.puspqsd.usp.br/gabinete/

[3] J.H. Newman, *The Idea of a University Defined and Illustrated : In Nine Discourses Delivered to the Catholics of Dublin*, Gutenberg ebooks, 2008 www.gutenberg.org/ebooks/24526.

[4] R.D. Anderson, *European Universities from the Enlightenment to 1914*, Oxford University Press, Oxford, 2004.

[5] R.P. Dober, *Campus Planning*, Reinhold, New York, 1964, p. 54.

[6] M.F. Schmertz, *Campus Planning and Design*, McGraw-Hill, New York, 1972.

[7] University of Pennsylvania and Sasaki Associates, *Penn Connects: A Vision for the Future*, University of Pennsylvania, Philadelphia, 2006.

[8] ANU, *Campus Master Plan 2030,* Acton, 2011, In: B. Cleveland and K. Fisher, 'The evaluation of physical learning environments: a critical review of the literature', *Learning Environments Research*, 17(1), 1–28. doi:10.1007/s10984-013-9149-3.

[9] B. Cleveland and K. Fisher, 'The evaluation of physical learning environments: a critical review of the literature', *Learning Environments Research*, 17(1), 1–28.

[10] G. Davis, *The Republic of Learning*, ABC Books, Pymble, NSW, 2010.

[11] S. Kaji-O'Grady, 'Melbourne School of Design', *Architecture Australia*, Vol. 104, issue 1, 2015, pp. 22–32.

[12] R. Lenzner and S.S. Johnson, 'Seeing things as they really are', *Forbes*, Vol. 159, issue 5, 1997, pp. 122–28.

[13] See note 8.

[14] R.P. Dober, *Campus Planning*, Reinhold, New York, 1964.

[15] A. Markusen, 'Sticky Places in Slippery Space: A Typology of Industrial Districts', *Economic Geography*, Vol. 72, issue 3, 1996.

[16] Case Western Reserve University, *Masterplan Summary,* 2005, B. Cleveland and K. Fisher, 'The evaluation of physical learning environments: a critical review of the literature', *Learning Environments Research*, 17(1), 1–28.

[17] University of Melbourne, 'The University of Melbourne Strategic Plan 2015–2020: Growing Esteem', *University of Melbourne*, http://about.unimelb.edu.au/__data/assets/pdf_file/0006/1462065/11364-GROWING-ESTEEM-2015-FA-WEB.pdf, 2015 (accessed 2 February 2016).

MASTERPLANNING

[18] M.P. Chapman, *American Places: In Search of the Twenty-First Century Campus*, Praeger, Westport, CT, 2006.

[19] P. Turner, *Campus: An American Planning Tradition*, Architecture History Foundation, Cambridge and London, 1996.

[20] J. Coulson, P. Roberts and I. Taylor, *University Trends: Contemporary Campus Design*, Routledge, Abingdon, 2015, p. 26.

[21] W. Whyte, *'Redbrick: A Social and Architectural History of Britain's Civic Universities'*, Oxford University Press, Oxford, 2015.

[22] T. Birks, *Building the New Universities*, David and Charles, Newton Abbot, 1972.

[23] Higher Education Statistics Agency (HESA), 'Higher education student enrolments and qualifications obtained at Higher Education providers in the United Kingdom 2013/14', www.hesa.ac.uk, 2015 (accessed 2 February 2016).

[24] Higher Education Design Quality Forum (HEDQF), *Estates Matter! Report on survey of students' views of their universities' estates 2013*, Architecture PLB and London School of Economics, 2014.

[25] C. Landry, *The Art of City Making*, Earthscan, London, 2006, p. 5.

[26] P. Temple (ed), *The Physical University: Contours of Space and Place in Higher Education*, Routledge, Abingdon, 2014.

[27] See also: R. Olcayto, 'Masterplanning', *Architects' Journal*, 13 October 2011, pp. 35–39; and E. Harwood et al, *Twentieth-century Architecture 11: Oxford and Cambridge*, Twentieth Century Society, London, 2014.

[28] *Architects' Journal*, issue 35, *RIBA Awards*, June 2015.

[29] Gunning Principles: Prior to 1985 in the UK little consideration had been given to consultation but in a landmark case in that year (R v London Borough of Brent ex parte Gunning) Mr Stephen Sedley QC propounded a set of fundamental consultation principles that were adopted by the presiding judge. These Gunning (or Sedley) principles were confirmed as applicable to all public consultations by the Court of Appeal in 2001 (Coughlan case) and must underpin every public consultation that takes place in the UK.

[30] Michael Serginson and Professor Steve Lockley, 'BIM for Facilities Management – University Campus', *OpenBIM – Case Studies*, www.openbim.org/case-studies/university-campus-facilities-management-bim-model (accessed 29 January 2016).

[31] University of California, Office of the President, 'Presidential initiatives: Carbon Neutrality Initiative' www.ucop.edu/initiatives/carbon-neutrality-initiative.html (accessed 29 January 2016).

[32] C. Kerr, *The Uses of the University, Godkin Lectures*, Harvard University Press, Boston, MA, 1963, p. 31.

PART 2

TEACHING AND LEARNING SPACES

[1] J. Biggs and C. Tang, *Teaching for quality learning at university*, Open University Press, London, 2011.

[2] J. Nordquist and K. Sundberg, An educational leadership responsibility in primary care: ensuring the physical space for learning aligns with the educational mission, *Educ Primary Care*. 24(1): 45–49.

[3] P. Temple, *Learning spaces for the 21st Century: a review of the literature*, Higher Education Academy, London, 2007; J. Nordquist, 'Alignment Achieved? The Learning Landscape and Curricula in Health Professions Education', *Medical Education*, Vol. 50, 2015, pp. 61–68.

[4] J. Nordquist and A. Laing, 'Spaces for learning – a neglected area in curriculum change and strategic educational leadership', *Medical Teacher*, Vol. 36, 2014, pp. 555–56.

[5] S. Dugdale, 'Space strategies for the new learning landscape', *Educause (March/April)*, Vol. 44, issue 2, 2004, pp. 50–63; A. Thody, '"Learning Landscapes" as shared vocabulary for learning spaces', in A. Boddington and J. Boys (eds), *Re-shaping Learning: The Future of Learning Spaces in Post-Compulsory Education*, Sense Publishers, Rotterdam, 2011, pp. 121–36.

[6] J. Nordquist and A. Laing, 'Spaces for learning – a neglected area in curriculum change and strategic educational leadership', *Medical Teacher*, Vol. 36, 2014, pp. 555–56; J. Nordquist, K. Sundberg and A. Laing, 'Aligning Physical Learning Spaces with the Curriculum', AMEE Guide 107, *Medical Teacher*, 2016 (in press); J. Nordquist, 'Alignment Achieved? The Learning Landscape and Curricula in Health Professions Education', *Medical Education*, Vol. 50, 2015, pp. 61-68.

[7] 'Designing Spaces for the Networked Learning Landscape: Design of Learning Spaces'. *Medical Teacher* 2015; 37:337–343

[8] D. Oblinger, *Learning Spaces*, Educause ebooks, 2006, A. Harrion and L. Hutton, *Design for the Changing Educational Landscape: Space, Place and the Future of Learning*, Routledge, London, 2014; J. Nordquist, 'Alignment Achieved? The Learning Landscape and Curricula in Health Professions Education', *Medical Education*, Vol. 50, 2015, pp. 61–68.

CHANGING SPACES

[9] Andrew Harrison and Antonia Cairns, 'The Changing Academic Workplace', DEGW on Behalf of the University of Strathclyde, 2008. p. 38. Available to download from www.Exploreacademicworkspace.com.

PART 3

BRIEFING AND DESIGN FOR SUSTAINABILITY

[1] Exploring how the UK can meet the 2050 emission reduction target using the web-based 2050 Calculator, www.gov.uk/guidance/2050-pathways-analysis

[2] Doug King, May 2012, *The case for Centres of Excellence in sustainable building design*, The Royal Academy of Engineering, ISBN 1-903496-80-2, www.raeng.org.uk/publications/reports/the-case-for-centres-of-excellence-in-sustainable

[3] University carbon footprint figures from the Carbon Trust, available at www.carbontrust.com/resources/guides/sector-based-advice/further-and-higher-education/

[4] HEFCE *Sustainable development in higher education* December 2014/30 *Policy development Policy framework* www.hefce.ac.uk/workprovide/carbon

[5] www.keele.ac.uk/greenkeele keelehub/

[6] www.cereb.org.uk/

[7] Four UK universities have set up Centres of Excellence in Sustainable Building Design, in collaboration with the Royal Academy of Engineering. The new centres at Heriot-Watt University, Loughborough University, the University of Sheffield and University College London will form a national network to demonstrate and exchange best practice in teaching and research for a more sustainable built environment. www.raeng.org.uk/news/news-releases/2013/May/four-new-centres-of-excellence-for-sustainable-bui#sthash.FwZwznli.dpuf

[8] www.nottingham.ac.uk/estates/documents/developments/etb-flyers.pdf

[9] University of Nottingham University Architecture Department www.nottingham.ac.uk/creative-energy-homes/index.aspx

[10] CIBSE www.cibse.org/Knowledge/Building-Services-Case-Studies/PROBE-Post-Occupancy-Studies)

PART 4

VALUE

[1] Association of University Directors of Estates, 'Higher Education Statistics Report 2015', 2015, www.aude.ac.uk

[2] CABE, 'Design with Distinction – The Value of Good Building Design in Higher Education', 2005, ISBN 1-84633-001-7.

[3] The Russell Group, 'A Passion for Learning – The Student Experience at Russell Group Universities', 2014, www.russellgroup.ac.uk

[4] ZZA Responsive User Environments, (report on Findings for LSE), 'Perceived Quality of the LSE Campus: Baseline Research on Student Opinion', 2011.

[5] Julian Robinson, 'Estates Matter! – Report on Survey of Students' Views of their Universities' Estates', HEDQF, 2013, www.hedqf.org.uk

[6] John Elmes, 'Facilities Key to Students' University Choice, *Times Higher Education*, 30 July 2015.

BUILDING PERFORMANCE

[7] Note on the REF and NSS.

[8] www.dqi.org.uk

[9] Vitruvius, *The Elements of Architecture*, 1624.

[10] www.dqi.org.uk

[11] Economic and social sustainability are rarely considered and, as well as being hard to measure, are always hard to attribute to specific features of a building.

[12] www.usablebuildings.co.uk/

[13] www.hedqf.org

[14] Sebastian Macmillan (ed), *Designing Better Building: Quality and Value in the Built Environment,* Taylor & Francis, 2003.

[15] Martin Cook, *The Design Quality Manual: Improving Building Performance, Wiley Blackwell,* 2007.

[16] 'Delivering Value from the Higher Education Estate', phase 2 of the Diamond Review.

[17] www.hedqf.org

[18] AUDE, *Guide to Post Occupancy Evaluation*, Higher Education Funding Council for England, Bristol, 2006, available at www.aude.ac.uk/resources/goodpractice/AUDE_POE_guide/ (accessed 10 December 2015).

[19] AMA Alexi Marmot Associates, www.aleximarmot.com (Knowledge section).

[20] Leesman, http://leesmanindex.com/our-surveys/

[21] Per cent frequency × per cent occupancy = per cent utilization. For general teaching space, HEFCE suggests that over 35% is good, whereas less than 25% utilisation is poor. This cannot be applied to specialised spaces.

[22] www.usablebuildings.co.uk/WebGuideAL/AboutBus.html

[23] www.cibse.org/Knowledge/Building-Services-Case-Studies/PROBE-Post-Occupancy-Studies

[24] www.carbonbuzz.org/

[25] www.lse.ac.uk/intranet/LSEServices/estatesDivision/pdf/HEDQF-Booklet2.pdf

ACADEMIC PERFORMANCE

[26] Baldry, C. (1999). Space, the final frontier. Sociology, August 1999 v33.

[27] Fisher, C. & Singleton, G. (2015). Is 'the new academic workplace' an oxymoron? Reviewing the scholarly transformative evidence-based literature'. Paper presented at the TEFMA (Tertiary Education Facilities Management Association) conference, Cairns 2015.

[28] www.cdio.org, and Fisher and Newton 2014

[29] A. Whiteside, L. Jorn, A Duin and S Fitzgerald, "Using the PAIR-up model to evaluate active learning spaces." *Educause Quarterly*, 2009, Making the case for space: "Three years of empirical research on learning environments." *Educause Quarterly, 2010 33/3. 11,*

[30] E. Drake and D Battaglia, 'Teaching and learning in active learning classrooms: recommendations, research & resources'. Facit: Higher Impact Learning by Design. Michigan, Central Michigan University, 2014.

[31] B. de la Harpe, T. Mason, M. McPherson, K Fisher, W. Imms, K. Fraser, S. Thomson and D Taylor, 'Not a waste of space – professional development for staff teaching in New Generation Learning Spaces. Office for Learning & Teaching'. Canberra, Australian Government Office for Learning & Teaching, 2014.

[32] www.educause.edu/eli/initiatives - (accessed April 2016).

[33] R. Ellis, P. Goodyear, A. Marmot and K. Fisher, Modelling complex learning spaces. Australian Research Council Discovery Research Grant (2015-2019), 2015.

[34] D.Brooks, 'Space and consequences: The impact of different formal learning spaces on instructor and student behaviour'. *Journal of Learning Spaces*. Vol. 1, No. 2, 2012

[35] D. Baepler, C. Brooks and J. Walker, Active Learning Spaces: New Directions for Teaching and Learning, Number 137. Jossey Bass, 2014.

[36] O. Helmer-Hirshchberg, O. 1967. *Analysis of the Future: an Analysis of the Delphi Method*. Rand Corporation, 1967, www.rand.org/content/dam/rand/pubs/papers/2008/P3558.pdf (accessed April 2016).

[37] J. Boys, 2014. *Building better Universities*, Routledge, London, 2014.

[38] M. Bower, C. Howe, N. McCredie, A. Robinson and D. Grover, 'Augmented Reality in education – cases, places and potentials'. *Educational Media International*. Vol. 51, issue 1, 2013.

[39] K. Fisher and C. Newton, 'Transforming the twenty-first-century campus to enhance the net-generation student learning experience: using evidence-based design to determine what works and why in virtual/physical teaching spaces'. *Higher Education Research & Development Journal*, 33:5, 2014 10.1080/07294360.2014.890566.

[40] K. Fisher and R. Ellis, Adapting to Change in University Learning Space - Informing and Being Informed by Feedback from Senior University Leaders. HERDSA (Higher Education Research and Development). Cairns, 2014.

[41] S. Painter, J. Fournier, C. Grape, G. Grummon, J. Morellis, S. Whitmer and J Cevetllo, *Research on learning space design: present state, future directions*. Ann Arbour, Society for College and University Planning, 2012.

TECHNICAL PERFORMANCE

[42] www.wellcertified.com/well

[43] The Higher Education Environmental Performance Improvement (HEEPI) Project, 'Results of the HEEPI HE Building Energy Benchmarking Initiative 2003–4', August 2004, available at www.goodcampus.org/files/files/15-Final_report_on_03-4_HEEPI_benchmarking_v2[1].doc.

[44] AUDE 2015 Higher Education Estates Statistics report

[45] http://saves.unioncloud.org

CASE STUDIES

[46] ABP. 2009. Architectural design competition: new building for the Faculty of Architecture Building and Planning [Online]. University of Melbourne. Available: https://msd.unimelb.edu.au/competition/ [Accessed 31 July 2015].

[47] CONRAD-BERCAH, P. 2014. Melbourne School of Design. The Plan, 96-108.

[48] GREEN STAR AUSTRALIA. 2014a. Education rating tool [Online]. Available: www.gbca.org.au/green-star/rating-tools/green-star-education-v1/1762.htm [Accessed 26 February 2015].

[49] GREEN STAR AUSTRALIA. 2014b. University of Melbourne Faculty of Architecture Building and Planning building [Online]. Available: www.gbca.org.au/events.asp?eventid=32890 [Accessed 26 February 2015].

[50] MSD. 2015. New Building Media Coverage [Online]. Melbourne: University of Melbourne. Available: http://msd.unimelb.edu.au/new-building-media-coverage [Accessed 1 September 2015].

[51] Nordquist J, Laing A. Designing Spaces for the Networked Learning Landscape: Design of Learning Spaces. Medical Teacher 2015;37:337-343

[52] www.goodcampus.org/s-lab

[53] www.universities-scotland.ac.uk/uploads/publications/Working%20Smarter%20Progress%20Report%202014%20-%20final.pdf

[54] https://exploreit.sfc.ac.uk

[55] www.ucisa.ac.uk/learningspace

[56] www.terrapinbrightgreen.com/report/economics-of-biophilia

[57] HYPERLINK "www.sciencedaily.com/releases/2012/10/121025174631.htm" www.sciencedaily.com/releases/2012/10/121025174631.htm.

[58] Design Competition Brief – New Students' Centre (2009) Estates Division – London School of Economics

[59] *Saw Swee Hock Student Centre: Reaction and Reflection*, short film by Rod McAllister and William Pine, 2014. https://www.youtube.com/user/rodmcallister

[60] Saw Swee Hock Student Centre: Post Occupancy Evaluation, ZZA Responsive User Environments, 2014.

[61] Saw Swee Hock – *The Realisation of the London School of Economics Student Centre*, ed. by. Julian S Robinson, 2015 (ISBN 9 781908 967527),

BIBLIOGRAPHY

CONTEXT

Anderson, R. D., *European Universities from the Enlightenment to 1914*, Oxford University Press, Oxford, 2004.

ANU (2011), 'Campus Master Plan 2030' (Acton).

Case Western Reserve University (2005). Master plan summary, Cleveland, Ohio.

Cleveland, B., and Fisher, K. (2014), 'The evaluation of physical learning environments: a critical review of the literature', *Learning Environments Research*, 17(1),1-28.

Davis, G., *The Republic of Learning*, ABC Books, Pymble, NSW, 2010.

Dober, R. P., *Campus planning*, Reinhold, New York, 1964.

Kaji-O'Grady, S., 'Melbourne School of Design', *Architecture Australia*, 104(1), 22–32.

Lenzner, R. and Johnson, S. S. (1997), 'Seeing things as they really are' (cover story), *Forbes*, 159(5), 122–28.

Markusen, A., 'Sticky Places in Slippery Space: A Typology of Industrial Districts', *Economic Geography*, 72(3), 293–313, 1996.

Newman, J. H., *The Idea of a University Defined and Illustrated: In Nine: Discourses Delivered to the Catholics of Dublin, 1852.*

Schmertz, M. F., *Campus planning and design*, McGraw-Hill, New York, 1972.

University of Melbourne, 'The University of Melbourne strategic plan 2015–2020, growing esteem', http://about.unimelb.edu.au/__data/assets/pdf_file/0006/1462065/11364-GROWING-ESTEEM-2015-FA-WEB.pdf (accessed June 2016).

University of Pennsylvania and Sasaki Associates, *Penn Connects: A Vision for the Future*, University of Pennsylvania, Philadelphia, PA, 2006.

USP. *Prefeitura Quadrilátero*, retrieved from http://www.puspqsd.usp.br/gabinete/

Wilson, R.G., J.M. Lasala and P.C. Sherwood, *Thomas Jefferson's Academical Village: The Creation of an Architectural Masterpiece* (rev. ed.), University of Virginia Press, Charlottesville, VA, 2009.

MASTERPLANNING

Architects' Journal, 2015, Issue 37 'RIBA Awards', London.

Birks, T., *Building the new universities,* David and Charles, Newton Abbot, 1972.

Chapman, M.P., *American Places: In Search of the Twentieth-first Century Campus*, Praeger, Westport, CT, 2006.

Coulson, J., P. Roberts and I. Taylor, *University Trends: Contemporary Campus Design*, Abingdon, 2014.

Coulson, J., P. Roberts and I. Taylor, *University Planning and Architecture: The Search for Perfection*, Routledge, Abingdon (2nd ed), 2015.

Harwood, E., A. Powers and U. Saumarez-Smith (eds), *Twentieth-century architecture 11: Oxford and Cambridge*, Twentieth Century Society, London, 2014.

HEDQF, *'Estates matter! Report on survey of students' views of their universities' estates 2013',* Architecture PLB and London School of Economics, London, 2014.

HESA (Higher Education Statistics Agency),'Higher education student enrolments and qualifications obtained at Higher Education providers in the United Kingdom 2013/14', 2015 (www.hesa.ac.uk).

Kerr, C., *The Uses of the University*, 'Godkin Lectures', Harvard University Press, Boston, MA, 1963.

Landry, C., *The Art of City Making*, Earthscan, London, 2006.

Olcayto, R., 'Masterplanning', *Architects' Journal*, 13 October 2011: 35-39.

Temple, P. (ed), '*The Physical University: Contours of Space and Place in Higher Education*', Routledge, Abingdon, 2014.

Turner, P., Campus. *An American Planning Tradition*, Architecture History Foundation, Cambridge and London, 1995.

Turner, P. V., *Joseph Ramée: International Architect of the Revolutionary Era*, Cambridge University Press, Cambridge, 1996.

Whyte, W., *Redbrick: A Social and Architectural History of Britain's Civic Universities*, Oxford University Press, Oxford, 2015.

TEACHING FLAT ROOMS

Altenberger Interior Design and Consulting, 'Wu Campus Vienna Inside', http://elkealtenberger.at/en/wu-campus-vienna-inside/ (accessed 29 January 2016).

BDP, 'Edinburg Napier University, Business School', 2004, www.bdp.com/en/projects/a-e/napier-university-business-school/ (accessed 29 January 2016).

Batres, Silvia, 'The Investcorp Building for Oxford University by Zaha Hadid', *Metalocus Magazine / Revista*, June 2015 www.metalocus.es/content/en/blog/investcorp-building-oxford-university-zaha-hadid (accessed 29 January 2016).

Hall-Van Den Elsen,, Cathy, 'Teaching Excellence in Next Generation Learning Spaces', *The Teaching TomTom*, http://teachingtomtom.com/tag/teal/, (accessed 29 January 2016).

Hanna, Julia, 'The Digital Deck', *Harvard Business School – Alumni Stories*, June 2014, www.alumni.hbs.edu/stories/Pages/story-bulletin.aspx?num=3720 (accessed 29 January 2016).

Ip, Melissa, 'A place for social innovation: The PolyU Innovation Tower (Photos)', Social Enterprises Buzz – *Social Enterprise News and Discussion*, www.socialenterprisebuzz.com/2013/11/20/a-place-for-social-innovation-the-polyu-innovation-tower-photos/ (accessed 29 January 2016).

McKinney, Andrew et al, 'Technology Enabled Active Learning: Visualizing Electricity and Magnetism at MIT', *MIT Physics 8.02*, http://web.mit.edu/8.02t/www/802TEAL3D/teal_tour.htm (accessed 29 January 2016).

INNOVATION & INCUBATOR SPACES

'Accelerator London – Business Incubator in London', http://accelerator-london.com/. (accessed 28 January 2016).

Allen, Thomas J. and Günter Henn, *The Organization and Architecture of Innovation: Managing the Flow of Technology*, Elsevier/Butterworth-Heinemann, Amsterdam and Boston, 2007.

Bergek, Anna and Charlotte Norrman, 'Incubator Best Practice: A Framework', *Technovation*, 28, no. 1–2 (January 2008): 20–28.

doi:10.1016/j.technovation.2007.07.008.

Brooke, Rory, Greg Openshaw, Lucy Farrow, Fiona Scott, Gemma Drake, Rob Harris and Raj Ramanandi, 'Supporting Places of Work:

Incubators, Accelerators and Co-Working Spaces', Greater London Authority, London, 2014. https://www.london.gov.uk/sites/default/files/180%20IAC%20Report. Artwork_web.pdf.

Crescenzi, R., Rodriguez-Pose, A. and Storper, M., 'The Territorial Dynamics of Innovation: A Europe United States Comparative Analysis', *Journal of Economic Geography*, 7, no. 6 (17 May 2007): 673–709. doi:10.1093/jeg/lbm030.

Davies, Alice and Kathryn Tollervey, *The Style of Coworking: Contemporary Shared Work Spaces*, Prestel, New York, 2013.

Griffiths, A., 'Elevated Offices Loop around Secluded Plaza at Technology Park', *Dezeen*, 9 January 2015. www.dezeen.com/2015/01/09/jorge-mealha-obidos-technological-park-offices-portugal-plaza/ (accessed June 2016).

House of Commons Science and Technology Committee, 'Technology and Innovation Centres' Second Report of Session 2010–11', House of Commons, London, 17 February 2011. www.publications.parliament.uk/pa/cm201011/cmselect/cmsctech/619/619.pdf (accessed June 2016).

Mairs, J., 'Elemental Builds "Monolithic" Concrete Innovation Centre in Chile', *Dezeen*, 5 November 2014. www.dezeen.com/2014/11/05/elemental-innovation-center-uc-anacleto-angelini-university-concrete-santiago-chile/ (accessed June 2016).

McKnight, 'CHA:COL Creates Tech Incubator Space in California', *Dezeen* www.dezeen.com/2015/08/19/cha-col-technology-startup-incubator-space-kennel-k9-ventures-california-shipping-container/. (accessed 17 September 2015).

Meister, Jeanne C. and Karie Willyerd, *The 2020 Workplace: How Innovative Companies Attract, Develop, and Keep Tomorrow's Employees Today*, 1st edition, HarperBusiness, New York, 2010.

Moriset, Bruno 'Building New Places of the Creative Economy. The Rise of Coworking Spaces', 2013. http://halshs.archives ouvertes.fr/halshs-00914075/.

Rief, Stephan, Wolfgang Bauer, Klaus-Peter Stiefel and Agnes Weiss, *Faszination Coworking: Potentiale für Unternehmen und ihre Mitarbeiter = The fascination of coworking*, Fraunhofer Verl., Stuttgart, 2014.

Ryzhonkov, Vassily, 'The History of Business Incubation', *Entrepreneurship, Business Incubation, Business Models & Strategy* Blog, 22 March 2013.

https://worldbusinessincubation.wordpress com/2013/03/22/426/ (accessed June 2016)

UBI Global, 'UBI Global', *UBI Global - Incubation Impact & Network*, http://ubi-global.com/. (accessed 18 February 2016).

ACADEMIC WORK PLACES

Baldry, Chris and Alison Barnes, 'The Open-Plan Academy: Space, Control and the Undermining of Professional Identity', *Work, Employment & Society*, 26, no. 2 (2012): 228–45. doi:10.1177/0950017011432917.

den Heijer, Alexandra, 'Managing the University Campus', CELE Exchange, Centre for Effective Learning Environments, 1 April 2012. www.oecd-ilibrary.org/education/managing-the-university-campus_5k9b950gh2xx-en (accessed June 2016).

Gorgievski, Marjan J., Theo J. M. van der Voordt, Sanne G. A. van Herpen and Sophie van Akkeren, 'After the Fire; New Ways of Working in an Academic Setting', *Facilities*, 28, no. 3/4 (2010): 206–24. doi:10.1108/02632771011023159.

Harrison, Andrew and Antonia Cairns, 'The Changing Academic Workplace', *DEGW on Behalf of the University of Strathclyde, 2008.* www.architecture4e.com/symposium/facilities/facilities_paper2.pdf.

Harrison Andrew and Les Hutton, *Design for the Changing Educational Landscape: Space, Place and the Future of Learning*, Routledge, London, 2013.

HASSELL, 'The Future Academic Workplace', February 2014. www.hassellstudio.com/docs/140221_academicworkplacelitre view-(2).pdf (accessed June 2016).

HEFCE, 'Academic Workspace', www.academicworkspace.com/ (accessed 21 September 2015)..

Parkin, Jennifer, Simon Austin and Mark Lansdale, 'Research Environments for HE', Departments of Civil and Building Engineering and Human Sciences Loughborough University, 2006, www.lboro.ac.uk/eng/research/imcrc/knowledge-transfer-project/downloads/Research-Environments-for-HE.pdf (accessed June 2016).

Pinder, James, *The Case for New Academic Workspaces*, Loughborough University, Dept. of Civil and Building Engineering, Loughborough, 2009.

Space Management Group, 'Promoting Space Efficiency in Building Design', Space Management Group, March 2006, www.smg.ac.uk/documents/PromotingSpaceEfficiency.pdf.

Space Management Group, 'UK Higher Education Space Management Project', www.smg.ac.uk/documents/casestudies.pdf (accessed June 2016) (accessed 18 September 2015).

VIRTUAL LEARNING HUBS

'Coursera Learning Hubs', *Degree of Freedom*. http://degreeoffreedom.org/coursera-learning-hubs/ (accessed 17 September 2015).

'Introducing Coursera Learning Hubs: Global Participation, Local Access and Support!' http://blog.coursera.org/post/65596539008/introducing-coursera-learning-hubs-global (accessed 17 September 2015).

'New Learning Hubs Locations Hosted by The New York Public Library and Seven Other International Partners.' http://blog.coursera.org/post/84322385012/new-learning-hubs-locations-hosted-by-the-new-york (accessed 17 September 2015).

Onah, D.F.O., J. Sinclair and R. Boyatt, 'Dropout Rates of Massive Open Online Courses: Behavioural Patterns', EDULEARN14 *Proceedings*, 2014, 5825–34.

'Emerging Trends in Online Education: A Resource Guide to Massive Open Online Courses', Accessed September 30, 2015. www.internationalpeaceandconflict.org/profiles/blogs/emerging-trends-in-online-education-a-resource-guide-to-massive-o.

Simpson, Ormond, '"22%-Can We Do Better?"- The CWP Retention Literature Review Final Report', Open University, Milton Keynes, July 2010.

www.94669.mrsite.com/USERIMAGES/Retention%20literature%20review.pdf (accessed June 2016).

Simpson, Ormond, 'Student Retention in Distance Education: Are We Failing Our Students?' *Open Learning: The Journal of Open, Distance and E-Learning*, 28, no. 2 (June 2013): 105–19. doi:10.1080/02680513.2013.847363.

BUILDING PERFORMANCE

AMA Alexi Marmot Associates, www.aleximarmot.com (Knowledge section).

AMA (Alexi Marmot Associates), *Spaces for Learning: A review of Learning Spaces in Further and Higher Education*, Scottish Funding Council (SFC), Edinburgh, 2006.

AUDE, *Guide to Post Occupancy Evaluation*, Higher Education Funding Council for England, Bristol, 2006, available at: http://www.aude.ac.uk/resources/goodpractice/AUDE_POE_guide/ (accessed 10 December 2015)

Barber, M., K. Donnelly and S. Rizvi, An *Avalanche is Coming*, IPPR, London, 2013.

CABE, *The value handbook: Getting the most for your money*, The Commission for Architecture and the Built Environment, London, 2006.

Cook, M., *The design quality manual: Improving Building Performance*, Blackwell Publishing, Oxford, 2007.

HEFCE SMG, *Promoting Space Efficiency in Building Design*, 2006, available at www.smg.ac.uk/rep_efficiency.html (accessed on 10 December 2015).

Hodges, C. and M. Sekula, M., *Sustainable facility management: The Facility Manager's Guide to Optimizing Building Performance*, Vision Spots Publishing, Alexandria, VA, 2013.

Jaunzens, D. and P. Grigg, *Building performance feedback: getting started*, BRE bookshop, Garston, 2003.

JISC (Joint Infrastructure Committee Development Group), *Designing Spaces for Effective Learning: 21st Century Learning Space Design*, JISC, Bristol, 2006.

ACTIVITY BASED LEARNING

Leesman, http://leesmanindex.com/our-surveys/

Macmillan, S.(ed.), *Designing better buildings*, Spon, London, 2004.

Mallory-Hill, S., W. Preiser and C. Watson, E*nhancing building performance*, Wiley-Blackwell, Oxford, 2012.

Marmot, A., *Managing the Campus: Facility Management and Design, the Student Experience and University Effectiveness*, Ch. 4 'The Physical University', ed by P. Temple, Routledge, London, 2011.

Preiser, W. and J. Vischer, J., *Assessing Building Performance*, Elsevier, Oxford, 2005.

Preiser, W., A. Davis, A. Salama and A. Hardy, *Architecture Beyond Criticism: Expert Judgment and Performance Evaluation*. London: Routledge/Taylor & Francis Group, London, 2014.

Rabeneck, A., (2008), 'A sketch plan for construction built environment theory', *Building Research and Information*, 36:3, 269-79.

RIBA, *Client Conversations: Insights into successful project outcomes*, RIBA, London, 2013.

IMAGE CREDITS

5th Studio p.75

Petra Appelhof p.103

Tom Arban p.37

Architecture 00 pp.63 (3rd and 4th row),
64 (middle)

Images copyright Arup and Giles Rocholl
Photography p.109 (top)

Simon Austin, Loughborough University
pp.67, 69

Photo: Iwan Baan pp.29, 30 (left),
41 (top), 65

Richard Battye p.xii (bottom right)

BDP/David Barbour p.159

David Borland/VIEW p.40 (middle and
bottom right)

Buro Happold p.136

Buro Happold/Daniel Hopkinson p.143

Burwell Deakins Architects;
photographer: Christopher Heaney
p.40 (bottom left)

Reproduced by permission of Burwell
Deakins Architects; photographer Hufton+Crow.
p. 35 (J)

Ian Caldwell   p.xi (top right)

Central St Martins/Stanton Williams;
Photography: Hufton + Crow p.54 (top)

CHACOL, Inc. p.63 (2nd row)

Jonathan Cole, www.
jonathancolephotography.com;
courtesy of Queen Mary's University p. 34 (A)

Keith Collie p.35 (B)

Peter Cook/VIEW pp.72 (top, middle left,
middle right and middle far right)

Rupert Cook p.x (bottom right)

Heidi Corbet pp.52, 66

Tim Crocker pp.33 (1st row, right), (2nd row,
right), (4th row, left); 35 (F), 43 (bottom right),
47 (top left), 53 (middle left), 56, 64 (top), 68
(bottom), 74 (top)

Erik Cronberg pp.155 (top left and top right),
156-157

Wallpaper design by Lewis F. Day p.110
(middle far left)

Diller Scofidio + Renfro p.45 (top right)

Doublespace p. 35 (O), 40 (top left and
top right)

Fiona Duggan p.xii (middle left)

Duggan Morris Architects;
photographer: Jack Hobhouse pp.78-79

Photo: Mogens Engelund* p.33 (1st row, left)

Mike Entwisle p.xiii (bottom left)

Torben Eskerod p.73 (bottom left and right)

ETH Zürich/Heidi Hostettler p.xii (top left)

Liz Eve/fotohaus pp.33 (3rd row, right), 137

Factory Fifteen pp.22-23, 50 (bottom)

Feilden Clegg Bradley Studios pp.12, 72
(bottom and middle far left), 85 (middle
right), 97, 108 (top middle, top right and
bottom row), 109 (bottom), 110 (top left,
middle left and bottom left), 111 (right side),
119, 140 (top), 141 (bottom)

Kenn Fisher p.xiii (top right)

Forbes Massie p.50 (top)

Andy Ford p.xii (top right)

Futuregrowth p.74 (bottom)

Dennis Gilbert pp.144-145, 165 (top left),
165 (middle right and bottom right)

photographer: John Gollings p.149

Ian Goodfellow p.xi (bottom right)

Photographer: Roland Halbe p.150 (left)

Martine Hamilton Knight/Builtvision;
Associated Architects p.135

Martine Hamilton Knight/Builtvision;
Hopkins Architects pp.33 (2nd row, left), 142
(top right and bottom left)

Martine Hamilton Knight/Builtvision;
University of Nottingham p.98 (right)

hammeskrause architekten p.49 (top and
bottom)

Hawkins Brown p.32, 33 (1st row, middle),
53 (top left, top right, bottom left and bottom
right), 68 (top), 71 (bottom)

HLM Architects pp.160-161

HOK/Glowfrog Studios Limited p.16
(bottom)

Hornberger Architekten AG p.85 (top left,
middle left)

Hufton+Crow pp.34 (E), 35 (C), 47 (bottom
left), 54 (bottom left), 55 (right), 80-81, 101,
107, 110-111 (centre), 138, 140 (bottom)

Keith Hunter www.keithhunterphotography.
com pp.39 (top right), 71 (top)

Katie Hyams p.xi (bottom left)

João Morgado Architectural Photography
p.59

John Horner Photography p.35 (P)

Keele University p.98 (left)

Tom Kvan p.x (top left)

Joern Lehmann p.49 (middle)

Jens Lindhe p.73 (top right)

Sebastian Lomas p.xiii (middle left)

London Centre for Nanotechnology
p.85 (top right), 88

London Metropolitan University p.35 (G)

D.Luckhurst/Feilden and Mawson;
courtesy of Queen Mary University
p.19 (top right)

Luke Hayes Photography p.39 (bottom left
and bottom right)

Lundgaard & Tranberg Architects p.73
(top left)

Jason Mabelis / Rock Hunter Ltd p.51
(bottom)

Eleanor Magennis p.xiii (bottom right)

Manchester School of Art p.108 (top left and
middle row)

Melbourne School of Design p.150 (right)

Miralles Tagliabue/courtesy of the Scottish
Parliament – 2004 p.33 (4th row, far right)

Moore Ruble Yudell Architects & Planners
pp.44-45 (top left)

Stefan Müller, Berlin p.34 (M)

Designer: MVRDV; photographer Rob 't Hart
pp.31, 35 (L)

The National Gallery, London p.33 (4th
row, far left)

The Neighbourhood Design Limited p.61

Image courtesy of Nicholas Hare Architects
p.134 (top left)

Nicholas Hare Architects p.134 (bottom)

Nicholas Hare Architects © Alan Williams
photography p.134 (top left)

Philip Ogden p.x (top right)

OMA; Photographer: Philippe Ruault p.54
(bottom right)

Penoyre and Prasad p.43 (top and bottom
left),

Photographer: Paul Philipson pp.112-113

Queen Mary University p.19 (top right)

Queen Mary University, photographer:Morley
von Sternberg p.19 (bottom left and bottom
right)

Regent Street Cinema p.57

Renzo Piano Building Workshop pp.0-1, 14

Richard+Schoeller Architectes;
photographer: Sergio Grazia p.33 (3rd
row, left)

RIBA p.93

Julian Robinson p.xiii (top left)

Nico Saieh p.60

ScanLAB Projects Ltd p.53 (middle right)

Science Gallery, Trinity College Dublin p.77

Shepley Bulfinch p.30 (top right)

Tim Soar pp.84, 85 (bottom)

Eric Soltan p.47 (right)

Spaces That Work/Robert Baker p.35 (D)

Stanford d.school p.55 (left)

Nigel Stead pp.164,
165 (top right and bottom left)

Photo courtesy of Steelcase p.35 (K)

Studio TILT; photographer: Jill Tate
pp.63 (top left), 64 (bottom)

Studio TILT; photographer: Patrick Quayle
p.63 (top right)

Paul Tahon and R & E Bouroullec
p.33 (4th row, right)

Ian Taylor p.17

David Tett for King's College London
p.30 (right)

Adrian Toon www.
architecturalphotographic.co.uk
p.141 (top left and top right)

Uniform www.uniform.net
pp.99 (bottom), 139

University of New South Wales
p.41 (bottom left)

University of New South Wales;
photographer: Peter Bennetts pp.33 (3rd
row, middle), 41 (middle and bottom right)

University of Nottingham / CampbellRowley
p.99 (top)

View Pictures Ltd/ Alamy p.35 (H)

VINCI Construction UK p.30 (top middle and
bottom middle)

Visualisation One p.51 (top)

Vitra; photographer: Eduardo Perez p.34 (I)

Copyright Wadsworth3d/Courtesy of HOK
with PLP Architecture p.16 (top)

WilkinsonEyre p.142 (top left and
bottom left)

© 2016 Wolfgang Tschapeller ZT GmbH
p.35 (N)

Nigel Young/Foster + Partners
p.33 (2nd row, middle)

Stefan Zimmerman pp.xi (top left),
155 (bottom)

*https://creativecommons.org/licenses/by-
sa/3.0/deed.en

INDEX

Note: page numbers in italics refer to figures and illustrated examples